Ashcliffe H

A tale of the last century

Emily Sarah Holt

Alpha Editions

This edition published in 2024

ISBN : 9789367247624

Design and Setting By
Alpha Editions
www.alphaedis.com
Email - info@alphaedis.com

As per information held with us this book is in Public Domain.
This book is a reproduction of an important historical work. Alpha Editions uses the best technology to reproduce historical work in the same manner it was first published to preserve its original nature. Any marks or number seen are left intentionally to preserve its true form.

Contents

I. OLD CICELY HAS HER THOUGHTS. .... - 1 -
II. A BAT BEHIND THE WAINSCOT. .... - 24 -
III. ALONE IN THE WORLD. .... - 42 -
IV. MY LADY INGRAM. .... - 58 -
V. THE HARRYING OF LAUCHIE. .... - 79 -
VI. THE TROUBLES OF GREATNESS. .... - 98 -
VII. THE NIGHT BOSWITH DIED. .... - 112 -
VIII. WANTED, DIOGENES' LANTERN. .... - 133 -
IX. INSIDE AND OUTSIDE. .... - 156 -
X. ANENT JOHN PATTERSON. .... - 176 -
XI. HOW PHILIP CAME BACK. .... - 194 -
XII. TRAITORS—HUMAN AND CANINE. .... - 209 -
XIII. LADY GRISELDA'S RUBY RING .... - 231 -

I.

OLD CICELY HAS HER THOUGHTS.

"I ask Thee for the daily strength
   To none that ask denied,
A mind to blend with outward things
   While keeping at Thy side;
Content to fill a little space
   So Thou be glorified."

Miss Waring.

In a large bedroom, on an autumn afternoon, two girls were divesting themselves of their out-door attire after a walk. They were dressed alike, though their ages were eleven and nineteen. Their costume consisted of brown stuff petticoats, over which they wore cashmere gowns of a white ground, covered with brown-stemmed red flowers, and edged with quillings of green ribbon. These dresses were high in the back and on the shoulders, but were cut down square in the front. The sleeves reached to the elbows, and were there finished by white muslin frills. The girls wore high-heeled shoes, the heels being red, and brown worsted stockings, which the petticoat was short enough to show plainly. On the dressing-table before them lay two tall white muslin caps, called *cornettes*, abundant in frills and lace, but having no strings. The hair of both girls was dressed high over a frame, standing up some three inches above their heads; and when the elder put on her cap, it increased her apparent height by at least three inches more.

The chamber in which they were dressing was long and low, two large beams being visible in the ceiling; and the casement, not two feet in height, ran nearly across the width of the room. There was a faint, delicate scent of lavender. The furniture comprised a large four-post bedstead, an unwieldy wardrobe, a washstand, a dressing-table, and two chairs. The carpet was only round the bed and washstand, the rest of the floor being left uncovered, and shining with age and use. The walls were wainscoted about half-way to the ceiling, the higher portion being painted a dull light-green. The girls turned to leave the room.

"O Lucy! your *cornette*!"

Lucy—aged eleven—made a dash at the dressing-table, and seizing her cap by its frills, to the severe detriment of the lace, stuck it on her head in the first way that occurred to her, and was about to rush down-stairs without further ceremony.

"That will not do, Lucy," said the elder girl. "You know what Henrietta will say. Go to the mirror and put your *cornette* on properly."

Muttering something which sounded like a statement that she did not care what Henrietta said, Lucy retraced her steps to the glass, pulled off the *cornette*, and stuck it on again, in a style very little better than before. This done, she joined her sister, who was half-way down the stairs. It was a fine old wooden staircase which the girls descended, "worn by the feet that now were silent,"[1] and at its base a long, narrow passage stretched right and left. Our young friends turned to the right, and after passing on for a few feet, entered a door on the left hand, which led to the family parlor. This room had already three occupants, two young ladies and a boy of fourteen. The two former were dressed like Lucy and her sister, except that the younger of them, who sat at a tapestry-frame in the corner of the room, wore broad pieces of brown velvet round her neck and wrists. The boy, who was equipped in out-door costume, part of which consisted of a pair of thick and pre-eminently splashed boots, sat on a low chair, staring into the fire, whistling, and playing with a riding-whip.

"Lucy! your hair!" was the shocked exclamation with which the new-comers were received.

"Oh, my hair is all right! I brushed it—this morning," said Lucy, the last words in a much lower tone than the rest; and then she asked of her whistling brother, "Have you heard anything, Charley?"

Charley shook his head without ceasing to whistle.

"Harry is not come yet?"

"No," said Charley, in a very discontented tone; "and he has taken Bay Fairy, and I can't go out. 'Tis enough to provoke a saint."

"That ben't you, Master Charley!" said a new and cheery voice, as an elderly woman appeared, carrying a little tea-tray, from behind the heavy, japanned screen which stood near the door. She was dressed in a black woollen gown, low in the neck, with a white muslin kerchief above, and a cap of more modest pretensions than those of the young ladies.

"What does the impertinent old woman mean by calling me a sinner?" inquired Charley, addressing himself to his boots.

"You ben't?" said old Cicely, setting down the tea-tray. "Well! stand up and let us look at you, do! You are the first ever I see that wasn't no sinner!"

To which cutting observation Charley replied only by banging the door between himself and the unwelcome querist.

"Ay, it ben't for none of us to set ourselves up i' thatn's!" meditatively remarked old Cicely, in her turn to the teapot. "Mrs. Henrietta, there's a poor old man at the yard-door, my dear, and I can't tell where to look for Madam; maybe you'd see to him, poor soul?"

Henrietta, the eldest sister, answered by quitting the room. Cicely arranged the tea-cups—large shallow cups of delicate china—on a small round table in the window.

"The tea is ready, Mrs. Bell," she said; "will you please to pour it?"

The decorated young lady who sat at the tapestry-frame rose languidly, and began to pour out the tea, while Cicely set four chairs round the little table; having done which, the latter calmly took one of them herself, and producing a large colored handkerchief from her pocket, carefully spread it over her black woollen dress.

"Well, truly," said she, for she was in a talkative mood this evening, "there is no end to the good in a dish of tea. I am sorry I ever said what I have done against it, my dears, and I wish Madam would drink it. 'Tis so heartening like! It is a new-fangled sort of drink, there's no denying; but surely, I wonder how we ever got on without it!"

"Cicely," said Henrietta, coming in, "I have told Dolly to give the poor man some meat and dry straw in the shed for to-night."

"Very good, Mrs. Henrietta," answered Cicely; "I'll see as he gets it. Mrs. Bell, I'll be obliged to you of another dish of tea."

There were only four tea-drinkers in this family, and, until a few months previous, there had been only three. The gentlemen despised what they considered a washy and exclusively feminine beverage, and the mistress of the house could by no means be induced to taste it. It was a new-fangled drink, she said, and new-fangled things, of whatever description, she abhorred. People never drank tea when she was a child, and why should they want it now? This was Madam Passmore's logic, and under its influence she drank no tea. Still she did not forbid her daughters' indulging in it. Young people, she allowed, were given to new-fangled things; and could be expected to be wiser only as they grew older. She was a little annoyed when the logic of the young people, adverse to her own, made a tea-convert of Cicely Aggett, who was about twenty-five years her senior; but Madam Passmore was a quiet, passive sort of woman, who never kept anger long, and was in her heart a fatalist. "What must be must be," she used to say; and many a time had she consoled herself with this comforting adage under troubles of various kinds. She said so when her son Harry went into the army; she said so when her husband broke his leg in fox-hunting; and she said so, but with tears, when her little daughter Margaret died. She had no political opinions but those of her husband, who was a fervent Whig; but deep down in her heart she was a profound Tory in all domestic matters, for she disliked change and novelty beyond everything. She never put down a new carpet until the old carpet was quite beyond endurance; not from any parsimonious motive, but simply because she liked best those things to which she was most accustomed. She never would have slept with comfort if her bed had been turned with its side to the wall instead of its back; nor would she ever have conceded that a new lamp burnt half so brightly as the old one. Her surviving family consisted of two sons and four daughters, who were remarkably alike in person—all but one. The neighbors who were sufficiently high in position to visit with Squire Passmore of Ashcliffe, often wondered how it was that Celia Passmore was so unlike every other member of the family. They were tall and stately in figure, she was small and slight; they had abundant light hair, hers was thin and dark; their eyes were blue or gray, hers brown. Most of all was she unlike her twin-sister, Isabella, who was considered the beauty of the family, and was very well aware of it. There was nothing remarkable about any of the others; but Celia, some said, was sadly plain, poor girl! and it must be a great mortification to Madam Passmore, who had been a country belle in her young days.

Cicely Aggett, whom we have seen seated at the table with her young mistresses, was one of a class wholly extinct in our days. She was a dependent, but not a servant. She had, some fifty years before this, been Madam Passmore's nurse, and she now filled a nondescript position in the family of her nursling. She was always ready to help or advise, and considered nothing beneath her which could add to the comfort of any member of the family; but she took all her meals in the parlor, and was essentially one of themselves. She was the confidante of everybody, and all knew that she never abused a trust. Madam Passmore would as soon have thought of turning the dog out of the room before making a confidential communication, as of turning out Cicely, simply because Cicely's dog-like fidelity was completely above suspicion.

The tea was now finished. Lucy, who had not yet arrived at the dignity of a tea-drinker, was roaming about the room as Cicely departed with the tea-tray.

"There is Harry!" she exclaimed, looking out of the window. "He must have some news—he is waving something above his head. Henrietta, may I run and meet him?"

Henrietta gave consent, and away went Lucy at the top of her speed down the broad avenue which led from the house through the park. The young officer was trotting up on Bay Fairy, with his spaniel Pero panting after him; but he reined in his horse as Lucy came up to him.

"A victory!" he cried. "A victory at Malplaquet! a glorious victory! Run, Lucy!—a race! who will tell Father first?"

Lucy—if it were possible; there was very little doubt of that. She ran back as fast as she had come, turning her head once to see how Harry was getting on. He was not urging his horse beyond a walk; it was evident that he meant to give her a chance of winning. She ran towards the stable-yard, where she knew that the Squire was, and at last, arriving triumphantly first at the yard-gate, burst suddenly into the arms of her father, as he was just opening the gate to come out.

"Hallo!" said the Squire, when this unexpected apparition presented itself. "Hoity-toity! What is the matter, Lucibelle?"

"A—victory!" was all that Lucy could utter.

"Where? who told you?" he asked, excitedly.

"Harry," said the panting Lucy. "Somewhere in—France, I think—'tis a—queer name."

"In France, Sir, at Malplaquet," said Harry, who now rode up quickly, having good-naturedly allowed his little sister the pleasure of winning the race; "a great victory under the Duke of Marlborough." And he handed the *Gazette* to his father.

"That is glorious!" said the Squire. "I will go in and tell Mother."

Not that Mother—that is, Madam Passmore—cared anything about victories, but she liked to see her husband pleased, and would have welcomed equally a victory or a defeat which had wrought that desirable end. Harry walked into the house with his father, and Lucy, having regained her breath, followed them.

"Why, Charley, where have you been?" asked the Squire, as that young gentleman made his appearance. "Here is a splendid victory over the French, and you are not here to cheer!"

"Where have I been?" repeated Charley, in a very glum tone. "Well, I like that! I have been at home, Sir, kicking my heels together for want of anything else to do: your party and Harry had taken all the horses."

"I did not know you wanted Fairy, Charley," said Harry, kindly. "I am sorry I took her."

"Come, my lad, no use in crying over spilt milk," said the Squire. "It is Saturday night, Charley, and people ought to be at peace on Saturday night."

"I hate Saturday nights, and Sundays too, and I don't want to be at peace!" said Charley, walking off.

On that afternoon, while Harry was riding home with the news of the victory of Malplaquet, an event was taking place in London Which the family at Ashcliffe little imagined, yet which very nearly concerned one of them.

In an upper room of a house in Holborn Bars sat half a dozen men in conclave. The door of the chamber was double, the inner of green baize, the outer of strong oak, barred and bolted, as if the conference were desirous to avoid eavesdroppers.

At one side of the table sat three men, all of whom had passed middle age. We have little to do with them, so they may be succinctly described as two short men and one tall one. Opposite stood three others, who were all young; and it is with one of these alone that we are intimately concerned.

He was about twenty-six years of age, tall and slight; he wore a black wig, and his eyes, also black, were peculiarly brilliant and penetrating. Yet his complexion was moderately fair, and he was not devoid of a fresh, healthy color. There was great quickness, combined with some natural grace, in all his motions; and he evidently comprehended the meaning of his elder and slower companions before their sentences were above half-finished.

"Here, Brother Cuthbert, are your instructions," the tall man was saying. "You remember, I am sure, the private orders which I gave you a week past, with reference to certain information to be gained and brought to the King?"

"Perfectly, Father—all of them," replied Cuthbert, in a clear, pleasant voice.

"Very well. Now listen to another order. My Lady Ingram writ to the General a month past, to send on an errand for her—(if it might be done with any other we should have)—one of our number, who could be trusted for secrecy, speed, diligence, and discretion. We have named you."

Brother Cuthbert bowed low in answer.

"This matter of her Ladyship's," pursued the tall man, "is, of course, of secondary importance, and may not, indeed, directly conduce to the interests of the Church. It must, nevertheless, be borne in mind, that should the sons die unmarried (as it is desirable the elder should), the daughter will become heir to the Ingram estates. I mentioned something of this to you last night."

Brother Cuthbert bowed again.

"Moreover, for other reasons known to the General, it was thought desirable to grant her Ladyship's request. Your destination, in the first place, is Exeter, where you will be met by my Lady Ingram's gentleman-usher, Mr. Gilbert Irvine, who is able to give you any information concerning her affairs which you may find it necessary to ask. From Exeter, you will proceed (after doing your business there) to Ashcliffe Hall, an old mansion on the road to Moreton Hampstead, belonging to one John Passmore, a Whig country gentleman. Here is a sealed paper, which you will open at Exeter. It contains further instructions, a plan of Ashcliffe Hall, and various notes which you may find useful. And here are ten guineas, which my Lady Ingram has transmitted. Mr. Irvine will accompany you to Ashcliffe; and you can employ or dismiss him at that place, as circumstances may arise. In the mean time, we recommend to you not on any consideration to neglect either the general and constant necessity of serving the Church, as the opportunity may present itself, nor the special secret service on which you go, touching the King and cause. If you require more money, apply to any one of us three. We rely upon you, not, on the one hand, to be more lavish of either time or money than is necessary, nor, on the other, to leave the work only half-finished."

"I will do my utmost, Father, to order myself by your instructions," replied Cuthbert, lifting his head.

"You will supply yourself with a surname, which even Mr. Irvine must not know not to be your real name. Select one which shall not be so uncommon as to attract notice, nor so common that letters would be likely to miscarry. You can consider this at your leisure, and let us know to-morrow of what name you have thought, since we shall not require you to set out before to-morrow evening."

"What say you to 'Stevens?'" suggested Cuthbert in a moment.

A grave consultation among the elder Jesuits followed, ending with the approval of Cuthbert's suggestion.

"You are very young, my Brother, to be trusted with so grave and important a matter as His Majesty's errands are," warned the elder priest in conclusion. "We have relied upon your ingenuity and devotion. Let us not have cause to regret choosing you."

"You will not do that, Father," answered Cuthbert, not so much proudly as coolly and confidently.

And making his adieux to the conclave, Mr. Cuthbert Stevens—for so we must henceforth call him—withdrew from the room.

We shall see him again shortly; but for the present we must return (rather more rapidly than he could travel) to Ashcliffe Hall.

"Celia!" said Lucy to her sister, a few hours later, as the latter tucked her up in bed, "do you think—is it very—did you hear what Charley said about Sunday?"

"Yes, dear. Charley was in a passion, and did not mean what he said, I hope."

"But do you think that it is—very wicked—to get so tired on Sunday?" asked Lucy, slowly, as if she were half afraid of bringing her thoughts to light. "For I do get dreadfully tired, Celia. Sermons, endless sermons all day long! for, as if the sermon in church were not enough, Father must needs read another at home on Sunday nights! Celia, do you think it is very wrong to get tired of sermons?"

"I suppose," said Celia, thoughtfully, "that must depend on the sort of sermon."

"I never seem to get a chance of hearing any sort but one," said Lucy; "and I can't understand them."

"Well, Lucy, it is not pleasant to be obliged to sit still and listen to what you do not understand," Celia admitted.

"Oh, I get so tired!" said Lucy, flinging herself on another part of the bed, as if the very thought of the coming Sunday fatigued her. "Don't take the light away just yet, Celia."

"No, dear; I have my clean ruffles to sew on for to-morrow," answered Celia, sitting down to her work.

"Celia, do you understand Dr. Braithwaite's sermons?"

"Not always. Remember what a learned man he is, Lucy; we must not expect very wise men to talk like you and me."

"I wish he did not know quite so much, then," said Lucy. "I could understand him if he would talk like you."

"Aught I can do for you, Mrs. Celia, my dear?" asked old Cicely, looking in. "Prithee give me those ruffles. You have been sewing all day."

"Cicely," asked Lucy, returning to the charge, "do you understand Dr. Braithwaite's sermons?"

"No, my dear, scarce a word," said Cicely.

"I wonder at your listening so quietly!"

"Well, you see, my dear, I has my thoughts," said Cicely, fitting the ruffle. "If aught goes on that I can't understand, why, I has my thoughts. When Master reads a sermon of an evening, well, sometimes I understand, and sometimes not. If I do, well and good; but if I don't, I can sit and think. And I think,

Miss Lucy, that there's a deal of difference between you and me; but there's a cruel deal bigger difference between either of us and Him up yonder. It must be a sight harder for us to understand Him than it is to understand Parson Braithwaite."

"But what has that to do with it, Cicely?" asked Lucy, wonderingly.

"Why, my dear, ben't that what all sermons is for—to teach us to understand God? Just the beginning, you know, must be hard; it always is. Why, when Madam had me learned to read—old Madam, your grandmother, my dears—do you think I liked learning the Christ-Cross-Row?[2] Wasn't it very hard, think you, keeping day after day a-saying, 'A, B, C, D,' when there wasn't no sense in it? But 'tis all through the Christ-Cross-Row that I've learned to read the Book. Eh! but I have thanked old Madam many a hundred times for having me learned to read the Book! Well, my dears, 'tis always hard at the beginning; and sure the beginning of learning Him must be harder nor learning to read."

"Why, Cicely, you are as bad to understand as Dr. Braithwaite!"

"Maybe so, my dear. If a little one asked you for to tell him what big A was like, I think you'd scarce make him understand without showing him. And if you want to know what He is like, I think you must read the Book. 'Tis like a picture of Him. I don't know any other way, without you read the Book."

"Do you mean the Bible, Cicely? But Dr. Braithwaite does not say much about that."

"I haven't got nought to say about Parson Braithwaite, Miss Lucy. But surely all that is good in any sermon or aught else must come out of the Book."

"But we could read that at home."

"So we could, my dear; more's the pity as we don't! But there's somewhat in the Book about that—as we ben't to stop going to church."[3]

"Where is that, Cicely? I never saw it."

"I haven't a good memory, not for particular words, my dear, and I can't tell you without I had the Book; but 'tis there, certain sure."

Celia had been quietly looking in her little book-case while Cicely was speaking. It contained many things beside books—baskets, pincushions, bottles of Hungary and lavender water, and other heterogeneous articles. But there were about half a dozen books absolutely her own, and one of them was a Bible—a Bible which she very rarely opened, she acknowledged to herself, with a feeling of shame. Looking for it, and bringing it out, she secretly wiped the dust from the covers, and offered it to Cicely.

"Here is one, Cicely; can you show us what you mean?"

"Not in your Book, Mrs. Celia. If I had my own Book, I could. My dear, 'tis choke-full of marks—bits of worsted mostly. I often have it lying open by me when I'm a-darning stockings or some such work, and if I finds a particular nice bit, why, down there goes a bit of worsted into him. Eh! but I have some fine bits marked with them worsted! My dears, if you haven't read the Book you don't know what nice reading there is."

"I think I will read it," said Lucy, gaping.

"You can't without you have glasses, my dear," said Cicely, quietly, finishing off the ruffle.

"Glasses! Why Cicely!" exclaimed Lucy.

"Yes, Miss Lucy, glasses," was Cicely's persistent answer. "Not such like as I works with, my dear: them is earthly glasses. But there is heavenly glasses, and you can't rend the Book without, and you must ask Him for them. He is sure to give them if you ask Him. I think I could find that bit, Mrs. Celia, if you will give me bold."

Celia passed the Bible to the old woman, and she, opening at the first chapter of St. Matthew, slowly traced the lines until she reached the passage which she wanted.

"Now, look here, Mrs. Celia. This is him."

Celia took the book, and read where Cicely pointed.

"'If ye, then, being evil, know how to give good gifts unto your children, how much more shall your Father which is in heaven give good things to them that ask Him?'"[4]

"Stop a bit!" said old Cicely; "that ben't just the one I meant. Let's look a bit on."

After a little more searching she discovered her text. "Read that, please, Mrs. Celia," she said.

Celia read in a low tone: "'If ye, then, being evil, know how to give good gifts unto your children: how much more shall your heavenly Father give the Holy Spirit to them that ask Him?'"[5]

Lucy seemed to have dropped asleep.

"Cicely," asked Celia, "how shall we know if we have the Holy Spirit?"

"Feel Him, my dear,—feel Him!" said Cicely, with a light in her eyes. "I reckon you don't want telling whether you are happy or not, do you?"

"No, indeed," replied Celia, smiling.

"No more you'll want to be told whether you have Him," resumed old Cicely, triumphantly.

"But how did you get Him given?" pursued Celia.

"Why, my dear, I wanted Him, and I asked for Him, and I got Him. 'Tis just so simple as that. I never knew aught about it till I read the Book. I'm only a very simple, ignorant, old woman, my dear. Maybe the reason why I don't know no more is just that I am such a dunce. He can't learn me no more, because I haven't no wits to be learned. You've got plenty of wit, Mrs. Celia—you try! Why, just think the lots of things you know more than me! You can write, and make figures, and play pretty music, and such like, and I know nought but sewing, and dressing meat and drink, and reading the Book. Mayhap the Lord gives me fine things to think about, just because I know so little of other things—a sort of making up like, you see. But you try it, Mrs. Celia, my dear!"

"I fear I scarce have your glasses, Cicely," answered Celia, with a sigh.

"I've done the ruffles now," said Cicely, rising. "You come to me into my little room when you've time, Mrs. Celia, and I'll show you some of them fine bits—any time you like. And as to the glasses, you ask for 'em. Good-night, Mrs. Celia."

Ashcliffe Hall was up at six on week-days, but when the Sunday came round, it was not its custom to rise before eight. Costumes were resplendent on that day, and took some time in assuming. On Sundays and special gala-days only, the young ladies wore hoop-petticoats and patched their faces.[6] Their attire to-day comprised quilted petticoats of light-blue satin, silk brocaded gowns, extremely long in the waist, *cornettes* of lace, lace-trimmed muslin aprons, white silk stockings, and shoes with silver buckles. Their gowns, too, had trains, which for comfort were fastened up behind, looking like a huge burden on the back of the wearer. They looked very stiff as they rustled down the stairs,—all except Lucy, whom no costume on earth could stiffen, though even she wore a graver and more demure air than usual, which perhaps was partly due to the coming sermons. The girls drank their tea, Lucy joining them in the meal, but using milk instead of the fashionable beverage. By the time they had done, Madam Passmore and the Squire were down-stairs; they always breakfasted in their own room on Sunday mornings. Then John, the old coachman, slowly drove up to the front door the great family-coach, drawn by two large, dappled, long-maned and heavy-looking horses. The coach held eight inside, so that it conveniently accommodated all the family, Cicely included, with the exception of Charley, who generally perched himself on the great box, which was quite large enough to admit him between John and the footman. The church was barely half a mile from the Hall, but none of the Ashcliffe family ever thought of walking there; such a proceeding would have involved a loss of dignity. It was a fine old Gothic edifice, one of those large stately churches which here and there seem dropped by accident into a country village, whose population has dwindled far below its ancient standard. The pews were about five feet high, the church having been recently and fashionably repewed. There was a great pulpit, with a carved oak sounding-board, an equally large reading-desk, and a clerk's desk, the last occupied by a little old man who looked coeval with the church. The Squire bestowed great attention upon the responses, which he uttered in a loud, sonorous tone; but when the psalm was over—one of Sternhold and Hopkins' version, for Ashcliffe Church was much too old and respectable to descend to the new version of Tate and Brady—and when the clergyman had announced his text, which the Squire noted down, that in the evening he might be able to question Charley and Lucy concerning it—no further notice did anything obtain from the owner of Ashcliffe Hall. Settling himself into a comfortable attitude, he laid his head back, and in a few minutes was snoring audibly. Madam Passmore generally made efforts, more or less violent, to remain awake, for about a quarter of an hour; and then, succumbing to the inevitable, followed her husband's example. Henrietta kept awake and immovable; so did Harry; but Isabella generally slept for above half the sermon, and Lucy would have followed her example had she dared, the fear of her eldest sister just opposite her keeping her decorous. The discourse was certainly not calculated to arouse a somnolent ear. Dr. Braithwaite generally began his sermon in some such style as this:—"That most learned doctor of the schools, styled by them of his age the Angelical Doctor,[7] whose words were as honey, yea, were full of sweetness and delight unto the ears of such as followed him, did in that greatest and most mellifluent of the writings wherewith he regaled his study, did, I say, observe, for the edification of the whole Church, and the great profit of them that should come after"—and then came a shower-bath of Latin dashing down upon the unlearned ears of his congregation. Greek he rarely quoted, since there was no one in the parish who understood it but himself; so that it was but seldom that he impressed the farmers with a due sense of the heights and depths of his learning by uttering a few words of that classic tongue; and whether his quotation were from Pindar or St. Paul, made no difference to them.

Until her conversation with Lucy and old Cicely on the previous evening, Celia had been in the habit of considering the sermon as something with which she had nothing to do, except to sit it out with patience and decorum. She was beginning to think differently now, and she tried hard to follow Dr. Braithwaite this morning through his discourse of an hour and three-quarters. But the sentences were long, the style involved, and the worthy

Doctor had got hold of a very unpromising subject. He was preaching upon the ceremony of baptism in the primitive Church, and its relation to the heresy of the Manichæans; and after half an hour, during which she felt confused amid a throng of exorcisms, white robes, catechumens, deacons, immersions, fire-worshippers, Arians, Pelagians, and Gnostics, Celia gave up her hopeless task. Old Cicely sat quite still, her eyes fixed on the closed prayer-book on her knee, a soft, pleased smile every now and then flitting across her countenance; and Celia longed to know of what she was thinking, which appeared to be so much more interesting than Dr. Braithwaite's Manichæans.

In a cheery, sunny little room, on the afternoon of the same Sunday, sat old Cicely, with her Bible on her lap. There were several unoccupied rooms in Ashcliffe Hall, and Cicely had chosen this as hers, where the evening sun came lovingly in, and dwelt for a season with lingering beams on walls and furniture. The same pleased smile rested on the old woman's lips, as she slowly traced the words with her finger along the page, for Cicely read with little fluency; and she said half aloud, though she was alone,—"'He hath made Him to be sin for us, who knew no sin; that we might be made the righteousness of God in Him.'[8] Ben't that good, now?"

"May I come in, Cicely?" asked a soft voice at the door.

"Surely, my dear, surely," was the answer. "I'm just a-looking over some of them fine bits where I has my marks. I'll set a chair, Mrs. Celia."

But the chair was set already, and Celia sat down by the old woman.

"Now show me what you like best," she said.

"Well, my dear, I do read most of these here four. 'Tis all good, you know—the very best of reading, of course; but I can understand these here best—Matthew, Mark, Luke, and John. There's nice reading in Luke—very pretty reading indeed; but the beautifullest of 'em all, my dear, that's John. He is up-and-down like, is John. You see I can't get used to the Book like as you would. There's five bits of John—two long uns and two little uns, and one middling. Now the last of 'em I don't understand; 'tis main hard, only a bit here and there; but when I do come to a bit that I can understand, 'tis fine, to be sure! But 'tis this piece of him after Luke that I reads mostly, and the next piece of him after that. Look!"

It was an old, worn book, bound in plain brown calf, which lay on Cicely's lap. The pages were encumbered with an infinitude of ends of worsted,—black, brown, and gray. These were Cicely's guide-posts. She was slowly pursuing the lines with her finger, till she came upon the passage which she wished to find.

"Now, my dear, you read that."

Celia read, "'And this is the promise which He hath promised us, even eternal life.'"[9]

"Wait a bit!" cried old Cicely; "there's another in this big piece—a rare good un. Let me find him!"

And turning hastily over the leaves of her book, she picked out, by the help of the worsteds, the verse she wished.

"Read that, Mrs. Celia."

"'And this is life eternal, that they should know Thee, the only true God, and Jesus Christ whom Thou hast sent.'"[10]

"Ben't that nice?" delightedly asked old Cicely.

"But how are we to know Him?" said Celia, wearily. "O Cicely! I wanted to ask you of what you were thinking this morning in the sermon which pleased you so mightily. You smiled as if you were so happy."

"Did I, my dear?" answered old Cicely, smiling again. "Well, I dare say I did. And I was cruel happy, that's sure! 'Twas just these two verses, Mrs. Celia, as I've been a-showing you. I'd read 'em last thing yesterday, and surely they did feel just like honey on my tongue. So, as I couldn't nohow make out what Parson Braithwaite were a-saying about them many keys, I falls back, you see, on my two verses. Well, thinks I, if He has promised us, sure we need not be afeard of losing none of it. If you promise somebody somewhat, my dear, mayhap afore you come to do it you'll feel sorry as you've promised, and be thinking of harking back, as Jack says; but there is no harking back with Him. I think, afore He promises, He looks of all sides, and you know, if he sees everything, no wonder He promises so sure. Well, then, I thinks again, what has He promised us? Eternal life. Why, that's another bolt, like, put on the door. If 'tis eternal life, surely we can't never let it go no more."

"But, Cicely," interrupted Celia, "don't you feel that you are often doing wrong?"

"Of course I am so, my dear!" said Cicely. "Every day in the year—ay, and every minute in the day. But then, you see, I just go to the Book. Look what I was a-reading when you came in."

She pointed to the verse which had engaged her. "For He hath made Him to be sin for us, who knew no sin; that we should be made the righteousness of God in Him."

"Look there, Mrs. Celia! Here's One that did no sin, and yet bare the punishment that our sin must needs have. And if He bare the punishment that did no sin, then belike we must go free for whom He bare it. Don't you see? 'Tis just a matter of fair dealing. The law can't punish both—him as did the wrong and him as didn't. So the other must go free."

"But we must do something to please God, Cicely? We must have something to bring to Him? It cannot be that Jesus Christ hath done all for us, and we have but to take to ourselves what He hath done, and to live as we list!"

"Well, my dear," said Cicely, "I've got my thoughts upon that, too. You look here! I don't find as ever I did a thing to please God afore I took Him that died to stand for me. I never cared aught about pleasing Him; and do you think He'd be like to be pleased with such work as that? If He can see into our hearts, why, it must be just like talking. And do you think Madam would be pleased with me, however well I sewed and swept, if I just went saying forever, 'Tis not to please you I'm working; I don't care a bit about you?'"

"I think I do want to please Him," said Celia slowly.

"Don't you stick at thinking, child," said old Cicely, with a pleased look; "go on to knowing, my dear. Well, then, as to bringing something to Him, look here in this other part."

Cicely turned to Isaiah, and after a little search, pointed out a verse which Celia read.

"'But we are all as an unclean thing, and all our righteousnesses are as filthy rags; and we all do fade as a leaf; and our iniquities, like the wind, have taken us away.'"[11]

"If the Queen was a-coming this way, my dear, and we was all of us a-going out to see her, what would you think of me if you see me ransacking the house for all the foul clothes I could find, to tie up in a bundle, and saying, 'There! I'm a-going to give these to the Queen!' Wouldn't you think I was only fit for Bedlam? You see it don't say 'all our *iniquities* are as filthy rags;' we should be ready to own that. Dear, no! 'tis all our *righteousnesses*. Will you tell me, then, what we have to bring to Him that is above all Kings and Lords? Well, and last of all, as to living as we list. I do find that mostly when we have made it up like with Him, we list to live after His ways. Not always—surely not always!" she added, sadly shaking her head; "truly we are a pack of good-for-noughts, e'en the best of us; yet it do hurt to think as we've grieved Him when we come to see all He has done and will do for us. Them's my thoughts upon that, Mrs. Celia."

"Why did you never speak to me—to any of us—in this way before now, Cicely?" asked Celia, very thoughtfully and gravely.

"Truly, my dear, I take shame to myself that I never did," replied Cicely; "but you see there was two reasons. Firstly, 'tisn't so very long since I come to know it myself—leastwise not many years. Then, you see, when I did know, I hadn't the face, like, for a good while. Seemed so bold and brassy like for me to be a-talking i' thatn's to the likes of you, as knowed so much more than me. And somehow it never seemed to come natural till last night, and then it come all at once out of what Miss Lucy she said about Parson's sermons."

Celia remained silent for a minute. The mention of Dr. Braithwaite's sermons had opened up a vein of thought. She wondered if anywhere there were men who preached sermons of a different kind from his, such as she and even old Cicely might understand, and from which they could derive benefit. Was there any preacher who, instead of enlarging on the Angelical Doctor, was satisfied to keep to Jesus Christ and Him crucified? A wild desire sprang up in her heart to go to London, and hear the great men who preached before the Queen. She did not mention this to Cicely. Celia knew full well that it would appear to her not only preposterous, but absolutely perilous. Harry was the only member of the family who had ever visited the metropolis, and this by virtue of Her Majesty's commission. The Squire considered it a hotbed of all evil, physical, moral, and political. Had he walked down the Strand, he would honestly have suspected every man he met to be a Jesuit in disguise, or at the least a Jacobite, which he thought scarcely better. He believed that the air of the capital was close and pestilential, that all honesty and morality were banished from its borders, that all the men in it—with the exception of the Duke of Marlborough and the Whig Ministers—were arrant rogues, and all the women—excluding the Queen and the Duchess of Marlborough—were heartless and unprincipled. There was some ground for his belief, but he sometimes excepted the wrong persons.

All these facts and feelings floated through Celia's mind, and she felt that to bring her wishes to light would probably hinder their accomplishment. She sat silent and thoughtful.

"Cicely," she asked at length, rather abruptly, "do you not find some parts of the Bible very hard to understand?"

"A vast sight, my dear!" said Cicely; "a vast sight! Sure there's a deal that's main hard to a poor old ignorant body such as me."

"Then what do you do, Cicely, when you come to a piece that you cannot understand?"

"Leave it alone, my dear. There's somewhat about the middle of the Book—I can't say the words right, never has 'em pat—about the road being made so straight and smooth like that the very fools can't shape to lose the way. Well, I think the Book's a bit like that itself. For I am a fool, Mrs. Celia, and I won't go to deny it. Surely God will show me all I want, and all that's meant for me, thinks I; and so what I can't understand I think ben't for the likes of me, and I leave it to them 'tis meant for."

"Now all about those Jews, on their way to the Promised Land, and the forty years they spent in the wilderness,—I cannot see what that has to do with us."

"Eh! Mrs. Celia, my dear, don't you go to say that!" urged old Cicely, earnestly. "Wasn't they hard-hearted and stiff-necked folks? and ben't we hard-hearteder and stiff-neckeder?"

"But is it not very gloomy, Cicely, to be always thinking of death, and judgment, and such horrid things?" said Celia, with a little shudder.

"Never thinks about 'em, my dear," was old Cicely's short answer.

"Why, Cicely! I thought religious people were always thinking about them?"

"Don't know nought about religious people, as you call 'em," said Cicely; "never came across one. All I know is, *I* never thinks—not any while—about death, and judgment, and such like. You see, I haven't got to die just now,—when I have, it'll be a hard pull, I dare say; but there's dying grace, and there's living grace. He don't give dying grace—at least so I think—till we come to dying. So I leave that alone. He knows when I'm to die, and He'll be sure to see to it that I have grace to die with. And as to the judgment, my dear, I have no more to do with that than the other,—a sight less, it seems to me. For we have all got to die; but if I understand the Book right, them that trust in Him haven't no judgment for to stand. If He has taken all my sins away, what am I to be judged for? Don't you see, Mrs. Celia? Eh, no! 'tis not we need think over the judgment, but the poor souls that have to stand it—who will not take Christ, and have nought of their own."

Celia sat silently gazing out of the window on the fair sward and trees of Ashcliffe Park. She had not found any answer when Lucy burst in, with no previous ceremony, and with the exclamation, "What are you doing here, Celia? Didn't you hear the bell for the sermon? Oh, me! I wish it was over!"

Perhaps Lucy was not the only person who wished it. The Sunday-evening sermon at Ashcliffe was a rather fearful institution to more mature and sedate persons than she. First, one of the Squire's sons—Harry, when he was at home, Charley, if not—read the Psalms and Lessons for the day, and it was necessary that they should be read very loud. This was disagreeable when they contained a number of Hebrew names, which Charley, at least, had no idea how to pronounce. He was consequently reduced to make hits at them, which passed muster in all but very flagrant cases, as, fortunately for him, his father was little wiser than himself. This ordeal over, the sermon itself was read by the Squire, and commonly lasted about an hour and a half. It was never very entertaining, being most frequently a discourse on the moral virtues, in tone heathenish, and in style dreary beyond measure. After the sermon, the whole family repeated the Lord's Prayer,—any other prayers the Squire, being a layman, would have thought it semi-sacrilege to read. Then, all remaining in their places, Charley and Lucy were called up to repeat their catechism, each answering alternately, and standing in as stiff a position as possible. When this was over, they had to repeat the text of Dr. Braithwaite's sermon, and that one who remembered it best was rewarded with a silver groat. This was the last act of the drama, the young lady and gentleman being then pounced upon by Cicely and ordered off to bed, after saying good-night all round. The Squire finished the day with a bowl of punch, and a game of cards or backgammon, in which it never occurred to him to see any incongruity with his previous occupations. Later came supper, after which the ladies retired, leaving the Squire to finish his punch alone; and the whole household was in bed by ten at the latest.

The sermon this evening was a discourse upon covetousness—a vice to which none of the hearers were addicted; and after listening to a learned prologue concerning the common derivation of misery and miser, with a number of quotations and instances to show it, Celia's thoughts began to wander, and roamed off once more to her conversation with old Cicely.

"The *Gazette*, Sir!" said Harry, coming into the room in boots and spurs one morning about three months after the Sunday in question. "Great tumults in London regarding one Dr. Sacheverell,[12] who hath preached a Jacobite sermon and much inflamed the populace; and 'tis said the Queen will not consent to his being deprived. Likewise"—

"Hang all Jacobites!" cried the Squire.

"Likewise," pursued his son, "'tis said the Pretender will take a journey to Rome to speak with the Pope, and"—

"Hang the Pretender twice over, and the Pope three times!" thundered his father.

"Hardly necessary, Sir, though you might find it agreeable," observed Harry, in his courtly way. "Moreover, 'tis thought he is gathering an army, wherewith he means to come against our coasts, if any evil should chance to Her Majesty."

"Let him come!" growled the Squire. "We'll send him packing in half the time! Anything else?"

"I see nothing of import," replied Harry, handing the newspaper to him.

"Who is Dr. Sacheverell, Harry?" asked Celia from the window, where she sat with her work.

"There is but little regarding him," was the answer. "He is of Derbyshire family, and was sometime tutor at Oxford. 'Twas on the 5th of November, Gunpowder Plot day last, that he preached before the corporation of London, saith one of the newspapers—I brought the *News-Letter* as well as the *Gazette*—and speaking upon 'perils among false brethren,' which he chose for his discourse, he denounced the Bishops and the Lord Treasurer,[13] and spake of the Lords who aided in the Revolution as men that had done unpardonable sin."

"Where is all that in the *Gazette*?" asked the Squire, turning the little sheet of paper about, and looking down the columns to catch the name of the obnoxious preacher.

"Not in the *Gazette*, what I said last, Sir," answered Harry; "'tis in the sermon, whereof I brought a copy, thinking that you might wish to see it. The bookseller of whom I had it told me that a prodigious number had been sold. Methinks he said thirty thousand."

"Thirty thousand sermons!" exclaimed Lucy, under her breath.

"Leather and prunella!" observed the Squire from behind his *Gazette*.

"Maybe so, Sir," responded Harry, very civilly. "Yet a sermon sold by the thousand, one would think, should be worth reading."

"Hold your tongue, lad! men don't buy what is worth reading by the cart-load!" growled the Squire. "'Tis only trash that is disposed of in that way."

"Very likely, Sir," responded Harry as before. "Yet give me leave to ask how many prayer-books have been printed in England since the reign of Queen Elizabeth?"

The Squire only grunted, being deep in the *Gazette*, and Harry turned his attention elsewhere.

"I should like to have heard Dr. Sacheverell," said Celia, timidly.

"Nonsense, Celia!" answered Isabella from her embroidery-frame. "You don't want to hear a man preach treason!"

"I was not thinking of the treason," sighed Celia.

"Celia, why do you want to hear Dr. Sacheverell?" asked Charley, as he sat on the step of the dais which elevated the window above the rest of the chamber.

Celia hesitated, colored, and went on with her work without answering. She and Charley were alone in the room.

"If you wanted to hear what he had to say about what they call treason, you don't need to be afraid of telling *me*," said Charley. "I don't know whether I shall not take up with treason myself."

"O Charley!" exclaimed Celia. "Don't talk in that way. Think how angry Father would be if he heard you!"

"O Celestina!" exclaimed Charley in his turn. This was his pet name for his favorite sister. Had she possessed a long name, he would probably have abbreviated it; as she had a short one, he extended it. "O Celestina! I am so tired of being good! I am tired of Sundays, and grammar, and the catechism, and sermons, and keeping things tidy, and going to church, and being scolded, and—I'm tired of everything!" said Charley, suddenly lumping together the remainder of his heterogeneous catalogue.

"Charley!" said Celia, slowly and wonderingly.

"I am! And I am half determined to go off, and have no more of it! Father may say what he likes about treason, and hang the Pretender as often as he pleases; but I say 'tis a grand thing to think of the King's son, whom we have kicked out, living on charity in a foreign land, and trying with such wonderful patience to recover the throne of his fathers! I should like to be with him, and bivouac—isn't that what Harry calls it?—bivouac in forests, and march on day after day, always seeing something new, and then at last have a battle! Wouldn't it be glorious?"

"For you to fight with Harry, and one of you kill the other? No, I don't think it would."

"I didn't say anything about fighting with Harry," resumed Charley, a little sulkily. "No, I should not like that. But as to anything else, I just tell you, Celia, that if some day I am not to be found, you will know I am gone to St. Germains to fight for the King—the King!" And Charley drew himself up at least two inches as he said the last words.

"Hush, Charley, do!"

"I won't hush! And I really mean it!"

"Charley, I shall have to tell Father, if you talk any more nonsense like that!" said Celia, really alarmed.

"Celia, do you know what it is to feel downright wicked?" asked Charley, in a different tone.

"Yes—no—not as you mean, I fancy."

"No, I don't think you do. I wish you did."

"Charley!"

"Well, I mean, I wish I didn't! Father talks of hanging things; I feel sometimes as if I could hang everything."

"Me?" demanded Celia, smiling.

"No, I wouldn't hang you; and I wouldn't hang Mother," pursued Charley, meditatively. "Nor Bay Fairy, nor Lucy, nor the black cat; nor Harry—I think not; nor Cicely, except first thing in a morning when she rouses me up out of a nice sleep, or last thing at night when she packs me off to bed whether I will or not. I am not sure about Father. As to the rest, they would have to look out for themselves."

"Now, Charley!" said Celia, laughing.

"Celia, you don't know what it is to feel wicked. I wish I could get something to make me—not keep good, because I have to do—but make me want to be good."

Celia was silent for a moment. Then she said, very slowly and hesitatingly, "Charley, I suppose we shall only want to be good, when we want to please God, and to be like Jesus Christ."

"I don't know anything about that," said Charley, turning round to look at her.

"I know very little about it," said Celia, blushing. "But I have begun to think, Charley—only just lately—that we ought to care more about pleasing God than anything else."

"Is that what makes you such a darling of a sister?" said Charley. "I'll think about it if it be. You are always trying to please everybody, it seems to me. But I don't think I could keep it up, Celia. I don't care much about pleasing anybody but myself."

"Charley," said his sister, with a great effort, "there is a verse in the Bible which I was reading this morning—'Even Christ pleased not Himself.'" She spoke very shyly; but she loved this younger brother dearly, and longed to see him grow up a really great and good man. And she found it easier to talk to Charley, Lucy, and Cicely than to others. She would not have dared to quote a text to Henrietta.

"Well, but you know we can't be like Him," said Charley, reverently.

"We must, before we can go to heaven."

"Well, then, I might as well give up at once!" answered Charley, beginning to whistle.

"Oh no, Charley dear!" said Celia, so earnestly, that Charley stopped whistling, and looked up in her face. "He will help us to do right if we try. I do want you to grow up a good man, loving God and doing good to men. Won't you ask Him, Charley?"

"Well, perhaps—I'll see about it," said Charley, as his sister stroked the light hair affectionately away from his brow. "At any rate, I don't think I'll go to St. Germains just yet. You are a dear old Celestina!"

[1] Tennyson, "Idylls of the King"—Enid.

[2] The alphabet, which in the hornbooks was surmounted with a cross and the lines:

"Christ's cross be my speed
In these letters to my need."

[3] Heb. x. 25.

[4] Matt. vii. 11.

[5] Luke xi. 13.

[6] Patches, scraps of black court-plaster, or gummed velvet cut in shapes—stars, crescents, circles, lozenges, and even more elaborate and absurd forms—became fashionable about 1650, and remained so for many years. In the reign of Queen Anne, ladies showed their political proclivities by their patches—those who patched on one side of the face only being Tories, and on the other, Whigs. Neutrals patched on both sides.

[7] Thomas Aquinas bore this flattering epithet.

[8] 2 Cor. v. 21.

[9] John ii. 25.

[10] John xvii. 3.

[11] Isaiah lxiv. 6.

[12] Henry Sacheverell, born at Marlborough in 1672, began life as a Whig, but finding that unprofitable, became a fervid Tory and High Churchman. He was presented to St. Saviour's, Southwark, in 1705. His celebrated trial, which followed the

sermon noticed above, began February 27, and ended March 20, 1710. The Queen presented him to St. Andrew's, Holborn, in 1713; and after some years spent in comparative obscurity, he died on the 5th of June 1724.

[13] Sidney Godolphin, Earl of Godolphin.

II.

A BAT BEHIND THE WAINSCOT.

"He gazed on the river that gurgled by,
   But he thought not of the reeds;
He clasped his gilded rosary,
   But he did not tell the beads:
If he looked to the heaven, 'twas not to invoke
   The Spirit that dwelleth there;
If he opened his lips, the words they spoke
   Had never the tone of prayer.
A pious priest might the Abbot seem,—
   He had swayed the crosier well;
But what was the theme of the Abbot's dream,
   The Abbot were loath to tell."

                      W. M. PRAED.

"Harry!" said Celia, coming down with her cloak and hood on, one fine day in the following spring, "one of the pegs in the closet in our room is loose; will you make it secure for us while we are walking?"

The whole family were going for an excursion in the woods, as it was Lucy's birthday, and Harry's sprained ankle kept him at home. He could stand without pain for a short time, but could not walk far; and a horse would not have been able to carry him through the thick underwood. Delay was suggested; but, as Lucy very truly, if somewhat selfishly, asserted, another day would not have been her birthday. All things considered, the Squire had decided that the excursion should not be put off, and the party set out accordingly. After they were gone, Harry went up to Celia's room, to see what would be required. The setting to rights of the offending peg was soon effected. He was retiring from the closet, when he set his foot upon a little round substance, which he guessed to be the head of a nail sticking up from the floor of the closet close to one of the back panels.

"Ah!" observed Harry, apostrophizing the nail, "you must come out. You will be tearing Miss Lucy's gown, and she won't like having to mend it."

Harry accordingly proceeded to attempt the removal of the nail. But he found to his surprise that neither his hand nor his tools seemed strong enough to pull it out. Its position, close to the back of the closet, made it all the more difficult. Was it really a nail? He looked at it more closely. It had a brass head, and Harry came to the conclusion that it was a knob placed there on purpose. But for what purpose? It would go neither backwards nor forwards; but when Harry tried to pull it to one side, to his astonishment a little door flew open, so neatly fitted into the closet floor as to defy detection, the nail or knob being fixed in the midst. Below the little door appeared a tiny box, with a second brass knob fixed in it. At the bottom was a brass plate, from a small round hole in which the knob protruded.

"Now then," remarked Harry, "let me look at you. What are *you* for?"

He very soon discovered that upon touching it. The moment that the little knob was pushed inwards, the whole panel in the back of the closet suddenly sprang back, showing that it was in reality a concealed door, the catch closing it having been liberated by pressing the little knob in the tiny box. What was behind the door it was impossible to see without a candle, for the closet was a deep one, and the opening of its door cut off the light from the bedroom window. Harry quietly came out of the closet, locked the bedroom door, and went to his own chamber to fetch a taper and his sword. He was determined to follow up his discovery.

The light of the candle revealed no array of skeletons, but a narrow passage, which he saw, on stepping into it, to be the head of a very narrow spiral staircase. With the candle in one hand, and the sword in the other, Harry, in whose mental vocabulary fear had no place, calmly walked down the staircase. The excitement of the adventure overpowered any pain which he felt from his ankle. A faint smell of dried roses met him at the foot of the stairs. On the right hand stood a heavy door. Harry gave it a strong push, and being unlatched, it slowly opened and admitted him. He stood in a very small square chamber. There was no window. A table was in the middle, two chairs stood against the wall, and in one corner was a handsome chest on which two books were lying. All the furniture was of carved oak. Harry opened the books, and then the chest. The former were a Latin missal and breviary; the latter was occupied by a set of church vestments, a crucifix, a thurible, and sundry other articles, whose use was no mystery to the travelled discoverer.

"So you are a priest's hiding-place," said Harry, dryly, to the concealed chamber. "So much is plain. They say mass at this table. Well, I did not know we had one of these at Ashcliffe. I wonder how many years it is since this was inhabited? I protest!—upon my word, I do believe it is inhabited now!"

He had suddenly perceived that while on the stairs the dust lay thick, there was none resting on the furniture within the chamber. Books, chest, chairs, table—all bore evidence of having been used so recently, that no considerable accumulation of dust had time to gather on them. Harry looked coolly around, and descried another door, opposite to the one by which he had entered. Opening this, he found himself at the summit of a second spiral staircase, down which he went—down, down, until he fancied that he must be descending below the foundations of the house. At length the spiral form of the staircase ended, and a further flight of steps ran straight down. Harry wondered whether he was going into the bowels of the earth, but he kept onwards, until once more stopped by a door. This door opened readily, being unlatched like the others, and he looked out into darkness. Casting his eyes upwards, he saw, in the direction wherein he supposed the sky should be, a small round patch of blue.

"Well, you were a cunning fox who planned this hole!" thought he. "One end opens into the closet in Celia's room, and the other into the old well in the garden. There must be some means of climbing up out of the well, I presume, and the worthy gentleman who makes this his abode is probably well acquainted with them. I wonder if my father and mother know of this? If not, I had better make up the entrance, and not tell them. My mother would be too frightened to sleep in any peace if she knew that such a place was hidden in the house, and my father would rouse all Devonshire about it. I wonder, too, who they are that use it? Are they still priests, or Jacobite fugitives? or are they highwaymen? Whatever they be, I must make up this door, as soon as I am a little better able to exert myself."

Thus thinking, Harry withdrew from the secret chamber, and regained Celia's room. Pulling to the door, he found that the panel and the hidden box closed each with a spring. He left the bedroom, and went down-stairs meditating upon his discovery.[1]

A fortnight later, when his ankle had regained strength, he took the opportunity, when both the sisters were out, to make a second visit to the secret chamber. He found its arrangements slightly altered—a proof that its mysterious occupant had been there within a few days. The books were gone, and one of the chairs was now standing by the table. Harry dragged some ponderous logs of wood to the outer door which led into the well, and by means of these barricaded the door effectually against any return of the refugee.

During the interval he had taken the opportunity of asking a few questions of different persons, which might give him some idea whether they were aware of the existence of this concealed chamber.

"Mother," he asked, one evening, when Madam Passmore had been lamenting the sad fact that things wore out much sooner than when she was a girl, "had you ever any of that fine carved furniture like Madam Harvey's?"

"No, my dear, not a bit," said his mother.

"Bell," he asked, on another occasion, "do you ever hear rats or mice in your wainscot?"

"Oh, they tease me infinitely!" answered Isabella. "They make noises behind the wainscot till I cannot sleep, and for the last week I have put cotton wool in my ears to keep out the sound."

"Cicely," he inquired, lastly, "did you ever see a ghost?"

"No, Master Harry, I never have," replied Cicely, mysteriously, thus hinting that there might be some people who had done so. "I never see one, nor never want. But they do haunt old houses, that's a truth."

"How do you know that if you never saw one?" laughed Harry.

"Well, my dear!" exclaimed Cicely, "if you'd a been down with me in the scullery one night last week—I couldn't sleep, and I went down for to get a bit of victuals, and washed my hands in the scullery—I say, if you'd a-heard the din they made over my head, you might have thought somewhat."

"Who made it, Cicely?"

"Them!" said Cicely, in a mysterious whisper. "Nay, I never saw none, but my grandmother's aunt's mother-in-law, she did."

"Ah! she is a good way off us," said Harry, satirically. "But you know, this house is rather too new for ghosts. A fine old castle, now, with all manner of winding stairs and secret passages—that would be the place to see a ghost."

"Eh! my dear, don't you give me the horrors!" cried Cicely. "Why, I could never sleep in my bed if I lived in a place where them secret places and such was—no, never lie quiet, I couldn't! Nay, Master Harry, nobody never seed no ghosteses in this house. I've lived here eight-and-twenty year come Martlemas, and I ought to know."

"And pray, Cicely, who was your great-grandmother's first cousin's niece, or whatever she were? and what did she see?"

"My grandmother's aunt's mother-in-law, Master," corrected Cicely. "She see a little child in a white coat."

"How very extraordinary!" commented Harry gravely.

"Master Harry, I'm certain sure you don't believe a word of it, for all you look so grave," said old Cicely, shaking her head sorrowfully.

"I can't say that I do at present. But you see I have not heard the particulars yet."

"Then you shall, Master," said old Cicely, rather excitedly. "'Twas at Dagworth in Suffolk, in the house of one Master Osborne, where she served as chambermaid. He had been a while in the house, had the ghost, and nobody couldn't get to see him—no, not the parson, though he used to reason with him on doctrine and godliness. They oft heard him a-calling for meat and drink, with the voice of a child of one year, which meat being put in a certain place was no more seen. He said his name was Malke. And after a while, one day she spoke to him and begged him for a sight of him, promising not to touch him. Whereupon he appeared to her as a young child in a white coat, and told her that he was a mortal child, stole by the good-folk,[2] and that he was born at Lanaham, and wore a hat that made him invisible, and so, quoth he, doth many another. He spoke English after the manner of the country, and had many roguish and laughter-stirring sayings, that at last they grew not to fear him."[3]

"How long did he stay there?"

"Now you are asking me more than I know, Master. But don't you never go to say again that there's no such things as ghostesses, when my grandmother's aunt's mother-in-law seen him with her own two eyes!"

"And Mr. Osborne kept no dogs, or cats, I suppose?"

"Master Harry, you don't believe it! Well, to be sure, I never did! You'll be saying next thing that there's no such things as the good-folk, when I've seen their dancing-rings on the grass many a hundred times! I'm sore afeared, Master Harry, that it haven't done you no good a-going for a soldier—I am."

And Harry found that all his arguments produced no further effect than the conviction of old Cicely that he had been in bad company. From the information thus gained, however, he formed these conclusions:—First, His mother knew nothing about the secret chamber. Secondly, Cicely was equally ignorant. Thirdly, It was situated, as he had surmised—above the scullery or behind it—probably both—and below his sister Isabella's bedroom. Fourthly, It had been inhabited as recently as the preceding week. All the more reason, he thought, for stopping up the means of ingress; and all the more for not revealing to old Cicely that her ghost was in all probability a Popish priest.

On the evening of the spring day upon which Harry thus barred the refugee out of his hiding-place, Celia was strolling through the park alone. She fed the fawns and the swans on the ornamental water, and wandered on with no definite object, until she reached the boundary of her father's grounds. She sat down on the grass near a large laurel, and became lost in thought. There happened at this place to be a small gap in the hedge near her, through which her position was plainly observable from the road. She started as she heard a sudden appeal made to her:

"Young Madam, pray you a penny, for the love of God!"

Celia turned and looked at the speaker. He was a dark, good-looking man, dressed in clothes which had once been handsome, but were now ragged and thread-bare. His eyes, dark, sunken, and very bright, were fixed earnestly upon her. She held out to him the penny for which he asked, when he said, abruptly:

"Your pardon, Madam! but are you Squire Passmore's daughter?"

"Yes, I am Celia Passmore," she replied, thinking nothing of the query.

"Be not too certain of it," answered the stranger, softly. "God and our Lady bless you!"

And gently taking the offered coin from Celia's hand, he withdrew before she could recover from her horror at the discovery that she had been conversing with a Papist. When she recovered herself, his words came back to her with strange meaning. The blessing she took to be merely his way of thanking her for the alms which she had bestowed. But had he not told her not to be too sure of something? Of what? Had she said anything to him beyond telling her name? Celia concluded that the poor fellow must have been wrong in his head, and began to feel very compassionate towards him. She sauntered back to the house, and into old Cicely's room, where she found its occupant mending stockings, with her old brown Bible lying open on the table before her.

"Cicely, I have had such an odd adventure."

"Have you so, Mrs. Celia? What was it, my dear?"

"Why, a poor man begged of me over the hedge, and said such strange things!—asked me my name, and told me not to be too sure of it! Was it not droll?"

Instead of a laugh rising to her lips, as Celia expected, a strange light sprang to old Cicely's eyes as she lifted her head and gazed at her. Not a glad light— far from it; a wild, startled, sad expression, which Celia could not understand.

"Ay, sweetheart!" said the old woman, in a voice not like her usual tones. "Did he so? And what manner of man?"

"Oh, not bad-looking," answered Celia. "A comely man, with black hair and eyes. His clothes had been good, but they were very bad now, and he was a Papist, for he said, 'Our Lady bless you.'"

"A Papist!" cried old Cicely, in a voice of horror.

"Yes," said Celia, smiling at her tone. "Why, Cicely, are you afraid of being murdered because there is a Papist in the county?"

"Eh no, my dear," answered old Cicely, slowly; "that's not it. Poor soul! God comfort you when you come to know!"

"Come to know what, Cicely?"

"What you've never been told yet, my dear—and yet he told you, if you did but know."

"I don't understand you, Cicely."

"I am glad you don't, my dear."

"But tell me what you mean."

"No, Mrs. Celia. Ask Madam, if you must. Tell her what you have told me. But if you'll take my counsel, you'll never ask her as long as you live."

"Cicely, what riddles are you talking?" replied Celia. "I will ask Mother."

The opportunity for doing so came the next day, about an hour after dinner. Madam Passmore sat knitting peacefully in her especial chair in the parlor. Henrietta was absent, superintending household affairs; and Isabella, with the velvet ornaments tied round her neck and arms, was occupied as usual with her endless embroidery-frame.

"We shall have an assembly on Monday," observed Madam Passmore, speaking to nobody in particular.

"That is right!" said Isabella, rather less languidly than usual. "I am so glad! Who are coming, Mother?"

"Dr. Braithwaite and his wife, Squire and Madam Harvey, and Squire and Madam Rowe."

"Nobody else?" asked Isabella, in a disappointed tone.

"Well, that I don't know, child," answered her mother. "Maybe some of the young folks may come from over the hill."

"Are they coming to dinner?"

"No, for the afternoon. Put on your blue satin petticoats, girls, and your best gowns; and Bell, bid Harry to have ready the basset-table in the corner. We will draw it out when 'tis wanted."

"But you will have dancing, Mother?" said Isabella, in a tone which indicated that her enjoyment would be spoilt without it.

"Please yourself, child," said Madam Passmore. "I don't know who you'll dance with, unless Johnny and Frank Rowe should come. The old folks will want no dancing, I should think; they would rather have a quiet game."

"How tiresome!" said Isabella.

"Well, I don't think so," replied Madam Passmore. "When you come to my time of life, you won't want to be sent spinning about the room like so many teetotums. Yet I was reckoned a good dancer once, to be sure."

"And you liked it, Mother?" asked Celia.

"Yes, I suppose I did. I was young and foolish," said Madam Passmore, with a little sigh. "But really, when you come to think it over, 'tis only fit for children, I think. I would rather have a good game of hunt-the-slipper—there is more sense in it, and quite as much moving about, and a great deal more fun."

"So very vulgar!" sighed Isabella, contemptuously.

"Very vulgar, Madam!" bowed Harry, who had entered while his mother was speaking; "almost as vulgar as eating and sleeping."

"I wish you would go away, Harry. I don't like arguing with you."

"By all means, Madam," said Harry, bowing himself out of the parlor.

Madam Passmore laughed. "Well, girls," she said, "I think I shall have to give the ladies some tea, though it is a new-fangled drink; and as you are used to pour it for your sisters, Bell, you had better take the charge of it."

"Very well, Mother."

"And, Celia, can you get some flowers and bits of green from the evergreens? They will look better than nothing in the jars. That great laurel at the other end of the park can spare some, and as you take long walks, I leave that to you."

"O Mother!" suddenly cried Celia, in a voice which showed that her thoughts were on anything but evergreens, "I want to tell you something. Yesterday I was sitting by that great laurel, when a man begged of me through the hedge. I gave him a trifle, and he asked me if I were Squire Passmore's daughter. I told him yes, my name was Celia Passmore; and he told me in answer not to be too certain of it. Was it not droll? But the thing yet more strange was, that when I told Cicely of it, she said I had better tell you—no, she said I had better not tell you—but that you could tell me what it meant if I asked you. So very strange! What did it mean, Mother?"

Madam Passmore was silent for a few moments. When she spoke, it was to say, in quite another tone, softer and tenderer than her previous one, "Thou art nineteen, Celia, my dear."

"Yes, Mother," answered Celia, rather surprised at the information. "I was nineteen on the third of June."

"Ay, born the same year as Bell," said Madam Passmore, gravely, and Celia thought a little sadly. "Well, I will tell thee, my dear, for thou oughtest to know, and thou art now a woman grown. Ay, I will tell thee, but wait until Tuesday. After the assembly will be better."

Squire Passmore was riding leisurely home, after having himself carried the invitation to his old friends Mr. and Mrs. Harvey of Ellersley. He had nearly reached his own gates, when he suddenly pulled up to avoid running over a pedestrian. The latter met him as he turned a corner, and was apparently too deeply engaged in his occupation—that of searching into a portfolio in his hand—to see any one coming. He was a young man of some six-and-twenty years, and the brightness of his dark, penetrating eyes struck the Squire as he looked up and hastily drew to one side with an apology.

"Your servant, Sir! I beg your pardon for my carelessness."

"Another time," said the Squire, in his hearty voice, "I should advise you to delay looking into your portfolio till you are round the corner."

"Thank you for your advice, which I shall certainly take," returned the young man. "Might I ask—can I be mistaken in thinking that I am addressing Squire Passmore, of Ashcliffe Hall?"

"My name is John Passmore," said the Squire, "and I live at Ashcliffe. Do you want anything with me?"

"I thought I could not be mistaken," answered the young man, with a very deferential bow. "My object in addressing you, Sir, is to request the very great favor of your permission to take a few sketches of your fine old Hall. I am sketching in this neighborhood in the employ of Sir Godfrey Kneller, the great London painter—you have surely heard of him—and if"—

"A good sensible Whig," interrupted the Squire. "If you want to sketch the Hall for him, you shall have leave to draw all the four sides; if you like. You are a painter, are you? I thought you must be some sort of a moonstruck fellow—painter, author, or what not—that you did not see me coming."

"Permit me to express my very great obligations," said the artist. "Might I venture so far as to ask your leave to take one sketch inside? I have been told there is a fine carved oak staircase"—

"Come and dine with me," replied the Squire, heartily, "and sketch the staircase by all means. We dine at twelve o'clock—old-fashioned folks, Mr.—
—I have not the pleasure"—

"Stevens, Sir—Cuthbert Stevens, at your service—and very much"—

"Ah! odd name, Cuthbert, but an old name—yes, a good old name. To-morrow at twelve, Mr. Stevens—very glad to see you."

And away rode the hospitable and unsuspicious man, leaving on the face of Cuthbert Stevens a look of amused contempt.

"'Moonstruck!'" he whispered to himself. "We shall see which is the cleverer, John Passmore, Esquire—we shall see."

"Lucy, my dear," said the Squire to his wife when he came in, "I have asked a gentleman to dinner to-morrow;—a painter—making sketches for Sir Godfrey Kneller—monstrous clever fellow!—take your portrait in no time—wants to draw the Hall."

When the Squire conveyed his information in this abrupt and detached style, Madam Passmore knew from experience that he was not altogether satisfied with his own act, and desired to justify himself in his own eyes. He was, in truth, beginning to feel rather uneasy. Though he called the artist a "monstrous clever fellow," he had not seen a single sketch; he had taken the man on his own word, and at his own valuation; he had yielded to the charm of his voice and manner; and now that this was withdrawn, he began to doubt whether he had done well in introducing a complete stranger into the bosom of his family. So Madam Passmore, seeing this, and also acting on her favorite maxim of "what must be, must," quietly said, "Very well, John," and left her husband to his own devices.

Noon came, and with it Mr. Cuthbert Stevens. The Squire inspected him as he entered, and could find nothing with which to be dissatisfied. His taste in dress was excellent, his manners were faultless; and the Squire began to think his first thoughts had been the best. Dinner passed without a single *contretemps*. The stranger talked with the Squire about hunting and poaching, and was quite alive to the enormities of the latter; to Charley upon snaring rabbits and making rabbit-hutches; to Henrietta and Isabella upon the fashions and London life (with which he seemed perfectly familiar); and told Madam Passmore of a new method of distilling cordial waters of which she had not previously heard. Of Celia he took little apparent notice. The family began to think that they had lighted on a very agreeable and accomplished man; and when dinner was over, and the sketch of the staircase made—(which latter the Squire, though no artist, could see was a faithful copy, and pronounced "as like as two peas")—the stranger was pressed to remain longer, but this offer, with many thanks, Mr. Stevens declined. His time, he said, was growing short, and he must make all possible use of it. He had still several sketches to complete before quitting the neighborhood; but he could assure Mr. Passmore that he would never forget the kindness shown him at Ashcliffe, and would inform Sir Godfrey of it on his return to London.

"Well, Sir, if you will remain no longer," said Madam Passmore, her kind heart compassionating his probably precarious circumstances, "you will put one of these raised pies in your pocket for your journey? I think you liked them at dinner."

The artist gratefully accepted the offer. With a very respectful bow he took leave, Charley volunteering to accompany him to the gate. There was a good deal of conversation on the way through the park, chiefly on Charley's side, the stranger contenting himself with an occasional simple and careless query. At the gate they parted—Charley to run home at the top of his speed, and Mr. Stevens to walk rather quickly for half a mile in the direction of Exeter. Having so done, he turned aside into a coppice bordering on the road, and, slackening his pace, commenced whistling a lively air. The verse was still unfinished, when an answering whistle of the same tune was heard, and the man who had accosted Celia over the hedge came in view, advancing to meet him.

"Well, Gilbert!" was the artist's greeting, "any good news?"

"The same that I left you with, Father," said the elder man in reply; "and if you call it good news, you have the heart of a stone. I am all but famished, and sick-tired of being cooped up in that miserable hole."

"And the inquiries, Gilbert? You told me all that before, you know."

"And much you cared about it!" answered Gilbert, ill-humoredly, kicking some dead sticks out of his way. "Inquiries! no, of course nothing has come of them, except what we knew before: that she passes as the third daughter, and she is short and dark."

Stevens sat down on a green knoll. "What a surpassing clever man you are, Gilbert Irvine!" he observed.

"Well, Father Cuthbert, you are uncommon complimentary," remonstrated Gilbert, leaning back against a tree. "Seven mortal weeks have I been cooped up in that dog-hole, with as much to eat as a sparrow, and wearing myself out, dodging about to get a glimpse of this girl—all to please my Lady and you; never slept in a bed except just these four nights we have been at Exeter—and the only reward of my labors which I have seen anything of yet, is to be told I am an ass for my pains: because, of course, that is what you mean."

"My excellent Gilbert, your temper is a little below perfection. You shall see what a mistake you have made. Look at me. I have just been dining with Squire Passmore."

Gilbert's mouth opened for an exclamation, but shut again without one, as if his astonishment passed the power of words to express.

"Now why could not you have done the same? Seven weeks you have been here, as you say, and caught one glimpse of the girl; and I, who have not been here as many days, have already seen and spoken to her, and found out more about her than you have. And I have dined like a prince in addition, while you are pretty near starving, Gilbert."

"Nice consolation that is to give to a famished wretch!" snarled Gilbert. "Father Cuthbert, you have a heart of stone."

"Not quite so hard as that, my friend," answered Stevens, feeling in his pocket, and bringing out of it the pie. "I only wished to show you what a very ingenious fellow you were. Eat that."

"Where did you get it?" was all the thanks Gilbert vouchsafed.

"It was offered me, and I accepted it," said Stevens. "I never say 'No, thank you!' to anything good. Always take all you can get, Gilbert."

Gilbert was too busy with the pie to answer.

"Now listen, Gilbert. I was wise enough to take no notice of the girl that any could see: but I studied her quietly, and I sounded the youngest brother well. I am satisfied that none of them know who she is, and I imagine only the parents know any thing at all. She seems very comfortable, and well taken care of, and will probably be in no haste to leave; at least so I judge from what I can see of her disposition, which is quiet and timid. Then"—

"Father Cuthbert, I wish you would wait a minute. 'Tis ill talking between a full man and a fasting.' Do let me finish this pie in peace."

"Finish it, Gilbert, and much good may it do you."

"But how did you get in?" was the question that followed the last mouthful of the pie.

"I represented myself as an artist, in the employ of Sir Godfrey Kneller "—

"Did you ever see him?"

"I once had him shown to me in London. And I asked leave to draw the Hall, and the staircase inside. I knew, after that, Mr. Passmore would ask me to dinner."

"Can you draw?"

"If I could not, my friend, I should have been unwise to take that character. I can do a good many things."

"You are a more ingenious man than I am, Father."

"You are not far wrong there, Gilbert," complacently assented the disguised priest.

"But I cannot believe, Father," pursued Gilbert, "that you came over from France only to see Sir Edward's daughter."

"I protest, Gilbert, you are even more surpassing than I took you for! It must be your conversation with that Jezebel of yours which has dulled your wits. You were a sharper fellow once."

"You are welcome to revile my wife as much as you please, Father," said Gilbert, calmly. "I can't think how in the world I ever came to marry the daughter of an old, ranting, canting Covenanter. The devil must have set me up to it."

"Probably he did, my friend," was the reply of Cuthbert. "But to relieve your mind: I came here on secret service—you will not ask me what it was. Suffice it you to know that it was at once for Church and King."

"Well!" sighed Gilbert, "the Church is infallible—is she not?—and immortal: she will get along all right. But for the King"—

An expressive pantomime of Gilbert's hands and shoulders completed the sentence.

"Faint-hearted, Gilbert?" asked Stevens, with a smile.

"Faint-hoping, Father," said he. "The King will never 'have his ain again.' Ay! that song you were whistling by way of signal is to me the saddest of all our songs. 'Tis easy to chant 'It was a' for our richtfu' King,'—or I can even stand 'Lilliburlero;' but 'The King shall have his ain again'—it but saddens me, Father Cuthbert. He will never have it."

"Why, Gilbert, has your solitude made you hopeless? You used to have more faith in right, and in the final triumph of the good cause."

"The cause is lost, Father Cuthbert," said Gilbert, stooping to pick up one of the dry twigs which lay before him. "'Tis as dead and dry as this branch; and as easily to be broken by the Princess and her Ministers, or by the Elector of Hanover and his, as I can break this—so!"

And the broken twig fell at Stevens' feet.

"Come, Gilbert, come!" said Stevens, encouragingly. "Remember how many friends the King has throughout England, and Scotland, and Ireland."

"Friends! what are they worth?" asked the other. "Good to sing 'Awa' Whigs, awa'!' or to pass their glasses over the water-jug when they say, 'The King, God bless him!'[4] But how many of them are ready to put their hands in their pockets to maintain your good cause? How many are ready to melt down their plate, as their fathers and ours did for King Charles? How many would die for the King now, as for his grandfather then?"

"*That* cause triumphed, Gilbert," said Stevens, suggestively.

"Did it?" answered Gilbert, more suggestively still. "How much worse had we been off now, Father Cuthbert—how far different, if the one at St. James's had been called Richard Cromwell instead of Anne Stuart? Trust me, England will henceforth be constant but to one thing—her inconstancy. She will go on, as she hath gone, from bad to worse, with short reactions every now and then. First King Charles—then my Lord Protector—then a little fit of reaction, and King Charles again. Then comes King James, and wounds her pride by being really a King and not a puppet, and off she goes to Dutch William—my Lord Protector over again. And now, the Princess Anne"—

"And after her, Gilbert?"

"After her? The saints know!—at least I hope they do; for I am sure I don't. But if these fellows had the King in to-morrow, they would kick him out again the day after."

"Probably," rejoined Stevens, calmly. "However, it does not much matter to me. I have a safe refuge in France in either case—my Lady Ingram's income to draw upon if we succeed—and, if we fail—well, I have friends on the other side. And at the worst, the Jesuit College at Rome would provide me with a shelter for my old age."

"Yes, there is no fear for you, Father," said Gilbert. "But we poor wretches, who have not the good fortune to be of your Order—we are proscribed exiles. Should we have been anything worse under Oliver?"

"Why, you might very likely have been in the pillory," said Stevens, "and had an ear or two less than now. And you might have been at Tyburn."

Gilbert took no notice of this flattering allusion. He answered as if he were pursuing his previous train of thought:

"No, the King will never 'have his ain again.' There are two things that England has come to value above even her throne and her peace: these are her Protestantism and her liberties. For these, and these alone, she will fight to the death. Of course the two monsters cannot live long together; the one must devour the other in the end. And whether heresy will swallow liberty, or liberty eat up heresy,—our great-grandsons may see, but we scarcely shall."

"On what does it depend, Gilbert?" asked Stevens, who seemed at once curious to draw out his companion's ideas, and reluctant to present his own.

"On the man who holds the helm when the two engage in battle," said Gilbert, thoughtfully.

"That is a battle that may last long," hinted Stevens.

"And probably will," replied the other. "But when the present notions shall have come to their full growth, as they must do—when the King shall have permanently become the servant of the Minister, and the Minister the mere agent of the mob—when, instead of '*Ego et Hex mens,*' it shall have become '*Nos*' without any '*Rex*' at all—when all men shake hands over the sepulchre of their religious prejudices and political passions—Father Cuthbert, then will be the triumph of the Catholic Church. If only she knew how to use the interval!—to be patient, never to be in a hurry—to instil gently and unperceivedly into men's minds the idea that all are equal, have equal rights, and are equally right—to work very slowly and very surely; she needs but one thing more, and that is the man at the helm. Let her choose the man. He must be plausible—able to talk well—to talk in a circle, and come to no conclusion—to throw dust in Protestant eyes: the bigger cloud he can raise the better. Let him hold out openly one hand to Protestantism, and give the other behind his back to Rome. When the foundation is so laid, and the man stands at the helm—our work is finished, Father Cuthbert. But I doubt if any Stuart will be reigning then—nay, I doubt if any will reign at all."

"So much for England, then!" responded Stevens, with a rather dubious smile. "And Scotland?—and Ireland?"

"Scotland!" said Gilbert, slowly. "I am a Scot, Father Cuthbert, though 'tis years since I saw Scotland. And I tell you, as a nation, we are hard-headed and long-sighted; and we do not as a rule take up with anything before testing it. But just as the sweetest-tempered man can be the most terrible when he is angry, so, when you can throw dust in a Scotchman's eyes, you make him blind indeed."

"And Ireland?" repeated Stevens.

"The cause was lost there, Father, on a certain 1st of July, more than twenty years ago. And as yet Ireland has been rather too busy setting her own house in order to have much leisure left to meddle with ours."

"You forget one thing, Gilbert," said Stevens, gravely. "Think how many Catholic emissaries we have in Ireland and Scotland, and how Catholic the Gaelic heart once was, and the Erse heart has ever been."

"Father Cuthbert, how many members of the Society of Jesus were in Oliver Cromwell's army?"

"A good many," admitted Stevens.

"Hundreds," resumed Gilbert.[5] "And do you think they did the cause any good?"

"Well, it scarce looked so at the time," said Stephens. "But in the end it seemed more like it."

"'Liberty' is our watchword now," said Gilbert. "Liberty to do anything and everything: which, of course, in six cases out of every ten, means to do wrong. So long as the Church is uppermost—despotism: she can allow no liberty. But let the Church be undermost, and she must set herself to obtain it by all means. Liberty for the sects, we ought never to forget, means liberty for the Church. And to the Church it is not of much consequence whether she herself, or her friend Liberty, devour the dying monster, Protestantism. When the Church sits once again on the throne of Great Britain, the first dish served up to her at her coronation banquet will be the dead body of her jackal, Liberty."

"Gilbert!" said Stevens, rising from his grassy seat, "you are not so stupid as I thought you. Unfortunately, your talents do not lie in the particular path which circumstances have marked out for you. But you have parts, Gilbert. Let us return to Ashcliffe."

"And go back to that dog-hole?" inquired Gilbert, suddenly subsiding into his former discontented self.

"I fear, my son Gilbert," said Stevens, placidly, "that the dog-hole will have to be your habitation for a few days longer. But be comforted, Gilbert. As soon as I can, I will take your place there."

"Hope you may enjoy it!" muttered Gilbert, as they emerged on the Exeter road.

---

[1] Evidence of twenty-one such concealed chambers will be found in *Notes and Queries* alone. They exist all over England, in old houses built between the time of Henry VIII. and that of James II.—possibly later still. I append the descriptions of the two which appear to have been most cleverly concealed and best preserved.

The first chamber is at Ingatestone Hall, Essex, which was anciently a grange belonging to the Abbot of Barking, and was in possession of the Petre family from the reign of Henry VIII. to about 1775. "The secret chamber at Ingatestone Hall was entered from a small room on the middle-floor, over one of the projections of the south front. It is a small room, attached to what was probably the host's bedroom.... In the south-east corner of this small room, on taking up a carpet the floor-boards were found to be decayed. The carpenter, on removing them, found a second layer of boards about a foot lower down. When these were removed, a hole or trap about two feet square, and a twelve-step ladder to descend into a room beneath, were disclosed.... The use of the chamber goes back to the reign of James I.... The hiding-place measures 14 feet in length, 2 feet 1 inch in width, and 10 feet in height. Its floor-level is the natural ground-line. The floor is composed of 9 inches of remarkably dry sand, so as to exclude damp or moisture."—*Notes and Queries*, 1st S., xi. 437.

The other example is at Irnham Hall, Lincolnshire. "The situation of this ingeniously-contrived place had been forgotten, though it was well known to exist somewhere in the mansion, till it was discovered a few years ago. In going round the chimney-stacks, it was observed that one of the chimneys of a cluster was without any smoke or any blackness, and as clean as when the masonry was new. This led to the conjecture that it was not in reality a chimney, but an open shaft to give light and air to the priest's hiding-place; yet so forming one of a group of chimneys as to obviate all suspicion of its real purpose. It was carefully examined, and the conjecture fully borne out by the discovery of the long-lost hiding-place. The opening into it was found by removing a beam behind a single step between two servants' bed-rooms. You then come to a panel which has a very small iron tube let into it, through which any message could be conveyed to the occupant of the hiding-place. This panel being removed, a ladder of four steps leads down into the secret chamber.... The hiding-place is 8 feet long by 5 feet broad, and just high enough to allow of standing upright."—*Notes and Queries*, 1st S., xii.

Other instances occur at Oxburgh Hall, Norfolk; Sawston Hall, Cambridgeshire; Coldham Hall, Suffolk; Maple Durham, Watcomb, and Ufton Court, Berkshire; Stonyhurst and Berwick Hall, Lancashire; Bourton, Gloucestershire; Henlip, Worcestershire; Chelvey Court, Somerset; Nether Witton, Northumberland; Paxhill, Sussex (built by Sir Andrew Borde, jester of Henry VIII., and the original of "Merry Andrew"); Treago, Hereford; Weybridge, Surrey; Woodcote, Hampshire; and elsewhere. In several of these instances the secret chamber was formed in the roof of the house, and in two cases at least it was accompanied by a small chapel.

[2] Fairies.

[3] The reader can appraise this ghost-story at what he thinks it worth. It is not the produce of the author's imagination, but may be found reported in the translation of the *Chronicon Roberti Montensis*, by John Stowe, Harl. MS., 545, fol. 190, *b*.

[4] In this way the more timid of the Jacobites drank the toast of "The King over the water."

[5] Dean Goode's "Rome's Tactics," pp. 50-53.

III.

ALONE IN THE WORLD.

"Speechless Sorrow sat with me;
I was sighing wearily:
Lamp and fire were out; the rain
Wildly beat the window-pane.
In the dark we heard a knock,
And a hand was on the lock;
One in waiting spake to me,
     Saying sweetly,
'I am come to sup with thee.'

"All my room was dark and damp,—
'Sorrow,' said I, 'trim the lamp;
Light the fire and cheer thy face;
Set the guest-chair in its place.'
And again I heard the knock;
In the dark I found the lock,—
'Enter, I have turned the key—
     Enter, stranger,
Who art come to sup with me.'

"Opening wide the door, He came,—
But I could not speak His name;
In the guest-chair took His place,—
Though I could not see His face:
When my cheerful fire was beaming,
When my little lamp was gleaming,
And the feast was spread for three,—
     Lo! my Master
Was the Guest that supped with me.
    HARRIET M'EWEN KIMBALL.

Grand beyond expression was Madam Passmore that Monday afternoon whereon her party was held. Her hair stood at the very least six inches above her head. Her petticoat was of crimson quilted satin, and she wore a yellow satin gown, edged with rich old point-lace. Large silver buckles decorated her shoes, and a lace *cornette* was perched upon the summit of her hair. A splendid fan, and a handkerchief nearly all lace, shared her left hand; and in her pocket, alas! dwelt a silver snuff-box. Her four daughters were dressed alike, in their blue satin petticoats and brocaded trains, with coral necklaces, and cherry-colored top-knots of ribbon instead of *cornettes* stood on the summit of their hair. They also displayed fans, Isabella making all manner of use of hers, and held handkerchiefs not quite so elaborate as their mother's. Their trains were not gathered up this evening, so that when they walked a grand display of brocade was made on the floor. About four o'clock, Dr. Braithwaite and his wife made their appearance. Mrs. Braithwaite was a modest, retiring little woman, holding in high reverence her big learned husband, but the fact of being constantly kept under the sound of quotations which she did not understand, gave her a scared, bewildered look which did not improve her countenance. She was quietly dressed in black, with lace tucker and ruffles, and a white top-knot on her hair, which, in comparison with that of Madam Passmore, was dressed quite low.

"Good-even, Madam, and the young ladies!" said Mrs. Braithwaite, courtesying nervously. "I hope I see you well in health?"

"Madam," said the Doctor, bowing low over the hand which Madam Passmore extended to him, "that most marvellous and mellifluent writer of poesy, of whom among the Grecian dramatists the fame hath transcended"—

"Squire and Madam Harvey!" said Robert, in a tone which drowned the Doctor's elaborate Greek compliment.

This lady and gentleman lived in the "great house" of the next parish. They were quiet people, who, having no children, had grown somewhat prim and precise; but they had honest and kindly hearts, and greeted their old friends, if somewhat stiffly, yet cordially. Squire and Madam Rowe, Mr. John Rowe, and Mrs. Anne Rowe, were next announced; and after a general salutation, the party sat round the fire in high-backed chairs, very stiff and uncomfortable. The table in the window held the tea-tray, and Cicely, who entered with the tea-pot, was welcomed by all parties, to whom she courtesied with "Hope I see you all well, Sirs and Madams!" Isabella, her train trailing after her, now approached the little table and poured out the tea. Cicely stood holding a waiter, on which, as each cup was filled, she carried it in turn to the person for whom it was intended. Nothing was eaten with the tea. Tea was tea in 1710, and nothing else.

Mr. John Rowe, *alias* Johnny, was a slim youth of eighteen, who had come to the party with the view of making himself agreeable to Isabella. He would scarcely have felt flattered if he had known how she regarded him. She despised him supremely, both on account of his slight juniority, and of his taste in dress. At this moment he wore yellow silk stockings, green breeches, a white waistcoat embroidered in blue, a gray silk coat heavily laced with silver, and a very large full-bottomed wig, of flaxen color, though his natural hair was almost black. As he had also dark eyes and black eyebrows, his wig certainly was not in the best taste. Isabella all but shuddered at his combination of colors as he advanced to salute her, and did not receive him by any means warmly—a calamity which he, poor innocent fellow, humbly set down to his want of personal merit, not knowing that it was caused by the deficiencies of his costume. Squire Passmore was nearly as smart as his young guest, but he was dressed with much better taste, in a dark green coat and breeches with silver lace, white waistcoat, and white silk stockings. The party sat still and sedately on their row of chairs round the fire—Mrs. Braithwaite eclipsed and silent, for Madam Passmore was on one side of her, in the yellow satin, and Madam Rowe on the other, attired in emerald green: these two ladies were talking across her. Further on was Madam Harvey in dark crimson, conversing with Mrs. Anne Rowe, who was dressed in simple white, and Henrietta, next to Squire Rowe. The younger daughters of Squire Passmore were out of the group, and so were John Rowe and Charley. As Celia crossed the room just behind the assembled elders, Madam Rowe's hand detained her.

"Come and talk with me, my dear. 'Tis an age since I saw you. You don't grow any taller, child!"

"I have done growing," said Celia, with a smile.

"Well, so I suppose. How different you are from all your sisters, to be sure! I am sure Mrs. Bell must be a head taller than you are."

"Not quite so much as that," said Celia, still smiling.

"Short and sweet, Madam Rowe!" observed Squire Harvey, who overheard her.

"Ay, I won't contradict you there," she said. "And how old are you now, my dear? Seventeen?"

"Nineteen, Madam."

"Dear me! well, how time does go! To be sure, you and your sister are just a year older than Johnny, I remember. You should hold yourself up more, my dear: always make the best of yourself. You don't bridle so well as you might, either.[1] Really, you use not all your advantages."

"Madam Rowe, that is what I am always telling her," said Isabella, with a faint assumption of energy, "and she takes no more notice"—

"Well, my dear," answered Madam Rowe, administering a dose of flattery, "you know we cannot all be as handsome as you."

Isabella bridled, colored, and remained, though silent, evidently not displeased.

Supper followed about six o'clock, and afterwards the basset-table was wheeled out by Harry, and the three Squires sat down with Dr. Braithwaite to enjoy their favorite game. After basset came prayers. As Dr. Braithwaite was present, of course he officiated; and, casting aside his cards, gravely took the Bible in his hand instead of them. A prayer followed—long, prolix, involved, and stony: more like a sermon than a prayer, nor a very simple sermon neither. The party now took their leave. Dr. and Mrs. Braithwaite walked to the vicarage, which was very near. As it was only a short distance from Ellersley to Ashcliffe, Squire Harvey and his wife came and returned in their coach; the distance to Marcombe was longer, and the Rowes were on horseback. Harry went out and assisted the ladies to mount, Mrs. Rowe riding behind her son, and Anne behind her father.

"Now, Miss Lucy, my dear, come you away to bed," said Cicely, taking sudden possession of that personage. "What could I have been thinking of not to come for you before, I should like to know? To think of you being up at this time! A quarter to nine, I do declare!"

"I don't know what you were thinking of, but I wish you would think about it every night!" answered Lucy, resigning herself to fate in the person of Cicely.

"Well, I shall go to bed also," said Isabella, yawning, and rising from the embroidery-frame. "I protest I am as tired as if it were Sunday evening! That John Rowe is the most tedious young man."

"You had better all go, my dears," responded Madam Passmore. "Good-night to you all. Good-night, Celia."

Celia fancied that her mother repeated the greeting to her with a tenderness in her voice which was scarcely usual with her. Was she thinking of the coming revelation?

She found Cicely helping Lucy to undress.

"Cicely," she asked, sitting down, "how do you pray?"

"Oh, that horrid Dr. Braithwaite!" cried Lucy. "I nearly fell asleep before he had half done."

"Make haste, Miss Lucy, my dear. You'd ought to have been a-bed long ago. How I pray, Mrs. Celia? Why, just like anybody else."

"Like Dr. Braithwaite? Oh, me!" said Lucy, parenthetically.

"No; not like Parson Braithwaite, my dear. Why, I couldn't even follow Parson, he said such hard words."

"I never tried," said Lucy, calmly. "I'm too sleepy to talk any more. Good-night." And she composed herself on the pillow and closed her eyes.

"You don't pray like Dr. Braithwaite, I am sure, Cicely," said Celia. "But how do you pray?"

"Well, my dear, the prayers my mother taught me, there was three on 'em—the 'Our Father,' and the 'I Believe,' and 'Matthew, Mark, Luke, and John.' I says the 'Our Father' yet, and 'I Believe' now and then; but I've left off to say Matthew and them, for when I comes to think, it sounds like the Papishes; and I don't see no prayers like it in the Book neither. I mostly prays out of the Book now, just the words that David did, and Moses, and the like of they; unless I wants somewhat very particular, and then I asks for it quite simple like, just as I'd ask you for a drink of water if I couldn't get it for myself."

Celia lay silent and thoughtful, but "Matthew, Mark, Luke, and John," roused Lucy in a minute.

"What's that about Matthew, Cicely?"

"Well, my dear, I'm not sure that 'tis more than foolishness. But my mother taught it me, and I used to say it a many years:

'Matthew, Mark, Luke, and John,
Bless the bed I lie upon;
Four parts around my bed,
Four angels guard my head.
I lay me down upon my side,
I pray that God my soul may guide;
And if I die before I wake,
I pray that God my soul may take.'"[2]

"O Cicely!" exclaimed Lucy, laughing.

"It does sound rather like praying to the apostles, Cicely," suggested Celia; "but the end of it is better."

"That's where it is, Mrs. Celia; and that's why I dropped it. Now don't you begin talking to-night—go to sleep, there's dears. There'll be as many hours in to-morrow as to-day. Eh! but, my dear, did you ask Madam, as I said?"

"Yes, Cicely," said Celia, half-rising. "She will tell me to-morrow."

The troubled look in old Cicely's face deepened. But she only said, as she took up the light, "Go to sleep, dear hearts!"

"I ask your pardon, Madam!" said Cicely, courtesying low, as Madam Passmore opened her bedroom-door in answer to her tap. "But could I have a minute's speech with you, if you please?"

"Come in, Cicely, and sit down. Is anything the matter?"

"Well, Madam," said Cicely, glancing round the room, as if to make quite sure there were no listeners, "I'm afeared there's somewhat up about Mrs. Celia. This afternoon, as I was a-going down the lane to Mally Rihll's, with the cordial water and jelly you was pleased to send for sick Robin, there was a fellow met me, that I didn't half like the looks of. I should know him again, for he stopped me, and began to talk;—asked the way to Moreton (and I doubt if he really wanted to go, for he took the t'other turning when he come to it), and asked whose the Park was, and if Master was at home; and was going on to what family he had, and such like impudent questions. 'If you want to know all that,' says I, 'you'd better go up and ring the bell, and ask Squire his own self,' I says. Well, he didn't ask me no more questions after that, but went shuffling on his way, and took the wrong turning. But when I got to Mally's, and while we sat a bit, she tells me that my gentleman had been there asking for a drink of water, and a lot more impertinence. And asked her right out if there warn't a young lady at the Park of the name of Celia, and how old she were, and when her birthday were, and all on like that. And Mally—(you know, Madam, she's but a simple soul)—I could hear from her story, she up and told him everything he asked, and maybe more than he asked, for aught I know. And what does he do but (seeing, no doubt, what a simple soul she was) outs with a table-book, and actually sets down in black and white what she was a-telling of him. 'The impudent rascal!' say I to Mally, when I hears that: 'and why couldn't you have given it him hot and strong, as I did?' I says. And she says he looked so like a gentleman, for all his shabby coat, with nigh a quarter of a yard of lace pulled off the bottom, and all a-flapping about in the wind, as is both full and cold to-day, as she hadn't the heart to say nothing impertinent, says she. But 'Impertinent!' says I; 'I think, after all the impertinence he'd given you, you might have give him a dose without hurting of him much,' says I. So I thought I'd come and tell you, Madam, at once."

"You have done right to tell me, Cicely," said her mistress. "I think—I am afraid—there will be some inquiry for the dear child, before long."

"Well, Madam, and that's what I'm afeared on, too," said Cicely. "And to see Mrs. Celia sitting there so innocent like!"

"She must know, Cicely—she must know soon."

"If I was you, Madam, I'd tell her now," said Cicely,—"asking your pardon for being so bold as to say it to you."

"Yes, Cicely, so I shall," replied Madam Passmore, in a very despondent tone.

"Madam," said Cicely, suddenly, "would you be offended with me if I said a word to you?"

"My good Cicely, why should I? Speak your mind."

"Seems to me, Madam," said Cicely, confidentially, "as you haven't asked the Lord about this trouble. And though He knows all things, yet He likes to be asked and told about 'em: He says so somewheres. Now, if I was you (asking your pardon, Madam), and didn't like for to tell Mrs. Celia (and I'm sure I shouldn't), I'd just go and tell Him. It'd come a sight easier, would telling her, after that. You see, Madam, the Lord don't put troubles on us that He don't know nothing about. He's tried 'em all Himself, and He knows just where they pinches. And when He must needs be bring one on us, or we shall be running off down the wrong road like so many chickens, He whispers like with it, 'Don't be down-hearted, child; I've tried it, and I know.'"

"Cicely, how did you come to know all this?" inquired her mistress in astonishment.

"Bless your heart, Madam, I don't know nothing!" humbly disclaimed Cicely,—"never did, nor never shall. 'Tis with the Lord's lessons like as with other lessons;—takes the like of me a month or more to spell out a word, where there be folks'd read it off plain. I knows nothing, only I knows the Lord."

Madam Passmore made no answer, but in her secret heart she wondered, for the first time, whether the one thing which Cicely owned to knowing were not worth a hundredfold all the things which she knew.

"Sit down, Celia, my dear. I will now tell you all I know."

Madam Passmore spoke rather sadly, and Celia sat down with a beating heart.

"Celia," said her mother again, "would you like me to tell you right at once, or by degrees?"

"At once, if you please, Mother. Let me know the worst."

"I am not sure that I know that, my dear," sighed the lady. "However, I will say the worst I know. Celia! you are not my daughter."

"Mother!" was Celia's inconsistent but very natural exclamation.

"I have told the truth," said Madam Passmore, gently.

"But who—who are my father and mother?" asked Celia, in a bewildered tone.

"I know not, my dear Celia. Only you are not our child, nor akin to us. I will tell thee all about it. It was on the 10th of June, my dear, when Bell was seven days old, nineteen years ago"—

"Is Bell not my sister, then?"

"No. I know nought of any of thy kindred. But hark!"

"I beg your pardon, Mother. Please go on."

"My husband came up into my chamber, where was only Cicely beside with the babe on her lap; and he said, 'Lucy, my dear, there is a strange thing happened at the Park gates. A little babe lies there all alone,—it would move thy motherly heart to see it. Shall we send and take the poor little soul in?' I said, 'Send Cicely to see and fetch it.' So Cicely brought it in—a poor, weak babe that had scarce strength to breathe. It was lapped in fine white linen, laced with real point, and there was a gold pin fastening a paper on its little coat, with but one word—'Celia.' Well, to be sure, Cicely had some work to bring it round! For hours we feared it would die. But at last it seemed a little easier, and we thought it breathed stronger. And when my husband next came up he said, 'Well, Lucy, shall we send the babe away?' But I said, 'Nay, John, it seems fairly to ask pity from us: let us keep it, and bring it up as our own, and call it Bell's twin-sister. It will never harm us—perchance bring a blessing with it, for truly it looks as if God Almighty had sent it to us.' So we did that. I do not know, my dear, whether it was quite right of us to call you Bell's twin-sister: I am afraid not, for certainly it is not true. But as to your having brought a blessing with you, that's true enough. But that is how it was."

Celia sat still and silent, feeling crushed and cut off from all she loved by this disclosure.

"You have no thought," she said slowly, at last, "who I was, nor whence I came?"

"Well, my dear, my husband thought you might be the child of some Jacobite forced to fly, who must needs leave you behind. 'Twas plain you were not forsaken because your father was too poor to keep you, for he must have been well to do, to judge from the lace on your clothes and the gold pin. Mayhap some nobleman, for aught I know."

"Mother," said Celia, with a great effort, "think you that my parents, whosoever they were, could be—Papists?" The last word was scarcely more than whispered. It conveyed to the Passmore mind the essence of all that was wrong, cruel, and fearful.

"I trust not, indeed, my dear," replied Madam Passmore, kindly, but evidently struck and distressed by Celia's question, "for I know nought. Now, Celia, child, don't take this to heart. Remember thou art as much our daughter, bound to us by every bond of love and custom, as before I spoke a word regarding this. There is ever a home for thee at Ashcliffe, child; and truly I scarce love my own better than I do thee. Let it not trouble thy mind. Go and chat with Harriet and Bell, to keep off the vapors.[3] Farewell, my dear!"

Madam Passmore kissed Celia, and let her go. She did not follow her advice to go and chat with her sisters, but walked very slowly along the passage which led to her own room. She felt as if all around her were changed, and she herself were isolated and lost. Heretofore the old house and its furniture had seemed a part of herself: now they felt as if suddenly placed at an immense distance from her. Even the portrait in the passage of the Squire Passmore who had fought at Edgehill, brandishing his sword fiercely—even the china dragons which faced the hall-window—old familiar objects, seemed to scowl at her as she went by them. She would be Celia Passmore no longer. At another time she would have smiled at the superstitious fancy—only natural now—that these disowned her as a daughter of the house. She turned aside sadly, mechanically, into the little room where old Cicely sat sewing and singing. Her joint occupations ceased when she saw Celia's face.

"Eh, my dear! I see Madam's told you. Come hither and sit down a bit. Is it very sore, dear heart?"

"Cicely, do you know any more?" Celia asked, without answering her question.

"I know nought more than Madam," said Cicely. "I went and fetched you, sweet heart, and a nice little babe you was, though you did keep crying, crying on for everlasting. Such beauties of clothes as they'd wrapped you in! I never see a bit of finer lace than was on them, nor never want; and the cambric was just beautiful! I have them laid by, if you'd like to see."

"Oh! let me see them, Cicely! I meant to have asked Mother."

What a mockery the last word seemed now!

Cicely unlocked one of her cupboards, and produced the clothes, very handsome ones, as she had said, yellow with time, and edged with rich point. The gold pin was still there, with the paper, on which a manly, yet delicate, Italian hand had written the one word which alone remained to Celia of her unknown origin. She wondered whether it were her father's writing.

"Cicely," she said, suddenly, "was I ever baptized?"

"Whether afore we had you or not, Mrs. Celia, I can't say," replied old Cicely, quietly. "Madam thought this here"—pointing to the paper—"meant as you wasn't, and they'd like you to be christened 'Celia;' and Master thought it meant as you was christened already. So old Parson Herring—him as was here afore Parson Braithwaite—he christened you in church, as it stands in the prayer-book, 'if thou hast not been baptized,' or what it is. Squire thought that'd do either way."

"And you saw nothing when you went to fetch me, Cicely?"

"Nothing at all, my dear. There might have been somebody a-watching, you know—the place is so thick with trees—but I see nought of any sort."

The long pause which followed was broken by Cicely, who perceived that Celia's handkerchief was coming surreptitiously into requisition.

"If I was you, Mrs. Celia, I wouldn't trouble, my dear. Very like nobody'll ever come after you; and if they did, why, a grown lady like you might sure say where you'd be—without your own father and mother asked you; I'd never counsel you to go again them; though it would be a sore job parting from you, to be sure. You see, my dear, you've lived here nineteen years, and never a word said."

"But that man, Cicely!" said Celia, under her breath.

"Well, that man, my dear," repeated Cicely doubtfully, "he's very like of no kin to you, only somebody as knowed who you be."

"He was a Papist," said Celia, in the same tone. "But even so, Cicely, should I make no search for my father and mother? I am theirs, whoever they were; even if they were Papists." And the handkerchief came out openly.

"Cry it out, my dear; you'll be all the better for it after. And if you'll list me, Mrs. Celia, you'll never trouble no more about this by yourself, but just go and tell the Lord all about it. He knows who they be, child, and He made you their child, knowing it. And, my dear, I do find 'tis no good to carry a burden to the Lord, so long as I just get up and lift it on again. I'm very much given to lifting on again, Mrs. Celia, and perchance you be. But when I find that, why, I just go and go again, till I can lay it down and come away without it. Takes a deal of going sometimes, that do! But what would you think of me, if I says, 'Mrs. Celia, you carry this linen up-stairs, if you please;' and then goes and walks off with it myself?"

Old Cicely's homely illustration was just what Celia wanted.

"Thank you, Cicely," she said; "I will try to leave the burden behind."

Father Cuthbert Stevens sat in his lodging at Moreton, complacently turning over the contents of his portfolio. To his landlady he had told the same tale as to Squire Passmore, representing himself as an artist in the employ of Sir

Godfrey Kneller; and had, to her thinking, verified his story beyond all doubt, by producing in part-payment of his debt a new shop-sign, representing a very fat and amiable-looking lion, standing on one leg, the other three paws flourishing in the air, while the eyes of the quadruped were fixed on the spectator. Mrs. Smith considered it a marvellous work of art, and cut off a large slice of Mr. Stevens' bill accordingly. Mr. Stevens passed his sketches slowly in review, tearing up the greater part, and committing them to the safe custody of the fire. But when he came to the staircase at Ashcliffe, he quietly placed that in security in a special pocket of the portfolio. He was too wise to speak his thoughts aloud; but had he done so he would have said:

"I have not done with this yet. To-morrow I propose to pay a visit to Marcombe, and this will secure me an unsuspected entrance into Mr. Rowe's family, where I may obtain some further information, on which a little paper and lead will be well spent."

Gilbert Irvine had rather remonstrated on Stevens' telling the same tale to Mrs. Smith as to the Squire at Ashcliffe, reminding him that it was well to have two strings to one's bow. Stevens answered, with that calm confidence in his own wisdom which never forsook him, "It is sometimes desirable, my good Gilbert, not to have too many strings to one's bow. This is my official residence. Mr. Passmore, or some other country gentleman, may find that I am lodging here. What do I gain, in that case, by representing myself to this excellent woman as a retired sea-captain or an officer on leave of absence? No; I am an artist at Ashcliffe, and I am an artist at Moreton. My private residence is——elsewhere. I am a citizen of the world. I am not troubled by any inconvenient attachment to country or home. I can sleep on a feather-bed, a green bank, or a deal board; I can eat black bread as well as *pâté aux truffes*."

"Ah! but can you do without either?" growled Gilbert, in reply.

To return from this episode. Mr. Stevens was now alone, having, as we saw, parted with Gilbert that afternoon, the latter returning to the hiding-place at Ashcliffe, very much against his inclination. The former worthy gentleman had supped on a hashed partridge, obtained in an unsportsmanlike manner which would have disgusted Squire Passmore; for while Stevens could talk glibly against poaching or anything else, when he required a savory dish, he was not above setting a snare on his own account. He had just placed safely in the pocket of the portfolio such sketches as he deemed it politic to retain, when a slight noise at the door attracted his attention, and looking up, he saw Gilbert Irvine, with white face and dilated eyes, standing in the doorway.

"We are betrayed!" hissed the latter.

Mr. Stevens, rising, quietly closed the door behind Gilbert, and set a chair for his excited visitor.

"Don't be rash, Gilbert," observed he, calmly tying the strings of the portfolio.

"Bash!" muttered Gilbert, between his closed teeth. "I tell you, they have discovered the hiding-place!"

"Have they? Then it was fortunate that I thought of dining to-day with Mr. Passmore."

"Father Cuthbert, do you care for nothing on earth?" said Gilbert, raising his voice.

"Gilbert," remarked Mr. Stevens, in his most placid manner, "I have already desired you not to be too rash. Allow me to remind you, that calling me 'Father Cuthbert' in a Protestant house, and especially in that tone of voice, is scarce likely to advance our interests. As to my caring for nothing on earth, I shall care to hear your information, when you can deliver yourself of it in a reasonable manner."

Gilbert, with some difficulty repressing his indignation, came to the conclusion that the being before him was inaccessible to feeling.

"When I arrived at the well," said he, "I was very near falling into it. I"—

"Ah! rash, as usual," commented Stevens, affectionately patting the portfolio.

"I lighted safely on the ledge of the door," pursued Gilbert, "but when I gave the necessary push, I found that it refused to stir. It had been made up from the inside."

"Something underneath the door, which stuck, of course," said Stevens.

"I took out my knife," replied Gilbert, "and with great difficulty steadied myself so that I could pass the blade under the door. There was nothing underneath, but the door refused to stir."

"What did you do then?"

"Came back to you directly, to ask you whether we ought to leave the country."

"You did not try at the other end?"

"In broad daylight? Mr. Stevens, what can you be thinking of?"

"The interests of the cause, my friend."

"Ah, well! I have the greatest respect for the interests of the cause, but I have also a slight disposition to attend to the interests of Gilbert Irvine."

"That is precisely your bane, my excellent Gilbert. And there are other defects in you beside."

"And pray, what excuse could you have devised to gain entrance?"

"Gilbert, I wonder at your marvellous incapacity for lying. Now it comes quite natural to me."

"Seems so," said Gilbert, grimly.

"Well, as your disposition to attend to the interests of Gilbert Irvine is so strong, I will not require more of you than to attempt the entrance by night. I noticed when I left the house that one of the drawing-room windows was unfastened. You can get in that way, and pass through Mrs. Celia's chamber."

"I'm blessed if I'll try that style of putting my neck in a noose for you more than this once!" Gilbert burst forth.

"I don't ask it of you more than this once," replied Stevens.

"And suppose they have fastened the window since you were there, as is probably the case?"

"If you cannot get in, come back to me. We must find out whether they have discovered the hiding-place. But I will take the next chance myself; and, Gilbert, it shall be in broad daylight."

Gilbert stared at him, and shook his head with an incredulous laugh.

"You are a poor conspirator, Gilbert," lamented Stevens. "Can you plaster a wall?"

"No," said Gilbert.

"I can. Can you mend a harpsichord?"

"Not I, indeed."

"I can. And can you make a tansy pudding?"

"Holy Mary! such women's work!"

"Women are useful, my friend, in their way—occasionally. And it is desirable, now and then, even for the nobler sex, to know how to do women's work. Now I dare say you have not the least notion how a shirt is made? I can sew beautifully."

"By the head of St. Barbara!"—Gilbert began.

"Avoid Catholic oaths, Gilbert, if you please. And never be above learning. Pick up all you can—no matter what. It may come in use some time."

"I wish you would tell me how you mean to get in?"

"Mr. Passmore was observing at dinner that he wanted a new under-footman. I shall offer myself for the place."

Gilbert's eyes and mouth opened rather wide.

"I can carry coal-scuttles, my friend," said Mr. Cuthbert Stevens, insinuatingly. "And I could black a boot. In a week (or as soon as my purpose was served) I should have a bad cough, find that the work was too hard for me, and leave."

"Father Cuthbert, you are a clever fellow!" said Gilbert, slowly.

Father Cuthbert made no attempt to deny the impeachment.

"And where am I to be, while you are blacking your boots and carrying your coal-scuttles?"

"Quietly pursuing your inquiries between here and Exeter, and keeping out of scrapes—if you can. You will find me here again this day month."

On the evening of the next day, Squire Passmore saw and engaged a new under-footman.

"A tall, personable fellow," said he to his family; "very well-spoken, and capable, he seems. He comes from Exeter, and his name is George Shepherd."

And much vexed was he, for he had taken a fancy to his new servant, when, four days later, Robert announced to him that George had such a bad cough, and found the work so hard for his weak chest, that he wished to leave at the end of the month.

"It ben't always the strongest-looking as is the strongest," observed Cicely on the subject; "and I'm a-feared, Madam, that George is but weakly, for all he looks so capable."

Madam Passmore, who felt very sorry for poor George, tried diet-drinks, linseed tea, and lozenges, but all were to no purpose; and at the end of the month the new footman left.

"What *are* you doing, Mr. Stevens?" demanded Gilbert Irvine, as he entered the lodger's room at Moreton on the same evening that the under-footman's place at Ashcliffe Hull was again left vacant.

"Good-evening, Gilbert," responded Mr. Stevens, without looking up. "Only making my official shirts into a rather smaller and neater bundle. They may serve again, you know."

"And what news?" asked Gilbert.

"You were right," said Mr. Stevens. "They have found it out, and have made up the well-door. But Mrs. Celia knows nothing about the hiding-place, though she sleeps in the chamber."

"Well, and why couldn't you believe me at first? What have you gained by all your trouble?"

"Why could I not believe you?" repeated Stevens. "Because you are rash, as I always tell you. And what have I gained? A month's board and lodging, and thirteen and fourpence. Look at it."

"Ugh!" said Gilbert to the shillings. "Well, I would not have blacked a lot of dirty boots for you, if you'd been twice as many!"

"A mistake, Gilbert! a sad mistake!" said Stevens, tying up his bundle. "Never be above doing anything for the good of the Church."

"Nor telling any number of lies," responded Gilbert. "Well, and where are we to go now?"

"Back to France, and report to my Lady Ingram as quickly as possible."

"And what then?"

"That is for her to say. I should think she will come and fetch the girl."

"And how are we to live meanwhile?"

"You, as you please. For me, being now so well equipped and in good practice," answered Mr. Cuthbert Stevens, with an insinuating smile, "if I found it impossible to get any other sort of work, I *could* take another place as footman!"

Time passed calmly on for some months after Madam Passmore's disclosure to Celia. The latter gradually lost the fear of being claimed by strangers, and devoted herself to the very diligent study of the Scriptures. The Squire and Madam Passmore became slowly grayer, and Cicely Aggett a little whiter than before. But nothing occurred to break the quiet tenor of events, until Henrietta's marriage took place in the summer of 1711. The bridegroom was the heir of a family living in the adjoining division of the county, and the day was marked at Ashcliffe by much splendor and festivity. The bride showed herself quiet and practical on this occasion, as on all others; and as she had made her mark but little, she was comparatively little missed. Cicely cried because she thought it was the first break in the family, and Dolly because she fancied it was the proper thing to do; but Henrietta herself would have scorned to run the risk of spoiling her primrose silk by tears. Everything was done *en règle*—wedding and breakfast, throwing the slipper, dancing, and a number of other small observances which have since been counted tedious or unseemly. And when the day was over, and Henrietta Carey had departed to her new home, things sank down into their old groove at Ashcliffe Hall.

When the year 1712 dawned, only the three younger sisters of the family were at home. Harry had rejoined his regiment, and Charley was away on a visit to his eldest sister and her husband.

So matters stood at Ashcliffe Hall on that New Year's Day when what Celia dreaded came upon her.

[1] The peculiar drawing up of the chin towards the throat, known as bridling, was a very essential point of fine breeding at the date of this story.

[2] Of *La Petite Patenôtre Blanche* there are as many versions as lines. The one I give in the text rests on oral tradition. There is another known to me, probably an older version, which I should have preferred if I could have been quite sure of the words. It was used by a woman who died in 1818 at the age of 108, and who therefore was born four years before the death of Queen Anne. It was repeated to me when a child of eight, and the only copy I can recover is my own record at the time. I give this for what it is worth:

"Matthew, Mark, Luke, and John,
Bless the bed that I lie on;
Four corners to my bed,
Four angels at their head,—
One to read and one to write,
And two to guard my bed [at night.]"

[3] "The vapors" were pre-eminently the fashionable malady of the reign of Queen Anne. The name answered to the sensation now known as *ennui*: but doubtless, as Miss Strickland suggests in her "Lives of the Queens of England," it was frequently used when its victim was suffering from nothing more remarkable or novel than a bad temper.

IV.

MY LADY INGRAM.

"She had the low voice of your English dames,
Unused, it seems, to need rise half a note
To catch attention,—and their quiet mood,
As if they lived too high above the earth
For that to put them out in anything:
So gentle, because verily so proud;
So wary and afraid of hurting you,
By no means that you are not really vile,
But that they would not touch you with their foot
To push you to your place; so self-possessed,
Yet gracious and conciliating, it takes
An effort in their presence to speak truth:
You know the sort of woman,—brilliant stuff,
And out of nature."
                    ELIZABETH BARRETT BROWNING.

The Tories were in power in the winter of 1711-12. The Duke of Marlborough's credit at home had long been sinking, and he was now almost at the lowest point in the Queen's favor. On that very New Year's Day of which I have spoken, for the first time in the annals of England, a Ministry had endeavored to swamp the House of Lords by a wholesale creation of Peers. Politically speaking, Squire Passmore was anything but happy, for he was a fervent Whig. He sat in the parlor that morning, inveighing angrily against the Earl of Oxford and all who followed or agreed with him—the Queen herself of course excepted—for the edification of Madam Passmore—who was calmly knotting—Isabella, and Celia.

"'Tis pity, John," said Madam Passmore, quietly, "that you have no Tories to list you."

"I wish I had—the scoundrels!" exclaimed the Squire.

"O Mother!" cried Isabella, rising hurriedly from her seat in the window, "sure here is some visitor of quality. There is a carriage at the front door with arms on the panels."

"What arms?" asked her father.

"I don't understand anything about arms," said Isabella, "and one of the coats I cannot see rightly. The one nearer here is all cut up into little squares, and in one part there is a dog on his hind legs, and in another a pair of yellow balls."

The Squire came to the window to see for himself. "Dog! balls!" cried he. "A lion rampant and bezants—the goose!"

"Well, Father, I told you I did not understand it!" remonstrated Isabella, in an injured tone.

"Madam, my Lady Ingram!" announced Robert, in a voice of great importance.

The Squire turned round directly, and offered his hand to conduct the visitor to a seat, like a well-bred gentleman of his day,—Madam Passmore rising to receive her, and her daughters of course following her example.

The stranger was a tall, commanding woman, with great stateliness of carriage, and much languor of manner. She had evidently been very handsome, but was now just past her prime. Her eyes and hair were dark, her voice low and languishing. Altogether it struck Celia that she was very like what Isabella would be in a few years, allowing for the differences in color. She took the chair to which the Squire led her, and addressed herself to Madam Passmore. There was a little peculiarity of distinctness in her pronunciation.

"You wonder to see me, Madam," she began.

"Madam, I am honored by your Ladyship's visit."

"I am the widow of Sir Edward Ingram, who held a commission under His Majesty King James. I come to speak with you on business."

"With *me*?" asked Madam Passmore, a little surprised.

"You are Madam Passmore, of Ashcliffe Hall?—Yes."

"Pray continue, Madam."

"Your daughters, Madam?" inquired the visitor, with a languid wave of her hand towards the young ladies.

"Yes; does your Ladyship wish to see me without them?"

"Not at all—oh! not at all. Which is Mademoiselle Celia?"

"The woman's French!" exclaimed the Squire, under his breath.

Celia's blood rushed to her face and neck, and then ebbed, leaving her white and faint, as she rose and came slowly forward. "Is this my mother?" she was asking herself, in a mental tumult.

"Ah! that is you? Stand a little farther, if you please. I wish to look at you."

"No; this is not my mother!" said Celia, to her own heart.

"Not by the half so tall as I should like—quite *petite*!" said Lady Ingram, scanning Celia with a depreciatory air. "And so brown! You cannot bridle—you have no complexion. Eh! *ma foi!* what an English-looking girl!"

The Squire had almost arrived at the end of his patience. Madam Passmore said quietly, "I ask your Ladyship's pardon, but perhaps you will tell me why you make these remarks on my daughter?"

"I beg yours," said Lady Ingram, languidly. "I thought I had told you. She is a foundling?—Exactly. *Et bien*, she is my daughter—that is, my husband's daughter."

"Thank Heaven, not yours!" growled the Squire, heard only by Isabella.

"My husband was married twice," pursued the visitor, unconscious of his rising anger. "His first wife was an Englishwoman—short, I suppose, and brown, like this girl. I am the second wife, *née* Mademoiselle de La Croix, daughter of Monsieur the Marquis de La Croix. *Tu peux m'embrasser ma fille.*"

Celia would have obeyed somewhat reluctantly, had she understood her step-mother. She stood still, unaware that she had been addressed at all, since she had never learned the language in which Lady Ingram had spoken to her.

"Well, you will not?"

"I beg your pardon, Madam," answered Celia, speaking for the first time, and in a very tremulous voice. "I did not understand what you said."

"You speak French?"

"No, Madam."

"*Possible!*" exclaimed Lady Ingram. "You have never taught her to speak French? She speaks only English? *Ma foi, quelle famille!*"

"I could scarce teach her what I knew not," replied Madam Passmore, with quiet dignity.

"*C'est incroyable!*" drawled Lady Ingram, "Well, child, come here and kiss me. How awkwardly you stoop! Your carriage is bad—very bad. Ah, well! I shall see to all that. You will be ready to return with me on Thursday?"

This was only Tuesday. Celia heard the question put with a sinking of dismay. How should she go? yet how should she refuse?

"My Lady Ingram," said Squire Passmore, coming forward at last, "if you were this child's own mother, or if her father were yet alive, I could not of course set myself against your taking her away. But you tell us that you are only her step-mother, and that her father is dead. It seems to me, therefore, that she is at least as much our child as yours—rather more, indeed, seeing that we have brought her up from her cradle, and you have never cared to see her until this day. Moreover, I hope your Ladyship will not take it ill of me, if I ask you for some proof that you really are the child's step-mother."

"What proof shall I give you, Mr. Passmore?" asked Lady Ingram, quietly. "I have every wish to satisfy you. If you desire to see proofs that I am really Lady Ingram, ask the servants my name, or look here"—

She drew a letter from her pocket, and held it out to the Squire. The direction was—"To my Lady Ingram."

"Madam," said the Squire, returning the letter with a bow, "I do not in the least doubt that I have the honor of addressing my Lady Ingram. But can you satisfy me that you are Celia's step-mother?"

"If my word is not enough to satisfy you, Mr. Passmore," answered Lady Ingram, not at all annoyed, "I know of nothing that will do it. The marriage-registers of Celia's parents, or my own, would give you no information concerning her: and she has no register of baptism. I believe, however, that her name was written on a paper left with her, in Sir Edward's hand. If you will produce that paper, I will show you more of his writing, which you can compare with it. I think the fact of my knowledge on the subject ought to prove to you that I am the person whom I represent myself to be."

The writing on the two papers, when compared, tallied; and Squire Passmore felt that Lady Ingram was right, and that she could not produce any proof of her relationship so strong as the mere fact of her knowledge of Celia's name and origin. If she really were Celia's step-mother, he had no wish to prevent his adopted daughter from making acquaintance with her own family: and he saw nothing for it but to take Lady Ingram at her word.

"I am satisfied, Madam, that you have some relation to Celia," said he. "And as to her visiting you—for I cannot consent to her being taken entirely away—let the child choose for herself. Sure she is old enough."

"Ah!" said Lady Ingram, shrugging her shoulders slightly. "Very well. You shall decide, *chère* Celia. At the least you will visit me?"

"I will visit you, Madam, with pleasure," answered Celia, a little to the damage of truth; "but these dear friends, who have had a care of me from my childhood, I could not leave them entirely, Madam." The sentence ended in tears.

"I am not an officer of justice, *ma belle*!" said Lady Ingram, laughing faintly. "Ah, well! a visit let it be. You will come with me—for a visit—on Thursday?"

"I will attend your Ladyship."

"You live near, Madam?" asked Madam Passmore, wondering whether she could live so far away as the next county.

"I live in France," was the unconcerned answer,—"in Paris in the winter, and not far thence in the summer."

The Squire almost gasped for breath. "And where is your summer dwelling, Madam? I think, if you please, that I have a right to ask."

"Oh! certainly. At St. Germain-en-Laye."

"St. fiddlesticks-and-fiddlestrings!" roared the Squire.

"Sir!" observed Lady Ingram, apparently a little startled at last.

"Pope, Pretender, and Devil!" thundered the exasperated Whig.

"Ah! I only know one of the three," said Lady Ingram, subsiding.

"And pray which is that, Madam?" grimly inquired he.

"*Le Roi Jacques*—you call the Pretender," said she calmly, drawing on her glove.

"If you please, Madam," asked Celia, with an effort, "do you know what was my mother's name?"

"White, Black—some color—I know not whether Red, Green, or Blue. She was a nobody—a mere nobody," replied her successor, dismissing Celia's insignificant mother with a graceful wave of her hands.

"Have I any brothers or sisters, Madam?"

"Sisters! no. Two brothers—one son of your mother, and one of mine."

"They live with you, Madam?"

"My son Philip does," said the Baronet's widow. "Your brother—Sir Edward now—is away on his travels, the saints know where. But he talked to me much about you before he went, and Philip teased me about you—so I came."

"Celia!" said the Squire, sternly, "this woman is an alien, a Tory, and a Papist. Will you still go?"

"Ought I not, Father?" she asked, in a low tone.

"Judge for yourself, child," he answered, kindly.

"I think I ought to go," said Celia, faintly.

"I am a Catholic, Mr. Passmore, it is true," remarked Lady Ingram, quietly; "yet you need not fear me. Sir Edward, my husband, was Protestant, and so is his son Edward: and I do not interfere. We are all surely going to heaven, and what matter for the different roads?"

"I think I ought to go," repeated Celia, but Madam Passmore thought, still more faintly than before.

"On Thursday, then," answered Lady Ingram, touching Celia's cheek with her lips. "Ah! *ma chère*, how I will improve you when I have you to myself!—how I will form you! That *bon ton*, that *aisance*, that *maintien!*—you have them not. You shall soon! Adieu!"

"Well, sure, 'tis sore to lose you, Mrs. Celia, my dear!" observed Cicely Aggett, as she sat sewing; "but more particular to a stranger—among them dreadful Papists—and such a way off, too! Why, 'tis nigh a hundred mile from here to Paris, ben't it?"

"I don't know how far it is," said Celia, honestly; "but I am sure 'tis a very long way."

"Well, anyhow, you'll not forget us, dear heart?"

"I shall never do that, Cicely. But don't talk as if I were going away altogether. 'Tis only a visit. I shall soon come back—in a year, at the longest."

"Maybe, my dear," answered Cicely, quietly; "and maybe not, Mrs. Celia. A year is a long time, and we none of us know what the Lord may have for us afore then. Not one of us a-going along with you! Well, you'll have Him with you, and He'll see to you a deal better than we could. But to think of you going among them wicked, cruel Papists! Don't have no more to do with none of them than you can help—don't, my dear! Depend upon it, Mrs. Celia, they ben't a bit better now than they was a hundred and fifty years ago, when they burned and tormented poor folks all over the country, as my grandmother used to tell me."

"What did she tell you about it, Cicely?"

"She were to Exeter,[1a] Mrs. Celia, and she lived till I was a matter of fifteen; and many a tale she's told me of their doings in them old times. But the one I always liked best was one her mother had told her. Her mother had been a young maid when the burnings was a-going on; she were to London,[1b] and was woman to a lady, one of them as was burnt."

"Tell me about it, Cicely," requested Celia, with feelings of curiosity and horror struggling for precedence.

"I'll tell you all I know about it, my dear. There! your ruffles is done. I'll take Mrs. Bell's next. Well, Mrs. Celia, her name, my great-grandmother's mistress, was Kyme; she was to Lincolnshire, leastwise her husband, for she was a London lady herself. An old family them Kymes be; they've dwelt in Lincolnshire ever since Moses, for aught I know. Mrs. Anne—that was her name—was a sweet, gentle lady; but her husband, Mr. Kyme, wasn't so likely: he'd a cruel rare temper, I've heard my grandmother say. Well, and after a while Mr. Kyme he came to use Mrs. Anne so hard, she couldn't live with him no longer, and she came back to her father and mother. She never went back to Lincolnshire; she took back her own name, and everybody called her Mrs. Anne Askew, instead of Madam Kyme. I never understood quite the rights of it, and I'm not sure my grandmother did herself; but however, some way Mrs. Anne she got hold of a Bible, and she fell a-reading it. And of course she couldn't but see with half an eye, when she come to read, that all them Papishes had taught her was all wrong, when she didn't find not one of their foolishnesses set down in the book. And by and by the priests came to hear of it. I don't just know how that were; I think somebody betrayed her, but I can't tell who: not my great-grandmother, I'm sure, for she held her lady dear. Ay, but there was a scrimmage when they knowed! Poor young lady! all turned against her, her own father and mother and all and the priests had their wicked will. They took her to Newgate, and tried first to talk her over; but when they found their talk was no good, but Mrs. Anne she held fast by what God had taught her, they had her into the torture-chamber."

Celia drew a long breath.

"Ah!" said old Cicely, slowly shaking her white head, "'tis easy to say 'God forgive them!' but truly I misdoubt whether God *can* forgive them that tear the flesh and rent the hearts of His saints! What they did to that poor young thing in that torture-chamber, God knoweth. I make no doubt 'tis all writ down in His book. But Mrs. Anne she stood firm, and not one word could they get out of her; and my Lord Chancellor, who was there, he was so mad angry with her, that he throwed off his gown and pulled the rack with his own hands. At last the doctors said—for they had doctors there, the devils! to tell them how much the poor wretches could bear—the doctors said that if Mrs. Anne had any more, she would be like to die under it. So then they took her down; but afore they let her be, they kept her two hours longer a-sitting on the bare floor, and my Lord Chancellor a-talking at her all that ever he could. Then at last, when they found her too much for them, they took her away and laid her to bed. 'As weary and painful bones,' quoth she to my great-grandmother, 'had I as ever had patient Job. I thank my Lord God therefor!'[2] And if that warn't a good Christian saying, my dear, I'd like to hear one. Well, for some months after that she laid in prison; the wicked priests for ever at her, wearying her life out with talk and such. So at the end of all, when they saw it was no good, they carried her out to Smithfield, there to die.

"They carried her out, really; for every bone in her was broken, and if she had lived fifty years after, she could never have set her foot to the ground again. But Mrs. Anne she went smiling, and they said which saw her, as joyful as if she were going to her bridal. There, at the stake, with the faggots round, they offered her, last thing, a pardon if she would come round to their evil ways. Ah! they knew not the strength within her! they saw not the angels waiting round, when that poor broken body should be ashes, to take up the glad soul to the Lord's rest. What was pardon to her, poor crushed thing? She had seen too much of the glory of the Lord to set any price on their pardons. So when they could do nought more with her, they burned her to ashes at the stake."

Old Cicely added no comment. Was any needed? But if she had known the words spoken at one such holocaust by the mother of the martyr, she might fitly have ended her tale with them:

"BLESSED BE JESUS CHRIST, AND HIS WITNESSES!"

"*Bon jour, ma chère.* You look a little better this morning—not quite so English. *Et bien!* you are ready to come?"

Celia had never felt so English as at that moment. She forced back the tears, which felt as if they would work their way out in spite of her, and said, in a very low voice, "I am ready, Madam."

"Let us lose no time, then," said Lady Ingram, rising, and allowing her hoop to spread itself out to its full width. "I wish you a *very* good morning, Madam."

She swept slowly and statelily across the room, leaving Celia to exchange passionate kisses with all the members of the family, and then, almost blinded by the tears which would come at last, to make her way to the coach which was standing at the door.

"There, there, my dear!" said Lady Ingram, a little querulously, when the coach had been travelling about five minutes; "that is quite enough. You will make your eyes red. There is nothing, absolutely nothing, so unbecoming as the red eyes. These people are not your family—not at all so good. I do not see anything to cry about."

"She does not mean to be unkind," thought Celia to herself. "She is only heartless."

True—but what an *only*!

Lady Ingram, having done her duty to her step-daughter, leaned back in the coach and closed her eyes. She opened them again for a moment, and said, "We arrive on Tuesday in London, I start for Paris not until the next Tuesday." Then the dark languishing eyes shut again, rather to Celia's relief. The ponderous vehicle worked its way slowly along the muddy roads. Celia sat by her step-mother, and opposite was Lady Ingram's maid, a dark-browed Frenchwoman; both were remarkably silent. Lady Ingram went to sleep, and the maid sat upright, stony, and passive, frequently scanning the young stranger with her black eyes, but never uttering a word. That evening the coach clattered into Chard, where they slept. The Friday saw them at Shaftesbury, the Saturday night at Andover, where they put up for the Sunday. On the Monday evening they reached Bagshot, Lady Ingram declaring that she must have the morning to pass Bagshot Heath, and adding a few anecdotes of her past troubles with highwaymen which terrified Celia. Two men travelling on horseback, who were staying at the inn, joined their forces to the carriage, and the heath was passed without any attack from the highwaymen. About ten o'clock, when they were a little past the heath, Lady Ingram desired Celia to keep her eyes open. "We are just entering Windsor," she said; "and though I have not time to stop and let you see the Castle, yet you may perhaps get a glimpse of it as we pass." They passed the Castle, and drove down the park. Suddenly the coach came to a full stop.

"The stupid man!" exclaimed Lady Ingram. "What does he?"

The question was very soon answered, for William, the footman, sprang from his perch, and presented himself at the carriage-window. Lady Ingram let down the glass.

"What is the matter?" she asked, testily.

"If you please, Madam," was the answer, "there is a coach coming with gentlemen on horseback, and two running footmen in attendance; and Shale thinks it must be the Queen's."

"Draw to one side immediately," commanded Lady Ingram, "and then open the door and we will alight."

All alighted except the coachman, and Lady Ingram took Celia's hand, and stood with her just in front of her carriage. The running footmen passed them first, carrying long wands, and dressed in scarlet and gold livery. Lady Ingram's practised eye detected at once that the liveries were royal. Then came three gentlemen, two riding in front, the third behind. The coach, a large, handsome, but very unwieldly vehicle, lumbered slowly after them. In it were seated three ladies—one alone facing the horses, the others on the opposite seat.

"Which is the Queen, Madam?" asked Celia, excitedly.

"The Princess Anne will sit alone, facing the horses," replied her stepmother.

The lady who occupied the seat of honor, and whom alone Celia noticed, was the fattest woman she had ever seen. She had a fat, round face, and ruddy complexion, dark chestnut hair, and regular features. Her eyes were gray, and the expression of her face, though kindly, was not indicative of either liveliness or intellect. She wore a black dress trimmed with ermine, and a long black hood lined with the same fur. Not until the Queen had become invisible to her did Celia notice her ladies on the opposite seat. One of them was remarkable for a nose not extremely beautiful, and abundance of curls of a dusky red streamed over her shoulders. Celia glanced at the other, and came to the conclusion that there was nothing particular about her.

"So that is Abigail Hill!"[3] said Lady Ingram, in a peculiar tone, when the coach had driven past. "I thought she had had more in her—at least to look at."

"Is that the lady with the red hair, Madam?"

"No, my dear—the other. The red-haired one is the Duchess of Somerset."[4]

Lady Ingram still stood looking after the royal carriage with a meditative air.

"I should like to see Abigail Hill," she said, as if to herself. "I cannot tell how to do it. But we must not delay, even for that. Get in, my dear."

Celia got into the coach, wondering what reason her step-mother could have for wishing to see Lady Masham, and also why she did not give her the benefit of her title. Lady Ingram resumed her own seat in silence, and leaned back in the carriage, apparently cogitating deeply. Mile after mile the travellers journeyed on, until the dusk fell, and at the little inn at Bedfont the coach pulled up. William appeared at the window.

"Please your Ladyship, we can cross the heath to-night," he said. "There's a regiment of Colonel Churchill's just before: the host says they haven't been gone five minutes."

"Then bid Shale hasten on, without stopping to bait," answered his mistress. "We must overtake them, for I do not mean to stop on the road another night, unless it cannot be helped."

The horses were urged on as fast as they could go, and in about a quarter of an hour they came up with the regiment, under whose guardianship they crossed the dreaded Hounslow Heath without fear of molestation. At Hammersmith the coach stopped again. After a little parley between William and the innkeeper, four men came out of the inn with torches in their hands.

Two of them placed themselves on each side of the coach, and they slowly journeyed on again. It was quite dark now. Gradually the road became busier and more noisy, and houses appeared lining it at intervals. At length they had fairly entered the metropolis. The coach worked its way slowly along the muddy streets, for it had been raining since they left Staines, and the shouts of the linkmen were almost deafening. As they proceeded, another coach suddenly appeared and attempted to pass them. This could not be permitted. The coachman whipped his horses, the linkmen screamed, the great coach swayed to and fro with the unusual pace. Lady Ingram opened the window and looked out, while the maid clasped her hands and shrieked in her own tongue that she was killed.

"Not at all, *ma bonne*," was the calm response of the mistress. Then turning to Celia, she asked, "You are not afraid?"

"Not unless you tell me there is something to fear, Madam," answered Celia, in the quiescence rather of ignorance than of courage.

"Ah! I like that answer," replied Lady Ingram, smiling her approval, and patting Celia's cheek. "There is good metal in you, *ma chére*; it is only the work that asks the polishing."

Celia wondered what the process of polishing would be, and into what kind of creature she would find herself transmuted when it was finished.

"William," said Lady Ingram, putting her head out of the window, "whose coach is that other?"

"Sir John Scoresby's, Madam."

"A baronet of three years later," observed Lady Ingram, quietly sinking back into her seat; "it is impossible to give way."

"Ah, Madame!" faltered the *bonne*, in a shrill key. "Madame will renounce her right? We shall be over! We shall be dead!"

"Impossible, my good Thérèse," was the placid answer. "I know what is due to myself and to others. To a baronet of one day earlier I should of course give place without a word; but to one of a day later—impossible!" replied Lady Ingram, waving her hands with an air of utter finality.

"But if we are all killed?" faintly shrieked Thérèse.

"Absurd!" said Lady Ingram. "But if I were, Thérèse, know that I should have the consolation of dying in the discharge of my duty. No soldier can do more."

"Ah! Madame is so high and philosophical!" lamented Thérèse. "Madame has the grand thoughts! *C'est magnifique!* But we others, who are but little people, and cannot console ourselves—hélas!"

Meanwhile the battle was raging outside the coach. Shouts of "Scoresby!" and "Ingram!" violent lashings of the struggling horses, oaths and execrations, at last the flashing of daggers. When things arrived at this point, Lady Ingram again let down the glass, which she had drawn up, and Celia, like a coward, shut her eyes and put her hands over her ears. Thérèse was screaming hysterically.

"Ah!" remarked the Baronet's widow, in a tone of satisfaction, replacing the window, "we shall get on now—William has stabbed the other coachman. Thérèse, give over screaming in that way—so very unnecessary! and Celia, my dear, do not put yourself in that absurd position—it is like a coward!"

"But the man, Madam!—the poor coachman!—is he killed?" questioned Celia, in a tone of horror.

"My dear, what does that signify?" said Lady Ingram. "A mere coachman—what can it matter?"

"But will you not ask, Madam?" pursued Celia, in a very pained voice.

"Impossible, my dear!" replied Lady Ingram. "I could not demean myself by such a question, nor must you. Really, Celia, your manners are so wanting in repose! You must learn not to put yourself into a fever in this way for every little thing that happens. Imagine! I, Lady Ingram, stopping my coach, and yielding precedence to this upstart Scoresby, to inquire whether this person—a man of no family whatever—has had a little more or less blood let out by my footman's thrust! Ridiculous!" And Lady Ingram spread out her dress.

Celia shrank back as far as she could into the corner of the coach, and spoke, not in words, to the only Friend she had present with her. "Oh! send me back to Ashcliffe!" was the strong cry of her heart. "This woman has no feelings whatever. Unless there be some very necessary work for me to do in Paris, send me back home!"

But there was very necessary work to be done before she could go home.

After another quarter of a mile spent in struggling through the mud, the coach drew up at the door of a large house. William, who seemed none the worse for his battle, opened the door, and held out his arm to assist his ladies in alighting. Lady Ingram motioned to Thérèse to go first, and the maid laid her hand on the arm of her fellow-servant.

"Ah, bah!" exclaimed she, as she reached the ground. "Why you not wipe de blood from de sleeve? You spoil my cloak—faugh!"

"You had better not use your dagger, William," observed Lady Ingram, as she stepped out, "unless it be necessary. It frightens Madam Celia." And with a peculiar smile she looked back at her step-daughter.

Celia followed Lady Ingram into a lighted hall, where servants in blue and gold liveries stood round, holding tapers in silver candlesticks. They seemed to recognize Lady Ingram, though Celia noticed that William's livery was different from theirs, and therefore imagined that the house she was entering must be that of a stranger. Lady Ingram walked forward in her usual stately manner until she reached the head of the staircase, closely followed by Celia and Thérèse. On the second step from the top stood a gentleman in full dress, blue and gold. A conversation ensued between him and Lady Ingram, accompanied by a great deal of bowing and courtesying, flourishing of hands and shaking of heads, which, being in French, was of course lost upon Celia; but could she have understood it, this was what she would have heard.

"You do me such honor, Monsieur?"

"It is due to you, Madame."

"The second stair, Monsieur! I am entitled only to the head of the staircase."

"Madame will permit me to express my sense of her distinction."

"You overwhelm me, Monsieur!"

"Pray let Madame proceed."

"Not until Monsieur has done so."

"Precedence to the ladies!"

"By no means before His Majesty's Consul!"

Here, then, appeared likely to be an obstacle to farther progress: but after a good deal more palaver, the grave point of precedence, which each was courteously striving to yield to the other, was settled by Lady Ingram and the Consul each setting a foot upon the top stair at the same moment. They then passed forward, hand in hand, Celia as before following her step-mother. The three entered a large, handsome drawing-room, where a further series of bowing and courtesying ensued before Lady Ingram would sit down. Celia supposed that she might follow her example, and being very tired, she seated herself at the same time as her step-mother; for which act she was rewarded with a glance of disapprobation from Lady Ingram's dark eyes. She sprang up again, feeling puzzled and fluttered, whereupon the Consul advanced to her, and addressed her in French with a series of low bows. Celia could only courtesy to him, and look helplessly at her step-mother. Lady Ingram uttered a few languid words in French, and then said in English to Celia, "Pray sit down. You have to be told everything."

So she sat, silent and wearied, until after a time the door flew open, and half a dozen servants entered bearing trays, which they presented first to Lady Ingram and then to Celia. The first tray contained cups of coffee, the second preserved fruits, the third custards, the fourth various kinds of sweetmeats. Celia mentally wondered whether the French supped on sugar-plums; but the fifth tray containing cakes, she succeeded in finding something edible. Lady Ingram, she noticed, after a cup of coffee and one or two cakes, devoted her attention to the sugar-plums.

"You are tired?" asked Lady Ingram, turning to Celia. "Very well, you shall go to bed. I will leave the forming of your manners at present; by and by I shall have something to say to you. Thérèse will dress your hair in the morning. Adieu! come and embrace me."

Thérèse appeared at the door, and after giving her some directions in French, her mistress desired Celia to courtesy to the Consul and follow Thérèse. The maid led Celia into a tolerably large room, with a French bed, which Thérèse informed her that she would have to herself.

"Ah! dat you have de hair beautifuls!" said Thérèse, as she combed it out. "I arrange it to-morrow. Mademoiselle like Madame?"

Celia liked no part of this speech. She knew that her hair was not beautiful, and felt that Thérèse was flattering her; while whatever might be her feelings on the subject of Lady Ingram, she had no intention of communicating them to her Ladyship's maid. Her answer was distant and evasive.

"Aha!" said Thérèse, with a soft laugh to herself. "Perhaps Mademoiselle shall like Monsieur Philippe. Monsieur Philippe love to hear of Mademoiselle."

Celia's heart warmed in a moment to her unknown brother. "How old is he?" she asked.

"Nineteen," said Thérèse.

"And my eldest brother, how old is he?"

"Sir Edward?" asked the French maid. "Ah! I see him very little. He is two, tree, five year older as Monsieur Philippe. He come never."

Celia resolved to question Thérèse no further, and the latter continued brushing her hair in silence.

"That will do, Thérèse," she said, when this process was completed. "I will not keep you any longer," she explained, seeing that the French girl looked puzzled.

"Mademoiselle undress herself?" asked Thérèse, with open eyes.

"Yes, thank you—I like it better. I wish to read a little first."

"De great ladies read never," laughed Thérèse. "Mademoiselle leave de book in Englands. Madame not like de read."

"I will never leave you in England," whispered Celia to her little Bible, resting her cheek upon it, when Thérèse was gone. "But oh! how shall I follow your teaching here? I know so little, and have so little strength!"

And a low soft whisper came into her heart,—"Lo! I am with you alway, even unto the end of the world."[5]

"When Mademoiselle is ready, Madame wish speak with her at her dressing-chamber."

This message was brought to Celia by Thérèse the next morning. She was already dressed and reading.

"Ah! dat Mademoiselle is early!" exclaimed Thérèse, lifting her eyebrows. "Mademoiselle read always."

There was a concealed sarcasm about everything this woman said to her, which was particularly distasteful to Celia. She rose and closed her book, only replying, "I will come to my Lady now."

Thérèse led her along the passage into a handsomely-furnished room, where, robed in a blue cashmere dressing-gown, Lady Ingram sat, with her long dark hair down upon her shoulders.

"Ah! good morning. Early!" was her short greeting to Celia, who bent down and kissed her.

"Now, my dear," pursued Lady Ingram, "please to sit down on that chair facing me. I have two or three remarks to make. You shall have your first lesson in the polishing you need so much."

Celia took the seat indicated with some trepidation, but more curiosity.

"Very well," said her step-mother. "Now, first, about blushing. You *must* get rid of that habit of blushing. There—you are at it now. Look in the mirror, and see if it does not spoil your complexion. A woman of the world, Celia, never blushes. It is quite old-fashioned and obsolete. So much for that."

"But, Madam,"—Celia began, and hesitated.

"Go on, my dear," said Lady Ingram. "You are not putting enough powder on the left side, Thérèse."

"If you please, Madam, I cannot stop blushing," pleaded Celia, doing it very much. "It depends upon my feelings."

"Well, it looks as if you could not," answered Lady Ingram, with a short, hard laugh. "But, my dear, you *must*. And as to feelings, Celia, a modish woman never has any feelings. Feeling is the one thing absolutely forbidden by the mode. Laugh as much as you please, but mind how you feel merry; and as to crying, that is not allowable except in particular circumstances. It looks well to see a girl weep for the death of her father or mother, and, within reasonable limits, for a brother or sister. But if you are ever left a widow, you must be very careful not to weep for the loss of your husband: that would stamp you instantly. And it is not *bien séant* for a mother to cry much over her children—certainly not unless they are quite babies. A few tears—just a few—may be very well in that case, if you have a laced handkerchief at hand. But you must never look astonished, no matter what happens to you. And, Celia, last night, when the Consul spoke to you, you absolutely looked perplexed."

"I felt so, Madam," said Celia.

"Is not that just what I am telling you?" replied Lady Ingram, with that graceful wave of her hands which Celia had seen before. "My dear, you must not feel. Feeling is the one thing which the mode cannot permit."

"Pardon me, Madam," answered Celia, looking perplexed now; "but it seems to me that you are trying to make me into a statue."

"Exactly so, my dear Celia—that is just it. A modish woman is a piece of live marble: she eats, she drinks, elegantly and in small quantities—she sleeps, taking care not to lie ungracefully—she walks, glidingly and smoothly—she converses, but must be careful not to mean too much—she distributes her smiles at pleasure, but never shows real interest in any person. My dear, a heart is absolute ruin to a modish woman! She may do anything she likes but feel. Now look at me. Have you seen any exhibition of feeling in me since you have known me?"

Celia felt herself quite safe in acquitting Lady Ingram on that count.

"No, of course not," continued her step-mother; "I hope I know myself and the mode too well. Now, as to walking, what do you think the Consul said to me last night when you left the room?"

Celia confessed her inability to guess it.

"He said, 'What a pity that young lady cannot walk!'"

Celia's eyes opened rather widely.

"It is quite true, you absolutely cannot walk. You have no idea of walking but to go backwards or forwards. A walk should be a graceful, gliding motion, only just not dancing. There—that will do for this morning. As to walking, you shall have dancing lessons; but remember the other things I tell you. You must not blush, nor weep, nor eat more than you can help—in public, of course, I mean; you can eat an ox in your own chamber, if you please—and above everything else, you must give over feeling. You can go now if you wish it."

"Madam, you order impossibilities!" said Celia, with tears in her eyes. "I will eat as little as you please, if it keep me alive; and I will do my best to walk in any manner you wish me. I will try to give over blushing, if I can, though really I do not know how to set about it; but to give over feeling—Madam, I cannot do it. I do not think I ought to do it, even at your command. I must weep when I am sorrowful—I must laugh when I am diverted. I will not do it more than I can help, but I cannot make any promise beyond that."

"Ah! there you are!" said Lady Ingram, laughing. "You island English, with your hearts and your consciences, every man of you a Pope to himself! Well, I will not be too hard upon you at first, *ma belle*. That will do for the present. By and by I shall exact more."

Celia had a request to prefer before she went.

"Madam," she asked, trembling very much, "if it pleased you, and you had no desire that I should do otherwise, would you give me leave to hear Dr. Sacheverell preach on Sunday?"

"*Ma chère!*" said Lady Ingram, "how can I, a Catholic, choose between your Protestant teachers? You shall go where you like. The Consul has been so good as to place one of his carriages at my disposal, and as I shall remain here all the day, I place it at yours. I will bid William ask where your great Doctor preaches."

Celia went slowly back to her own room, feeling very strange, very lonely, and very miserable, though she hardly knew why. As soon as she reached it, she proceeded to contravene all Lady Ingram's orders by a good cry. She felt all the better for it; and having bathed her eyes, and comforted herself with a few words out of her Book, she was ready when Thérèse came to summon her to go down to breakfast with her step-mother. They breakfasted in a room down-stairs, the Consul and his wife being present; the latter a voluble French woman, who talked very fast to Lady Ingram. The days passed drearily to Celia; but she kept looking forward to the Sunday, on which she hoped to hear a sermon different from Dr. Braithwaite's. When the Sunday arrived, the carriage came round after breakfast to take Celia to hear Dr. Sacheverell, who, William had learned, was to preach at St. Andrew's that morning. To Holborn, therefore, the coach drove; and Celia entered St. Andrew's Church alone. She was put into a great pew, presently filled with other ladies; and the service was conducted by a young clergyman in a fair wig, who seemed more desirous to impress his hearers with himself than with his subject. Then the pulpit was mounted by a stout man in a dark wig, who preached very fluently, very energetically, and very dogmatically, a discourse in which there were more politics than religion, and very much more of Henry Sacheverell than of Jesus Christ.

All the attention which Celia could spare from the service and the preacher was concentrated in amazement on her fellow-worshippers. They were tolerably attentive to the sermon, but on the prayers they bestowed no notice whatever. All were dressed in the height of the fashion, and all carried fans and snuff-boxes. The former they flourished, handled, unfurled, discharged, grounded, recovered, and fluttered all through the service.[6] Whenever the fans were still for a moment, the snuff-boxes came into requisition, and the amount of snuff consumed by these fashionable ladies astonished Celia. They talked in loud whispers, with utter disregard to the sanctity of place and circumstances; and the tone of their conversation was another source of surprise to their hearer.

"Do you see Sir Thomas?"

"I am sure he is looking this way."

"There is Lady Betty—no, on your left."

"Lady Diana has not come this morning."

"How modishly she dresses!"

"Look at the Duchess—what a handsome brocade!"

"That lace cost five guineas the yard, I am certain."

Then came a fresh flourishing of fans, varied by the occasional rising and courtesying of one of the ladies, as she recognized an acquaintance in the fashionable crowd. Did these women really believe themselves in the special presence of God? thought Celia. Surely they never could! There was one point of the service at which all their remarks were hushed, their fans still, and their attention concentrated. This was during the singing. Celia found that no member of the congregation thought of joining the psalmody, which was left to a choir located in the gallery. At the close of each chant, audible comments were whispered round.

"How exceeding sweet!"

"What a divine voice she hath!"

"Beautiful, that E-la!"

And when the prayers followed, the snuff-boxes and fans began figuring again.

On the whole, Celia was glad when this service was over. Even Dr. Braithwaite was better than this. And then she thought of her friends at Ashcliffe, and how they would be rumbling home in the old family-coach, as she stepped in her loneliness into the Consul's splendid carriage. Did they miss her, she wondered, and were they thinking of her then, while her heart was dwelling sadly and longingly upon them? She doubted not that they did both.

"*Et bien?*" said Lady Ingram, interrogatively, when she met Celia after dinner. "Did you like your great preacher?"

"Not at all, Madam."

"Not at all? Then I wonder why you went. You look disappointed, *ma belle*. You must not look disappointed—It gives awkward lines to the face. Here—take some of this cake to console you; it is particularly good."

Celia took the cake, but not the consolation.

"At eleven o'clock on Tuesday, my child, we depart for Paris. Do not give yourself any trouble. Thérèse will do all your packing. Only you must not walk in Paris, until you have some clothes fit to be seen. I will order stuffs sent in at once when we arrive, and set the women to work for you."

"Do you know, Madam, if you please"—Celia hesitated, and seemed a little uncomfortable.

"Go on, child," said Lady Ingram. "Never stop in the middle of a sentence, unless you choose to affect the pretty-innocence style. Well?"

"Do you know, Madam, whether there be any Protestant service in Paris?"

"I imagine there is a Huguenot *prêche* somewhere—or was one. I am not sure if I heard not something about His Majesty having stopped them. Do not put your Protestantism too much forward there—the Court do not like it."

"I have nothing to do with the Court, Madam," said Celia, with sudden firmness; "and I am a Protestant, and I cannot disguise my religion."

"Oh dear! your Protestant consciences!" murmured Lady Ingram. "But you have to do with the Court, my friend; it is to the Court that I am taking you. Do you suppose that I live in the atmosphere of a recluse? When I am an old woman of eighty, *ma chère*, very likely I shall repair to a convent to make my salvation; but not just now, if you please."

"I am not an old woman—" Celia was beginning, but Lady Ingram interrupted her.

"Precisely, *ma belle*. The very reason why it is so absurd of you to make a recluse of yourself, as I see you would like to do,—unless, indeed, you had a vocation. But, so far as I know, Protestants never have such things."

"What things, Madam?"

"Vocations, my dear—calls to the religious life."

"Madam!" exclaimed Celia, very much astonished, "ought we not all to lead religious lives?"

"You are so absurd!" laughed Lady Ingram. "You absolutely do not understand what is meant by the religious life. My dear child (for a child you are indeed), the life which we all lead is the secular: we eat, drink, talk, sleep, dance, game and marry. These are the seculars who do these things. The religious are those who, having a call from Heaven, consecrate themselves entirely to God, and deny themselves all pleasures whatever, and so much of necessaries as is consistent with the preservation of life. Their mortification is accepted by Heaven, when extreme, not only for their own sins, but for the sins of any secular friend to whom they may desire to apply the merit of it. Now do you understand? *Ma foi!* what a grave, saint-like conversation you provoke!"

"Not at all, Madam."

"Let me hear your views then."

Had Celia been left free to choose, Lady Ingram was about the last person in her little world to whom she would have wished to give a reason for the hope that was in her. But she felt that there was no choice, and she must make the effort, though not in her own strength. She lifted up her heart to God for wisdom, and then spoke with a quiet decision which surprised her stepmother.

"Madam, I believe all persons to be religious who love God, and whom God loves. Because God loved us, He gave His Son to die for us, that we who believe in Him might have eternal life. It is He who saves us, not we who make our own salvation; and it is because we love God that we wish to serve Him."

"Well, my dear," answered Lady Ingram, slowly, as if considering Celia's speech, "I can see very little difference between us, except that you would have all men hermits and friars instead of some. We both believe in Jesus

Christ, of course; and no doubt there is a certain sense in which the religious feel love to God, and this love inclines them to the cloister. I do not therefore see wherein we differ except on a few unimportant points."

Celia saw an immense distance between them, on points neither few nor unimportant; but the courage which had risen to a high tide was ebbing away, and her heart failed her.

"Well, this will do for to-day, my fair divine," said Lady Ingram, with a smile. "Now bring me my silk-winders, and hold that skein of red silk while I wind it—or stay, is that a matter of conscience, my little votaress?"

"On the Lord's Day, Madam, it is, if you please."

"Very well, let the silk alone; I can wind it to-morrow just as well. Would it be breaking the Sabbath for you to tell Thérèse that I wish to speak with her? Pray don't if you feel at all uncomfortable."

Celia gave the message to Thérèse, and then locked herself into her own room, and relieved her feelings by another fit of crying.

[1a] [1b]A Devonshire phrase, as well as an American one, signifying, in the former case, "she belonged to, or lived at," the place.

[2] Foxe's "Acts and Monuments," ed. Townsend, 1846, vol. v., p. 550.

[3] Abigail Hill was a cousin and dependent of Sarah Duchess of Marlborough, and supplanted her in the Queen's favor. She was a violent Tory. She married Samuel Masham, one of the Queen's pages, created Baron Masham, December 13, 1711.

[4] Elizabeth Percy, only child of Josceline Earl of Northumberland, and Elizabeth Wriothesley: born 1665-6; married (1) 1679, Henry Cavendish, Lord Ogle, (2) 1681, Thomas Thynne Esq., (3) 1682, Charles Seymour, Duke of Somerset; she died December 1722, and was buried in Salisbury Cathedral. The Duchess of Somerset succeeded the Duchess of Marlborough in the office of Mistress of the Robes to Queen Anne.

[5] Matt. xxviii. 20.

[6] For the meaning of these technical phrases in "the exercise of the fan," see the *Spectator* of June 27, 1711.

V.

THE HARRYING OF LAUCHIE.

"'Have I received,' he answered, 'at thine hands
Favors so sweet they went to mine heart-root,
And could I not accept one bitter fruit?'"

LEIGH HUNT.

"Now, use your eyes, my young anchorite—if it be not wicked to look out of the window: this is the Rue de Rivoli, the finest street in Paris. By the way, you ought not to have been ill in crossing the Channel—so very undignified. Here is my town-house—that with the portico. Till your manners are formed, I shall give you a private closet as well as a bedroom, and an antechamber where you can take lessons in French and dancing.—— Good evening, St. Estèphe! Is Monsieur Philippe here?"

"Monsieur Philippe is not at himself, Madame; he ride out with Monsieur Bontems."

Lady Ingram knitted her brows, as if the information were not agreeable to her. She alighted, and desired Celia to follow her up-stairs. Through suites of spacious rooms, splendidly furnished, and along wide corridors she led the way to a quiet suite of apartments at one end of the house—an antechamber, a bedroom, and a small but elegant boudoir.

"These are your rooms," she said. "I will give you a new attendant, for I must have Thérèse to myself now. These will be entirely at your disposal, within certain restrictions. I shall visit you every morning, to have your masters' opinions as to your improvement, and you will take a dish of coffee or chocolate with me in my boudoir at four o'clock every afternoon. Until you are formed, you must dine alone, except when I dine entirely *en famille.* Your masters will attend you in the antechamber every morning. No one must be permitted to cross the threshold of your boudoir, except myself and your brothers, your own attendant, or any person sent by me. Do you dislike that?"

"No, Madam; I am very glad to hear it."

"Ah! my Sister of St. Ursula!" said Lady Ingram, laughing. "But remember this is only until you are formed, and the sooner that happens the better pleased I shall be."

"I am anxious to obey your wishes in everything not forbidden by my conscience, Madam."

"Very well," said Lady Ingram, still laughing. "The conscience requires a little formation too, *ma belle*, as well as the manners. Farewell! I will send your attendant."

She sailed away with her usual languid stateliness, and Celia went forward into the bedroom. She was vainly endeavoring to find an unlocked drawer in which to place her hood and cloak, when a low, quiet voice behind her said:

"Here are the keys, Madam. Will you allow me to open them for you?"

Celia looked up into a face which won her confidence at once. Its owner was a woman of middle height, whose age might be slightly under sixty. Her dress was of almost Quaker simplicity, and black. Her hair and eyes were of no particular color, but light rather than dark; her face wore no expression beyond a placid calm. But Celia fancied that she saw a peculiar, deep look in the eyes, as if those now passionless features might have borne an expression of great suffering once.

"Oh, thank you!" said Celia, simply. "Is it you whom my Lady promised to send?"

"I am to be your woman, Madam. I am her Ladyship's sewing-woman; my name is Patient Irvine."

The "lady's woman" of the seventeenth and eighteenth centuries was the ancestress rather of the modern companion than of the maid. She was called by her Christian or surname, sewed for her mistress, and assisted her in dressing; but in every other particular the mistress and maid were upon equal terms. The "woman" was her lady's constant companion, and nearly always her *confidante*. She sat at her mistress's table, went with her into company, and appeared as a member of her family when she received her friends. As a rule, she was the equal of her lady in education, and not seldom her superior. Her inferiority lay in birth and fortune, sometimes in the latter only.

"And what would you like me to call you?—Patience or Irvine?" asked Celia of her new acquaintance.

"Patient, if you please, Madam."

"Patient—not Patience?"

"I was not baptized Patience, Madam. My father was a Scottish Covenanter, and he named me, his first-born child, 'The-Patient-Waiting-for-Christ.'"

"What a strange name!" involuntarily exclaimed Celia.

"Yes, Madam; very strange, I doubt not, to such as have never met with our Puritan practice of Scripture-text names. I have known divers such."

"Do the Puritans, then, commonly give their children such names?"

"Very often, Madam. I had an aunt who was called 'We-Love-Him-Because-He-First-Loved-Us.'"

"They called her Love for short, I suppose?"

"Yes, Madam," answered Patient, in her calm, passive manner.

Celia thought this very odd indeed, and turned the conversation, lest she should get comic associations with texts of Scripture of which she could not afterwards divest herself. She wondered that Patient did not feel the ludicrous strangeness of the practice, not knowing that all sense of the ludicrous had been left out of Patient's composition.

"And how long have you lived in France, Patient?"

"Since I was of the age of twenty years, Madam Celia."

"You know my name, then?" said Celia, smiling.

"I know you, Madam, much better than you know me. I have borne you about in mine arms as a babe of a few hours old. And just now, when I saw you, you looked to mine eyes as the very image from the dead of my dear Miss Magdalene."

"Patient! do you mean my mother?"

"Yes Madam. I ask your pardon for calling her such a name, but it ever sounds more natural to mine ear. She was my Lady Ingram for so short a time, and I knew her as Miss Magdalene when she was but a wee bonnie bairn."

"What was her name?"

"Magdalene Grey, Madam. She was the Minister's daughter at the Manse of Lauchie, where my father and I dwelt."

"Then she was a Scottish lady?"

"Yes, Madam, at least she was born in Scotland, and her mother was Scottish. Her father, Mr. Grey, was English by descent, though his fathers had dwelt in Scotland for three generations afore him."

"And where did my father meet with her? He was not Scottish?"

"He was not, Madam. And I will tell you all the story if it please you; but will you not dress now?"

"You can tell me while I comb my hair, Patient. I want to know all about it."

"May I do it for you, Madam? I can speak now, if that be your pleasure; but 'tis almost necessary that I tell mine own story in hers."

"Will it pain you, Patient?" asked Celia, kindly.

"No, Madam; I am far past that," answered Patient, in her calm, passionless voice.

"Then please to let me hear it."

"My father's name, please you," Patient began, "was Alexander Leslie, and he dwelt on Lauchie Farm, near to the Manse. And sith Mr. Grey, our Minister, wedded Mrs. Jean Leslie, of the same clan, it fell out that Miss Magdalene and I were somewhat akin, though in worldly goods she was much beyond us. For Mr. Grey was not one of our poor ministers of Scotland, but a rich Englishman, who made his way into what the English deemed our wild valleys, for no cause but only the love of Christ. Miss Magdalene being an only bairn, without brother or sister, it so fell that I and Roswith were called up whiles to the Manse to divert her."

"You and who?"

"Roswith, my sister."

"What strange names your father gave his daughters!"

"Ay, that was a strange name, and all said so. It came out of an old chronicle that he had, a very ancient book, and he deemed it a fair name, and gave it in the baptizing to his youngest-born. Those were evil days, Madam, on which we fell. Yet why should I call them evil, when they were days of growing in the truth, and of the great honor of suffering for the Lord's sake? Mr. Grey, your grandfather, Madam, was a very gracious man, and did preach most savory discourses. Wherefore, he was one of the first on whom the blow fell. And when King Charles sent his troopers into our parts, under command of Claverhouse,[1] bidding them hunt and slay all that would not conform unto his way, they came, one of the first places, into our valley. Many an humble and honest husbandman, that feared God, was hung up at his own door by the wicked Claverhouse and his troopers, and many a godly man and woman was constrained to dwell in caves and dens of the earth until this enemy was overpast. I could tell many a tale of those days that would stir your blood, Madam, if it pleased you to hear it. We were amongst those whom the Lord was pleased to honor by permitting them to suffer for His name's sake. Mr. Grey refused to fly. He was dragged down, one Sabbath morn, from the pulpit in Lauchie Kirk, Claverhouse himself being at the door. He had been preaching unto us a most sweet, godly, and gracious discourse of casting care upon the Lord, and standing firm in the truth. And just when he was speaking that great and precious promise of the Lord, 'Lo! I am with you alway, even unto the end of the world,' the troopers burst in. Then the whole kirk thronged around our Minister, and sought to free him from the evil men. Mine uncle Jock Leslie, fell, thrust through with the swords of the troopers, and many another. But at length they had their wicked will, and bound us, men, women, and children, two and two, with one strong rope, like a gang of slaves going to the market-place. I was greatly honored to have the next place to Mr. Grey, hand in hand with whom walked Miss Magdalene, a sweet young maid of scarce fourteen years. His godly wife was bound, just before, with Janet Campbell, an old wife of nigh eighty. So we were marched down eleven miles to the shore. Ah! but my heart ached for Miss Magdalene and Roswith ere we reached it! It was a grand comfort to find Roswith bound with me, for she was but a wee wean of eight years, and I a grown maiden of twenty. Doubtless this was the Lord's mercy. When we came to the sea, we saw a great ship lying afar off, and we were all thrust into boats to carry us thither. When we were aboard, the troopers, some of whom came with us, did drive us below, and shut down the hatches upon us: which, it being summer time, was hot and painful, and many women and children fell sick therewith. Whither we were to go we knew not, only Mr. Grey surmised that they thought either to sell us for slaves in Barbary unto the heathen there, or else to convey us unto the King's plantations in Virginia or those parts; though if they were bound unto Virginia he knew not wherefore they should set sail from the eastern part of the kingdom. For three days and nights we were thus kept under hatches, to our much discomfort, and the ship sailing northwards with all the speed the sailors could make. During which time we were greatly comforted with the thought of Christ our Lord, and the three days and three nights which He was in the heart of the earth. Likewise Mr. Grey did oft exhort us, and prayed us to bear all that should come upon us meekly and bravely, and as unto the Lord. Then some of us which were mighty in the Scriptures did say certain parts thereof for the comfort of the rest; in particular, old Jamie Campbell, Janet's guidman, and Elsie Armstrong, his sister's daughter. So passed these three days until the Wednesday even. And then arose a great and mighty tempest, with contrary winds, driving the ship down, so that, notwithstanding all the skill of the shipmen, she lost in one day and night more than she had gained in all the three. Verily she fled like a mad thing afore the violence of that wind. And on the Thursday night, a little on the hither side of midnight, she flying as thistledown afore the wind, we felt a mighty shock, and suddenly the water came in at our feet with a great rush. Mr. Grey said he thought the ship must have lighted on some rock, and that a hole was driven in her. Then the shipmen opened the hatches, and in dolorous voices bade us come up on deck, for we were all like to drown. Wherefore we ascended the ladders, thirty-five in all our company, I alway holding tight the hand of my wee sister. When we were upon deck, we found from the words of the shipmen that they were about to loose the boats. So when all the boats were loosed, the troopers filled two of them and the seamen the third, and no room was left for the prisoners. Then in this time we thought much on Paul and his shipwreck, and how the seamen were minded to kill the prisoners lest any should escape: and we marvelled if they counselled to kill us, seeing there was no room for us in the boats."

"O Patient! surely they laid no hands on any of you?"

"No, Madam; they left that to the wind and the sea. The three boats cast off, and we prisoners stood alone on the deck of the sinking ship. We had neither wit nor material to make any more boats nor rafts. And when we saw our death thus before us—for our ship, like Paul's, was stuck fast in the forepart, but the sea beat freely on the hinder—we stood like men stupid and amazed for a short season. But then above all the noise of the storm came Mr. Grey's voice, which we were used to obeying, saying, 'Brethren, in a few hours at most, perchance in a few minutes, we shall stand before God. Let our last hour be employed in His worship.' Then we gathered all around him, on that part of the ship which was fast on the rock, and he led the exercise with that Psalm:[2]

'O God, the heathen entered have
   Thine heritage; by them
Defiled is Thine house: on heaps
They laid Jerusalem.'

"After the Psalm there was an exhortation. Our Minister bade us remember that we were the Lord's freedmen—doubly so now, since our enemies had cast us away from them, and we were left only on the mercy of our God. Moreover, he recalled that of David, saying in his strait, 'Let me fall into the hand of the Lord, for His mercies are great.'[3] Then he prayed with us; and while the exercise yet lasted, and Mr. Grey was still praying, and entreating the Lord to deal with us in his mercy, whether for life or for death,—but if it should be death, as there seemed no other, to grant, if it so pleased Him, an easy dying unto the little children in especial—while he prayed, the ship parted asunder with a great crash, and the waves, leaping up on that part which stuck fast, swept every soul of us out into the boiling sea."

"O Patient, what a dreadful story! And how many were saved?"

"Four, Madam."

"Only four out of thirty-five!"

"Ah, Madam! the thirty-one were happier than any of the four!"

"Who were saved, Patient?"

"Miss Magdalene, and wee Jamie Campbell—old Jamie's grandson—and Roswith, and me.'

"And not one of the others?" said Celia, pityingly.

"Not one. They were carried by the angels into the rest of the Lord, and He would not grudge them the crown of martyrdom."

"And how did you get ashore?"

"That, Madam, I never knew. I mind falling into the water, and sinking down, it seemed to me, far and low therein; and then I was buoyed up again to the top, and I tried to make some little struggle for life. But the waters closed over me again, and I knew no more. The next minute, as it felt, I was lying with mine eyes shut, methought, in my little bed at Lauchie. I thought I had dreamed a bad dream, sith I felt stiff, and sore, and cold, and wet, all over: but as I awoke, I felt it was truly so: and at last I oped mine eyes and strove to sit. Then I saw that I sat on the sea-sand, and above me the blue sky, and I all alone: and an exceeding bitter cry rose to my lips as it came back upon me what had been. When I fancied I heard a bit groan no so far from me and I struggled up on my feet, and crept, rather than walked, wondering I had no bones broken, to a cleft of the rocks whence methought the groan came. And there was Jamie Campbell, lying sorely bruised and hurt; and when I stooped to him he lifted up his eyes, and saith, 'O Patient! I thought all were drowned, and that there was none here but God.' I said, 'Are you sore hurt, my poor bairn?' 'Yea,' quoth he, 'for I cannot move nor sit, and methinks I have some bones broke.' Poor laddie! he was in a sad way indeed. I tare mine own clothing to bind up his bruises, and promising to return to him, I set out to see if any other might have been saved from the wreck, ever hoping to find my father, my mother, or Mr. Grey. I walked upon the sand to the right hand, and saw no sign of any soul: then I turned to the left hand, and passing Jamie, walked far that way. Not a soul did I see, and I was about turning again in despair, accounting that he and I were the only two alive, when all at once I fancied I heard Roswith's voice. I stood and hearkened—sure enough it was Roswith's voice, for I never could mistake that. I could not hear whence it came, and so weak was I become with sorrow and weariness and fasting, that methought she was speaking to me from Heaven. Then I called, 'Roswith!' and heard her cry as in joy, 'Patient! O Miss Magdalene, Patient is alive! here is Patient!' And before I knew aught more, her little arms were around me, and Miss Magdalene, white and wan, stood at my side."

"How had they been saved?"

"They knew that no more than I did, Madam. Truly, Roswith, like a bit fanciful lassie, said she thought the Lord sent an angel to help her, and talked of walking over some rocks. I had not the heart to gainsay the bairn, and how did I know that the Lord had not sent His angel? Well, we all got back to Jamie Campbell, but what little I could do for him was no good; he died that forenoon. Then I said we would set forth and seek some house, for it was eleven hours gone since we had eaten food. But afore we could depart, the tempest, which was somewhat lulled, washed up two bodies at our feet, Mr. Grey's and Elsie Armstrong's. We poor weak maids could do nought for their burying; but Miss Magdalene cut off a lock of her father's hair, and kissed him, and wept over him. Then we set out to try and find some house near. When at last, after two hours' good walking, we reached a cot, we found to our sorrow that they spake a strange tongue. Miss Magdalene was the only one of us that could speak their speech, and she told us that the country where we were thus cast was the North of France."

"Patient! Patient Irvine, where are you?"

"Here, Sir," answered Patient to the voice without. "Your brother, Madam, Mr. Philip Ingram."

Celia was half-way across the room before she remembered that one side of her hair was still floating on her shoulders.

"I will take him into your closet, Madam," said Patient, as she left the room.

The colloquy outside was audible within.

"Mr. Philip, will you wait a few minutes? I have not ended dressing Madam's hair, but by the time you have changed your boots she will be ready to see you."

"Pray what is the matter with my boots?"

"They are splashed all over, Sir. My Lady would not allow you to come into Madam's closet with such boots as those, which you know."

"Leather and prunella! Never mind my boots nor my mother neither!"

"Sir!" responded Patient, in a tone which admitted of but one interpretation.

"Well, come, I don't mean——you are always making me say something I don't mean, you dear old tease!"

"Sir, I must obey my Lady's orders."

"Must you, really? Well, then, I suppose I must. Eh! Madam Patient?"

"If you will please to change your boots, Mr. Philip," quietly repeated Patient, "Madam will be ready to receive you in a few minutes."

"Very well, Madam Patient. I will obey your orders."

And the boots were heard quickly conveying their owner down the corridor. Celia's hair was soon put up, for she was very wishful to make the acquaintance of her half-brother; and she was in the boudoir waiting for him before Mr. Philip Ingram had completed the changing of his objectionable boots.

"Come in!" she said, with a beating heart, to the light tap at her door.

"Are you my sister Celia? I am very glad to see you—very glad. I must congratulate dear old Patient on having finished you sooner than I expected."

The first greeting over, Celia looked curiously at her half-brother. He was not like what she had anticipated, and, except for a slight resemblance about the eyes, he was not like Lady Ingram. He looked older than his years—so much so, that if Celia had not known that he was her junior, she would have supposed him to be her senior by some years. Philip Ingram was of middle height, inclining rather to the higher side of it, slenderly built, thin, lithe, and very active in his movements, with much quickness, physical and mental. He had dark glossy hair, brilliant dark eyes, and a voice not unmusically toned.

"Well, Madam!" he said at last, laughingly; "I hope you like me as well as I do you."

Celia laughed in her turn, and colored slightly. "I have no doubt that I shall like my new brother very much," she said. "Whom do you think me like?"

"That is just what I cannot settle," said Philip, gravely, considering her features. "You are not like Ned, except about the mouth; you have his mouth and chin, but not his eyes and forehead."

"Am I like my father?"

"Don't recollect him a bit," said Philip. "He died before I was three years old."

"Edward is not here, is he?"

"No; he is on his travels."

"Where has he gone?"

"The stars know where! He did not ask me to go with him, and if he had done, my Lady-Mother would have put an extinguisher upon it. I wish he were here; 'tis only endurable when he is."

"What is it that you dislike?"

"Everything in creation!" said Philip, kicking a footstool across the room.

"You speak very widely," replied Celia, laughing, and thinking of Charley Passmore.

"I speak very truly, as you will shortly find, Madam, to your cost. Wait until you have been at one of her Ladyship's evening assemblies."

"I am not to go until she is better satisfied with my manners," said Celia, simply.

Philip whistled. "You will not lose much," he answered.

"Don't you like them?"

"What is there to like?" asked Philip, dissecting the tassel of the sofa-cushion. "A thousand yards of satin and lace, or the men and women under them, whose hearts are marble and their brains sawdust! Celia Ingram, don't let my mother spoil you! From the little I see of you now, I know you are not one of them. Indeed, I guessed that from what my mother told me. She said you were absolutely without a scrap of fine breeding—which she meant as a censure, and I took as a compliment. I know what your grand ladies are, and what their fine breeding is! And I hope you are a true English girl, with a heart in you, and not one of these finnicking, fussy, fickle, faithless French-women!"

Philip let the sofa-cushion go when he had relieved his feelings by this burst of alliteration.

"I hope I have a heart, dear Philip," replied Celia. "But can you find no friends anywhere?"

"Just one," said Philip, "that is, beside Ned. You see, when Ned is here, he is master; but when he is away, I am not master: her Ladyship is mistress and master too."

"But surely, Philip, you do not wish to disobey your mother?"

"Disobey my mother!" answered Philip, reflectively, and resuming the sofa-cushion. "Well, Madam, I never get much chance of doing that. You don't know the sort of game my mother can play sometimes!"

"What do you mean, Philip?"

"I will tell you what I mean. Celia, there is a very, very pleasant prospect before you. Imprimis, Madam, you will be converted; that is, if she can manage it; and if she can't, it will show that you are a clever hand. In the latter case, the probability is that she won't think you worth the waste of any more time; but if she succeed in converting you, she will then proceed to form you. She will turn your feet out, and pinch your waist in, and stick your head up, and make you laugh when you are angry, and cry when you are pleased. She will teach you to talk without interruption for an hour, and yet to have said nothing when the hour is over. You will learn how to use your eyes—how to look at people and not see them, and *who* to see, or not to see. I can give you a hint about that, myself; a man who wears no orders is nobody—you may safely omit seeing him. A man of one order is to be treated with distant civility; a man of two, with cordiality; but a man who wears three is to be greeted with the most extreme pleasure, and held in the closest friendship."

"But if I don't like the man, I cannot make a friend of him," said Celia, in a puzzled tone.

"My dear, that doesn't come into consideration. You will have to learn never to look at the man, but only at his coat and decorations. A man is not a man in genteel society; he is a Consul, a Marquis, or a nobody. Never look at nobodies; but if a Duke should lead you to a chair, be transported with delight. You have a great deal to learn, I see. Well, after you have got all this by heart—I am afraid it will take a long while!—my mother will proceed with her work. The last act will be to take your heart out of you, and put instead of it a lump of stone, cut to the proper shape and size, and painted so as to imitate the reality too exactly for any one to guess it an imitation. And then, with a lot of satin and velvet and lace on the top, Mrs. Celia Ingram, you will be finished!"

"Oh dear! I hope not," said Celia involuntarily.

"So do I," echoed Philip, significantly.

"But, Philip, I want to ask you one thing—are you not a Protestant?"

"I?" asked Philip, with a peculiar intonation. "No."

"You are a Papist?" said Celia, in a very disappointed tone.

"No," said Philip again.

"Then what are you?" asked she, astonished.

"Neither—nothing," he answered, rather bitterly. "I am what half the men of this age are, Sister Celia;—nothing at all. I call myself a Catholic, just to satisfy my mother; and when I see her becoming doubtful of my soundness in her faith, I go to mass with her half a dozen times, to quiet her conscience—and perhaps my own. But, Catholic as I am—so far as I own to anything—I do not believe you have read more Protestant books, or heard more Protestant preaching, than I have. I have tried both religions in turn, and now I believe in nothing. I have lost all faith, whether in religion, in morality, in man, or woman. I see the men of this city, Protestant and Catholic, either bent on pursuing their own pleasures, or on seeking their own interests—thinking of and caring for themselves and nothing in the world else; and I see the women, such as I have described them to you. I find none, of either faith, any better than the rest. What wonder, then, that the fire of my faith—the old, bright, happy trust of my childhood—has blackened and gone out?"

"But, Philip, dear Brother," pleaded Celia in great pain, "surely you believe in God?"

"I believe in *nothing*," said he, firmly.

Celia turned away, grieved at her very heart.

"Listen to me, Celia," resumed Philip, now quite serious. "You will not betray me to my mother—I see that in your eyes. You see I can believe in *you*," he added, smiling rather sadly. "There was a time when I believed all that you do, and more. When I was a little child, I used to think that, as Patient told me, God saw me, and loved me, and was ready to be my Friend and Father. All that I noticed different from this in the teaching of my other nurse, Jeannette Luchon, was that she taught me to think this of the Virgin Mary, my patron saint, and my guardian angel, as well as of God. Had I been struck deaf, dumb, and blind at that time, I might have believed it all yet. Perhaps it would have been as well for me. But I grew up to what I am. I watched all these highly religious people who visit here. I heard them invoke the Virgin or the saints to favor—not to forgive, mind you—but, before its committal, to prosper—what they admitted to be sin. I saw my own mother come home from receiving the Eucharist at mass, and tell lies: I knew they were lies, I was taught that it was very wicked in me to tell lies, and also that, in receiving the Eucharist, she had received Christ Himself into her soul. How could I believe both the one and the other? I was taught, again, that if I committed the most fearful sins, a man like myself, sitting in a confessional, could with two words cleanse my soul as if I had never sinned. How could I believe that, when from that cleansing I came home and found it no whit the cleaner? I turn to Protestantism. I hear your preachers tell me that 'Without holiness no man shall see the Lord;' that God has 'purer eyes than to behold sin;' and many another passage to the like effect. The next week I hear that one of the pastor's flock, or perhaps the very preacher himself, has been guilty of some glaring breach of common honesty. Does the man mean me to believe—does he believe himself—what he told me from the pulpit only a few days earlier? Romans and English, all are alike. I find the most zealous professors of religion in both communions guilty of acts with which I, who profess no religion at all, would scorn to sully my conscience. I have seen only one man who seems to me really honest and anxious to find out the truth, and he is about where I am; only that his mind is deeper and stronger than mine, and therefore he suffers more."

"But Edward!"

"Oh, Edward! He is a Protestant after your own heart. But he could not enter into my feelings at all. He is one of your simple, honest folks, who believe what they are taught, and do not trouble themselves about the parts of the puzzle not fitting."

"Philip, I do not know what to say to you," answered his sister, candidly. "I do not think we ought to look at other people, and take our religion from what they do, or do not do, but only from God Himself. If you would read the Bible"—

"I have read it," he interrupted.

"And do you find nothing to satisfy you there?" asked Celia, in surprise.

"I will tell you what I find. Very ancient writings, and very beautiful language, which I admire exceedingly; but nothing upon which I can rely."

"Not in God's Word?"

"How do I know that it is God's Word? How can I be sure that there is a God at all?"

Celia was silent. Such questions had never suggested themselves to her mind before, and she knew not how to deal with them. At length she said—

"Philip, I believe in one God, who is my Father, and orders all things for me; and who gave His Son Jesus Christ to die for me, instead of my dying for my own sins. Is this so difficult to believe?"

"I believe that you believe it," said Philip, smiling.

"But you do not believe it yourself?" she asked, with a baffled feeling.

"I have told you," he said, "that I believe nothing."

"Philip," she answered, softly, "I do not understand your feelings, and I do not know what to say to you. I must ask my Father. I will lay it before Him to-night; and as He shall give me wisdom I will talk with you again."

So she closed the subject, not knowing that the quiet certainty of conviction expressed in her last words had made a deeper impression upon Philip than any argument which could have been used to him.

"Come in!" said Lady Ingram, that afternoon, in reply to Celia's gentle tap at her door. "I thought it was you, *ma chère*. I am glad you are come, for I have something to say to you."

"Yes, Madam," responded Celia, resigning herself to another lecture.

"When you have taken dancing-lessons for a month, so that your deportment is a little improved, I wish you to be present at my first assembly for this year. Do not be alarmed—I require nothing more of you than to dress well and sit still. I shall present you to my particular friends, saying that you do not yet speak French, and none of them will then address you but such as are acquainted with English. You must remain in a corner of the room, where your awkward manners will attract no notice; and I shall put you in Philip's charge, and desire him to tell you who each person is, and so on. You will then have the opportunity of seeing really fine breeding and distinguished manners, and can help in the formation of your own accordingly, as you will then understand what I require of you."

"Yes, Madam," said Celia again.

"I have ordered stuffs for you, and they are now in the house. My assembly will be on Thursday week. There is quite time enough to make you one dress; and you will not appear again until you are formed—at least, that is my present intention. Thérèse will take your measure this evening, and cut out the dress, which Patient can then make. I wish you to have a white satin petticoat and a yellow silk bodice and train, guarded with lace; and I will lend you jewels."

"Thank you, Madam," answered Celia, giving herself up to all her step-mother's requirements.

"When you feel tired—I dare say you are not accustomed yet to late hours—you may slip out of the room and retire to you own apartments. Nobody will miss you."

"No, Madam," meekly responded Celia again, to this not very flattering remark.

"I think that is all I need say," pursued Lady Ingram, meditatively. "I do not wish to encumber and confuse your mind with too many details, or you will certainly not behave well. I will instruct Patient how you must be dressed, and I will look at you myself before you descend to the drawing-room, to be sure that no ridiculous mistake has been made. Thérèse shall dress your hair. Now help yourself to the chocolate."

"Patient! will you bring your work into my closet? I want to hear the end of your story."

"If you please, Madam. I must try the skirt on you in a little while, by your leave."

So Patient and the white satin petticoat came and settled themselves in Celia's boudoir.

"You had just landed in France when you left off, Patient. I am anxious to know if you found friends."

"'Twould make it a very long tale, Madam to tell you of all that we did and suffered ere we found friends. It was a hard matter to see what we should do; for had I sought a place as woman to some lady, I could not have left Roswith alone; and no lady would be like to take the child with me. So I could but entreat the Lord to show me how to earn bread enough for my wee sister and myself. The woman of the house who took us in after the shipwreck was very good unto us, the Lord inclining her heart to especial pity of us; and she greatly pressed us to go on to Paris, where she thought we should be more like to meet with succor. Therefore we set out on our way to Paris. The Lord went with us, and gave us favor in the eyes of all them whom we had need of on our road. Most of the women whom we met showed much compassion for Roswith, she being but a wee bit wean, and a very douce and cannie bairn to boot. It was in the month of October that we arrived in Paris. Here the Lord had prepared a strange thing for us. There was an uncle of Miss Magdalene, by name Mr. Francis Grey, who was a rich gentleman and a kindly. He had been on his travels into foreign parts, and was returning through this city unto his place; and by what men call chance, Miss Magdalene and I lighted on this gentleman in the Paris street, we returning from the buying of bread and other needful matters. He was as if he saw her not, for he afterward told us that he had heard nought of the harrying of Lauchie, nor of our shipwreck. But she ran to him, and cast her arms about him, calling 'Uncle Francis!' and after a season he knew her again, but at first he was a man amazed. When he heard all that had come upon us, and how Miss Magdalene was left all alone in the world, father and mother being drowned, he wept and clipped[4] her many times, and said that she should come with him to his inn, and dwell with him, and be unto him as a daughter, for he had no child. Then she prayed him to have compassion upon us also, Patient and Roswith Leslie; who, as John saith, had continued with her in her tribulation, and, it pleased her to say, had aided and comforted her. Mr. Francis smiled, and he said that I, Patient, should be in his service as a woman for her; and for Roswith, 'She,' quoth he, 'will not eat up all my substance, poor wee thing! So she shall come too, and in time Patient must learn her meetly unto the same place to some other lady.' Thus it was, Madam, that at the time when we seemed at the worst, the Lord delivered us out of our distresses."

"Then you went back to Scotland?"

"No, Madam, we never went back. For when Mr. Francis heard all, of the harrying of Lauchie, and the evil deeds of the King's troopers, and the cruelty of Claverhouse, he said there could be no peace in Scotland more, and sent word unto his steward to sell all, and remit the money to him. He bought a house at Paris, and there we dwelt all."

"It was in her uncle's house, then, that my mother met my father?"

"There, Madam. Sir Edward took her to England, for they married in January, 1687, while King James yet reigned; and Sir Edward was great with the King, and had a fine land there. Her son, your brother, Madam, that is Sir Edward now, was born in London, in the summer of 1688."

"Patient, what kind of man was my father?"

"He was a very noble-looking gentleman, Madam, tall, with dark eyes and hair."

"Yes, but I mean in his mind and character?"

"Well, Madam," answered Patient, rather doubtfully, "he was much like other men. He had good points and bad points. He was a kindly gentleman, and open-handed. He was not an angel."

"You scarce liked him, I think, Patient."

"I ought not to say so, Madam. He was alway a good and kind master to me. Truly, he was not the man I should have chosen for Miss Magdalene; but I seldom see folks choose as I should in their places. Yet that is little marvel, since, fifteen years gone, Patient Leslie made a choice that Patient Irvine would be little like to make now."

Patient's dry, sarcastic tone warned Celia that she had better turn the conversation.

"And where was I born, Patient?"

"Well, Madam, you know what happened that summer your brother was born. He that was called Prince of Wales was born in the same month;[5] and in October King James fled away, sending his wife Queen Mary[6] and the babe to France. When King William landed, it was expected that he would seize all belonging to the malignants;[7] this was not so entirely, yet so much that Sir Edward was sore afeared to lose his. He kept marvellous quiet for a time, trusting that such as were then in power would maybe not think of him. But when King James landed in Ireland, he was constrained to join him, but he left my Lady behind, and me with her, at his own house in Cheshire. After the battle of Boyne Water,[8] whereat he fought, it happed as he feared, for all his property was escheated to the Crown. At this time Mr. Francis Grey came back into the country, and for a time Sir Edward and my Lady abode with him at a house which he had near the Border, on the English side: but Sir Edward by his work on the Boyne had made the place too hot for to hold him, and he bethought himself of escaping after King James to France. So about March, 1691, we began to journey slowly all down England from the Border to the south sea. Sir Edward was mortal afeared of being known and seized, so that he would not go near any place where he could possibly be known: and having no acquaintance anywhere in the parts of Devon, made him fix upon Plymouth whence to sail. It was in the last of May that we left Exeter. We had journeyed but a little thence, when I saw that my Lady, who had been ailing for some time, was like to fall sick unto death. I told Sir Edward that methought she was more sick than he guessed, but I think he counted my words but idle clavers and foolish fancies. At last she grew so very bad that he began to believe me. 'Patient,' he said to me one morn, 'I shall go on to Plymouth and inquire for a ship. Tend your Lady well, and so soon as she can abide the journeying, she must come after. If I find it needful, I may sail the first.' It was on a Monday that Sir Edward rode away, leaving my Lady and the little Master, with me and Roswith to tend them, at a poor cot, the abode of one Betty Walling."

"Betty Walling of Ashcliffe? Why, Patient, I know her!"

"Do you so, Madam? She knows you, I guess, and could have told you somewhat anent yourself. Not that she knew my Lady's name: I kept that from her. It was on the Friday following that you were born. Saving your presence, Madam, you were such a poor, weak, puny babe, that none thought you would live even a day. Betty said, I mind, 'Poor little soul! 'twill soon be out of its suffering—you may take that comfort!' I myself never reckoned that you could live. I marvel whether Madam Passmore would remember Betty Walling's coming unto her one wet even in June, to beg a stoup of wine for a sick woman with her? That sick woman was my dear Lady. It was the Saturday eve, and she died on the Sunday morning. I laid her out for the burying, which was to be on the Wednesday, and was preparing to go thence unto Plymouth afterward, with Roswith and the babes, when on the Tuesday night I was aroused from sleep by a rapping on the window. I crept to the casement and oped it, and was surprised to hear my Master's voice saying softly, 'Patient, come and open to me.' I ran then quickly and let him in; he looked very white and tired, and his dress soiled as if he had ridden hard and long. Quoth he, 'How fares Magdalene?' As softly as I could break it, I told him that she would never suffer any more, but she had left him a baby daughter which he must cherish for her sake. He was sore grieved as ever I saw man for aught. After a while, he told me much, quickly, for there was little time. He had not entered Plymouth, when, riding softly in the dark, another horseman met him, and aroused his wonder by riding back after him and away again; and this he did twice over. At length the strange horseman rode right up to him, and asked him plainly, 'Are you Sir Edward Ingram, holding King James's commission?' And when he said he was, then said the horseman, 'If you look to sail from Plymouth, I would have you know that you are expected there, and spies be abroad looking for you, and you will be taken immediately you show yourself. If you love your life, turn back!' Sir Edward desiring to know both who he was and how he knew this, the horseman saith, 'That I may not tell you: but ride hard, or they will be on your track; for they already misdoubt that you are at Ashcliffe, where if your following be, I counsel you to remove thence with all the speed that may be.' Sir Edward said that he had ridden for life all through three days and nights, and now we must move away without awaiting aught. 'And we will go,' quoth he, 'by Bideford; for they will expect me now, if they find I have given them the slip, to take passage by Portsmouth or Southampton, and will scarce count on my turning westward.' It grieved us both sore to leave my Lady unburied, but there was no help; and Betty passed her word to follow the body, and see that she was meetly laid in her grave. 'And how will I carry the babe?' quoth I. 'Nay, truly,' said he, sorrowfully, 'the babe cannot go with us; it will bewray all by its crying. We must needs leave it somewhere at nurse, and when better times come, and the King hath his own again, I will return and claim it.' For Master Edward was a braw laddie, that scarce ever cried or plained; while you, Madam, under your leave, did keep up a continual whining and mewling, which would have entirely hindered our lying hid, or journeying under cover of darkness. So I called Betty when it grew light, and conferred with her; and she said, 'Leave the babe at the gate of the Hall, and watch it till one cometh to take it.' Madam Passmore, she told us, was a kindly gentlewoman, that had sent word she would have come to see my Lady herself if she also had not been sick; and at this time having a little babe of her own, Betty thought she would be of soft heart unto any other desolate and needful babe. So I clad you in laced wraps, and pinned a paper on your coat with a gold pin of my Lady's, and Sir Edward wrote on the paper your name, 'Celia,' the which my poor Lady, as she lay a-dying, had felt a fancy to have you called. He said he had ever wished, should he have a daughter, to name her Grissel, which was my Lady his mother's name; 'But,' quoth he, 'if my poor Magdalene in dying had asked me to name the child Nebuchadnezzar, I would not have said her nay.' He was such a gentleman as that, Madam; in his deepest troubles he scarce could forbear jesting. So I carried you to the Hall, and laid you softly down at the gate, and rang the bell, and hid and watched among the trees. There first the Master rode up, looked strangely on you, though pitifully enough, but touched you not: and anon came out a kindly-looking woman of some fifty-and-five or sixty years, and took you up, and carried you away in her arms, chirping pleasantly unto you the while. So I was satisfied for the babe."

"That was Cicely Aggett," said Celia, smiling: "dear old Cicely! she told me about her finding me."

"The next hour," pursued Patient, "saw us thence. We got safe to Bideford, and away, the Lord aiding us, and after some tossing upon the sea, landed at Harfleur in fourteen days thereafter. Thence we came up to Paris, unto Mr. Francis Grey's house, which he had given unto my Lady in dowry; and Sir Edward bought another house at St. Germains, for he had had prudence to put some of his money out to interest in this land, so that all was not lost."

"And now tell me, Patient, how did he meet my step-mother?"

"I must pray you to leave that, Madam, for the time, and try on this skirt. Thérèse hath given me the pieces for the bodice."

---

[1] John Graham, of Claverhouse, Viscount of Dundee, was the eldest son of Sir William Graham and Lady Jane Carnegy his wife. He was a descendant of the royal line of Scotland, through his ancestress the Princess Mary, daughter of King Robert III. He fell at Killicrankie, July 16, 1689. In person he was eminently beautiful, in politics devoutly loyal; in character, a remarkable instance of the union of the softest and most genial manners with the sternest courage and most revolting cruelty in action. His least punishment as a General was death; and his persecution of the hapless Covenanters was restrained by no sense of humanity or compassion.

[2] Ps. lxxix.

[3] 2 Sam. xxiv. 14.

[4] Embraced.

[5] At St James's Palace, June 10, 1688.

[6] Maria Beatrice Leonora, only daughter of Alfonso IV., Duke of Modena, and Laura Martinozzi; born at Modena, October 5, 1658; married (by proxy) at Modena, September 30, and (in person) at Dover, November 21, 1673, to James Duke of York, afterwards James II.; died of cancer, at St. Germain-en-Laye, May 7, 1718, and buried at Chaillot.

[7] This name was given, both during the Rebellion and the Revolution, by each party to its opponents.

[8] Fought July 1, 1689.

VI.

THE TROUBLES OF GREATNESS.

> "Good Majesty,
> Herod of Jewry dare not look upon you,
> But when you are well pleased."
>
> SHAKESPEARE.

"Very fair! Turn round. Yes, I think that will do. Now, do you understand how to behave to people?"

"If you please, Madam, I do in England, but I don't know about France," said Celia, in some trepidation as to what her step-mother might require of her.

"Absurd!" said Lady Ingram. "Good manners are the same everywhere, and etiquette very nearly so. Now, how many courtesies would you make to a Viscountess?"

"I should only make one to anybody, Madam, unless you tell me otherwise."

"*Incroyable*! I never saw such a lamentable want of education as you show. You have no more fine breeding than that stove. Now listen, and remember: to a Princess of the Blood you make three profound courtesies, approaching a little nearer each time, until at the last you are near enough to sink upon your knees, and kiss her hand. To a Duchess, not of the Blood, or a Marchioness, three courtesies, but less profound, and not moving from your place. To a Countess or Viscountess, two; to any other person superior or equal to yourself, one. Inferiors, of course, you will not condescend to notice. Do you understand, and will you remember?"

"I will do my best, Madam, but I am afraid I shall forget."

"I believe you will, first thing. Now listen again: I expect to-night the Duchesses of Longueville and Montausier, the Marchioness de Simiane, and other inferior persons. What kind of seat will you take?"

"Will you please to instruct me, Madam?" asked Celia, timidly—an answer which slightly modified Lady Ingram's annoyance.

"You are very ignorant," said that Lady. "It is one comfort that you are willing to be taught. My dear, when we are merely assembled *en famille*, and there is no etiquette observed, you can sit on what you like. But if there be any person present in an assembly of higher rank than yourself, you must not sit on a chair with a back to it; and whatever be the rank of your companions, on no occasion must you occupy an arm-chair. You will take your place this evening on an ottoman or a folding-stool. You will remember that?"

"I will remember, Madam," replied Celia.

"Should any member of the Royal House condescend to honor me by appearing at my assemblies—I do not expect it to-night—you will rise, making three deep courtesies, and remain standing until you are desired to seat yourself."

"Yes, Madam."

"Very well. Now go down into the drawing-room, and find a stool somewhere in the corner, where nobody will see you."

Thus graciously dismissed, Celia retired from her step-mother's dressing-room, with a long look at Lady Ingram, whom she had never before seen so splendidly attired. She wore a blue robe, with a long sweeping train, robe and train being elaborately embroidered with flowers, in white, crimson, and straw-color; a petticoat of the palest straw-colored satin, a deep lace berthe, and sleeves of lace reaching to the elbow; long white gloves advanced to meet the sleeve, and jewels of sapphire and diamond gleamed upon the neck and wrists. Her hair was dressed about a foot above her head, and adorned with white plumes, sapphires, and diamonds. Celia descended to the drawing-room, feeling stiff and uncomfortable in her new yellow silk and white satin, and nervously afraid of losing her bracelets and necklace, of topaz and diamonds, which Lady Ingram had lent her for the occasion. In the drawing-room she discovered Mr. Philip resplendently arrayed in white and crimson, and occupied in surveying himself intently in the mirrors.

"O Celia!" said he, when she uttered his name, "I am glad you have come early. It is such fun to see the folks come in, and do all their bowing and courtesying; and I shall have some amusement to-night in watching your innocent astonishment at some things, my woodland bird, or I am mistaken. Please be seated, Madam; here is a place for you in a nice little corner, and I shall keep by your side devotedly all the evening. Has my Lady-Mother seen and approved that smart new gown of yours?"

Celia smiled, and answered affirmatively.

"That is a comfort!" quoth Mr. Philip. "Now, I liked the looks of you a good deal better in that brown cashmere. But I am an absolute nobody, as you will find very shortly, if you have not done so already."

"The brown cashmere will go on again to-morrow, and I shall not be sorry for it. But, Philip"—

"Stop! look out—somebody is coming."

A gentleman in dark blue led in a lady very elaborately dressed in pink. As they entered by one door, Lady Ingram came forward to receive them from another. She stood and made three courtesies, to which the lady in pink responded with one. Then Lady Ingram came forward, and, taking the hand of her guest, turned to Celia and Philip in the corner.

"*Bon soir, ma tante*," observed the latter unceremoniously from his station behind Celia's chair.

"Celia, this is my sister, the Duchess de Montausier," Lady Ingram condescended to say; and Celia, rising, made two low courtesies, having already forgotten the number of reverences due.

"Three," whispered Philip, too low to be overheard, thus saving his sister a scolding.

The Duchess returned the compliment with a single courtesy, Celia thought a rather distant one. But her astonishment had not yet left her at the meeting between the sisters.

"Is that really your aunt?" she asked of Philip.

"Yes, my mother's sister," answered Philip, smiling. "Why?"

"They courtesied so!" was Celia's ungrammatical exclamation.

"Ah! you think it unsisterly? The one, my dear, is a Duchess, the other only the widow of a Baronet. You must not consider the sistership."

Celia laughed within herself to think how the Squire and Madam Passmore would look, if they saw her and Isabella courtesying away at each other in that style.

"Now don't lose all these folks," resumed Philip, as more people entered. "That little man dressed in black, with a black wig, to whom my mother is courtesying now,—do you see him?"

"I was just looking at him," replied Celia. "I cannot say that I like him, though I have no idea who he may be."

"Why?—because he is so short?"

"Oh no! I hope I should never dislike a man for any natural infirmity. I thought he looked very cross."

"He has the happy distinction of being the crossest man in France," said Philip.

"Well, he looks like it," said Celia.

"But one of the most distinguished men in France, my dear. That is the great Duke de Lauzun,[1] who has spent ten years in prison for treason, who aspired to the hand of Mademoiselle, the King's own cousin, and whom King James trusted to bring the Queen and the Prince of Wales over here from England."

"I wonder he trusted him," observed Celia.

"I never wonder at anything," philosophically answered Mr. Philip Ingram. "Now look to your right! Do you see the lady in black, with fair hair, and blue eyes, who seems so quiet and uninterested in all that is passing?"

"I think I do."

"That is a cousin of my mother's, who would not have appeared here if it had not been a family assembly. She is a Jansenist. Thirty years ago she was a famous beauty, and a very fashionable woman. Now all that is over."

"What is a Jansenist, Philip?"

"Ah! there you puzzle me. I thought you would want to know that. You had better ask my Cousin Charlotte—she can tell you much better than I can."

"I do not like to speak to any one," said Celia, timidly. "Can you not tell me something about them?"

"Well, this much I can tell you—they are very bad people, who lead uncommonly holy lives—ergo, holiness does not make a saint."

"Philip, you are laughing at me."

"No, my dear; I am laughing at the Catholic Church, not at you. The Jansenists are a sort of heretic-Catholics, whom all real Catholics agree to call very wicked. They hold all manner of wrong doctrines, according to the Bishops and my Lady-Mother; and they lead lives of such austerity and purity as to put half the saints in the calendar to shame. Now this very Cousin Charlotte of mine, who sits there looking so quiet and saintly, with her blue eyes cast down, and her hands folded on that sombre black gown,—when my mother was a girl, she was the gayest of the gay. About fifteen years since she became a Jansenist. From that day she has been a very saint. She practices all kinds of austerities, and is behaved to almost as if she were a professed nun. Of course, in the eyes of all true Catholics, her Jansenism is her worst and wickedest action. I don't quite see myself how anything can be so very wrong which makes such saints of such sinners. But you see I am a complete *extern*, as the religious call it."

"I should like to know something more about these people, Philip. What doctrines do they hold?"

"Now, what a remarkable attraction anything wrong and perilous has for a woman!" observed Mr. Philip Ingram, with the air of a philosopher. "Well, my dear, I have only heard one; but I believe they have a sort of confession or creed, indicating the points whereon they differ from the Church. That one is, that there is no such thing as grace of congruity, and that men are saved by the favor of God only, and by no merit of their own."

"But, Philip, that is the Gospel!" exclaimed Celia, turning round to look at him. "That is what we Protestants believe."

"Is it, my dear? Well, I have no objection. (Now, return to your condition of a statue, or you will have a lecture on awkwardness and want of repose in your manners. Oh! I know all about that. Do you think I was born such a finished courtier as you see me?) As to merit, I have lived long enough to find out one thing, and that is, that people who are always talking of merit are generally least particular about acquiring it, while those who believe that their good deeds are worth nothing, have the largest stock of them."

"That is natural," said Celia, thoughtfully.

"Is it?" asked Philip again. "Well, it looks like the rule of contrary to me. But you see I have no vocation. Now look at the lady who stands on my mother's left—the one in primrose. Do you see her?

"I see her," said Celia. "I like her face better than some of the others. Who is she?"

"The Marchioness de Simiane,[2] daughter of the Countess de Grignan, and granddaughter of the late clever Marchioness de Sévigné. Her flatterers call her an angel. She is not that, but I don't think she is quite so near the other set of ethereal essences as a good many of the people in this room."

"What an opinion you have of your friends, Philip!"

"My friends, are they?" responded Philip, with a little laugh. "How many of them do you suppose would shed tears at my funeral? There is not one of them who has a heart, my dear—merely lumps of painted stone, as I told you. These are not men and women—they are only walking statues."

"Do you call that cross little man a walking statue?" asked Celia, smiling.

"He!—scarcely; he is too intensely disagreeable."

"I should rather like to see the lady to whom you said that man took a fancy, Philip. Is she here?"

"Ah! my Sister," answered Philip, in a graver voice than any in which he had yet spoken, "you must go to the royal vaults at St. Denis, and search among the coffins, to do that. She was buried twenty years ago.[3] She was so unfortunate as to have a heart, and he has a piece of harder marble even than usual. So when the two articles met, the one broke the other."

"I never can tell whether you are jesting or serious, Philip."

"A little of both generally, my dear. Don't lose those ladies who are going through the courtesying process now—they are distinguished people. The elder one is the Duchess du Maine,[4] one of the daughters of the Prince of Condé, who is emphatically '*the* Prince' in French society. The younger is Mademoiselle de Noailles,[5] the daughter of the Duke de Noailles—a famous belle, as you may see. She will probably be disposed of in a year or two to some Prince or Duke—whoever offers her father the best lump of pin-money. We don't sell young ladies in the market here, as they do in Barbary; we manage the little affair in private. But 'tis a sale, for all that."

"It sounds very bad when you look at it in that light, Philip."

"A good many things do so, my dear, when you strip off the gilding. His Majesty gave a cut of his walking-stick once to a gentleman with whom he was in a passion, and was considered to have honored him by that gracious notice. Now, if he had been the Baron's son, and the other the King, whipping to death would have been thought too good for him after such an insult to Majesty. We live in a droll world, my Sister."

"But, Philip, there must be differences between people—God has made it so."

"Aren't there?—with a vengeance! On my word, here comes Bontems, the King's head *valet-de-chambre*. Now we shall have some fun. You will learn the kind of differences there are between people—Louis XIV. and you, to wit."

"What do you mean by fun?"

"You shall hear. Here is a chair, Monsieur Bontems, and I am rejoiced to see you."

"Sir, I am your most obedient servant," responded a dapper little gentleman, dressed in black and silver, with a long sword by his side, and large silver buckles in his shoes. He sat down on the seat which Philip indicated.

"I trust that His Most Christian Majesty enjoys good health this evening?" began that young gentleman, with an air of the greatest interest in the reply to his question.

"Sir, I am happy to say that His Majesty condescends to be in the enjoyment of most excellent health."

"Very condescending of him, I am sure," commented Philip, gravely. "May I venture to hope that His Royal Highness the Duke de Berry[6] is equally condescending?"

"Sir," answered Monsieur Bontems, looking much grieved, "I regret exceedingly to state that Monseigneur the Duke is not in perfect health. On the contrary, he has this very day been constrained to take medicine."

"How deeply distressing!" lamented Mr. Philip Ingram, putting on a face to match his words. "And might I ask the kind of medicine which had the felicity of a passage down Monseigneur's most distinguished throat, and the honor of relieving his august sufferings?"

"Sir," answered Monsieur Bontems, not in the least perceiving that he was being laughed at, "it was a tisane of camomile flowers."

"I unfeignedly trust that it has not affected his illustrious appetite?"

"Sir," was the reply, always commencing by the same word, "I am much troubled at the remembrance that His Royal Highness's appetite at supper was extremely bad. He ate only two plates of soup, one fowl, fifty heads of asparagus, and a small cherry tart."

"Ah! it must have been very bad indeed," said Mr. Philip, with a melancholy air. "He generally eats about a couple of geese and half a dozen pheasants, does he not?"[7]

"Sir?" said Monsieur Bontems, interrogatively. "I am happy to say, Sir, that all the members of the Royal House have tolerably good appetites; but scarcely—two geese and six pheasants!—no, Sir!"

"Yes, I have gathered that they have, from what I have heard you say," answered Philip, gravely. "Monsieur Bontems, I am anxious to inform my sister—who speaks no French—of the manner in which His Majesty is served throughout the day. I am not sure that I remember all points correctly. It is your duty, is it not, to present His Majesty's wig in the morning, and to buckle his left garter?"

"The left, Sir?" asked Monsieur Bontems, somewhat indignantly. "The right! Any of His Majesty's ordinary valets may touch the left—it is my high office to attend upon the august right leg of my most venerated Sovereign!"

"I beg your pardon a hundred thousand times!"

"You have it, Sir," said Monsieur Bontems affably. "A young gentleman who shows so much interest in His Majesty's and Monseigneur's health may be pardoned even that. But you are a little mistaken in saying 'buckle.' His Majesty is frequently pleased to clasp his own garters; it is my privilege to unclasp them in the evening."

"Would you kindly explain to me, that I may translate to my sister, His Majesty's mode of life during each day?"

"Sir, I shall have the utmost pleasure," replied Monsieur Bontems, laying his hand upon his heart. "Madam," he continued, addressing himself to Celia, though she could understand him only through the medium of Philip, "first thing in the morning, when I rise from the watch-bed which I occupy in the august chamber of my Sovereign, having noiselessly dressed in the antechamber, I and Monsieur De St. Quentin, first gentleman of the chamber, reverently approach his royal bed, and presume to arouse our Sovereign from his slumbers. Then Monsieur De St. Quentin turns his back to the curtains, and placing his hands behind him, respectfully presents the royal wigs, properly curled and dressed, for His Majesty's selection."

"Pardon my interrupting you; I thought the King's attendants never turned their backs upon him?"

"Sir, His Majesty cannot be seen without a wig! Profanity!" cried Monsieur Bontems, looking horrified. "This is the only part of our service in which we are constrained to turn our ignoble backs upon our most illustrious Master."

"I beg your pardon, and understand you now. Pray proceed."

"When the King has selected the wig which he is pleased to wear, St. Quentin puts away the others; and then, His Majesty placing his wig on his august head with his own royal hands, he indicates to me by a signal that he is ready for the curtains to be undrawn. As soon as I have undrawn the curtains, there is the familiar *entrée*. This is attended by the Princes of the Blood, and by His Majesty's physicians. Then I pour into the hands of my Sovereign a few drops of spirits of wine, and the Duke d'Aumont,[8] first Lord of the Bedchamber, offers the holy water. Now His Majesty rises, and I present his slippers. After putting on his dressing-gown, if it be winter, His Majesty goes to the fire. The first *entrée* follows. The King shaves on alternate days. Monsieur De St. Quentin has the high honor of removing the royal beard, and washing with spirits of wine and water our Sovereign's august chin. I hold the glass, while His Majesty wipes his face with a rich towel. Then, while His Majesty's dresses, the *grande entrée* takes place. His Most Christian Majesty is assisted in dressing by the Grand Master of the Robes, Monsieur d'Aumont, a Marquis (graciously chosen by the Sovereign), Monsieur De St. Quentin, my humble self, three valets, and two pages. Thus, as you will see, many attendants of the Crown are allowed the felicity of approaching near to the person of our most illustrious Master."

"Too many cooks spoiling the broth, I should say," was the translator's comment. "Fancy ten people helping a fellow to put his coat on!"

"His Majesty's shoes and garters are clasped with diamonds. At this point the king condescends to breakfast. On an enamelled salver a loaf is brought by the officers of the buttery, and a folded napkin on another: the cup-bearer presents to the Duke d'Aumont a golden cup, into which he pours a small quantity of wine and water, and the second cup-bearer makes the assay. The goblet, carefully rinsed and replenished, is now presented to His Majesty upon a golden saucer. The napkin is offered by the first Prince of the Blood present at the *entrée*. His Majesty then intrusts to my hands the reliquary which he wears about his neck, and I carefully pass it to one of the lower attendants, who carries it to the royal closet, and remains there in charge of it. The royal shirt is then presented—by the Grand Master of the Robes, if no person of more distinction be present; but if any more august persons have attended the *entrée*, it is passed on till it reaches the first Prince of the Blood. I assure you, on frosty winter days, I have known it perfectly cold on reaching His Majesty (though always carefully warmed), the persons of distinction through whose hands it had to pass being so numerous."

"Ah! 'Pride costs more than hunger, thirst, or cold,'" observed Mr. Philip Ingram. "That is a copy I had set me ages ago. But what a very cool proceeding!"

"When His Majesty's lace cravat is presented, he is pleased himself to indicate the person who shall have the honor of tying it. Then I bring him the overcoat which he wore on the previous day, and with his own august hands he removes from the pockets such articles as he is pleased to retain. Lastly, Monsieur De St. Quentin presents to him, on an enamelled salver, two handkerchiefs laced with superb point. Now His Majesty returns to his *ruelle*[2] for his private devotions. Two cushions are placed there, upon which His Majesty condescends to kneel. Here he prays aloud, all the Cardinals and Bishops in the chamber following his royal accents in lower tones."

"I hope he learns his prayers by heart, then, or all his Cardinals following will put him out abominably!" was the interpolation this time.

"Oh dear, Philip!" murmured Celia, "it reminds me of Daniel and Darius."

"'Save of thee, O King?'[10] No, he is a little better than that."

"Our Sovereign," pursued Monsieur Bontems, "now receives the envoys of foreign powers, not one of which powers is worthy to compete with our august Master."

"I say, draw that mild!" objected Mr. Philip Ingram.

"Then he passes into his cabinet, and issues his orders for the day; when all retire but the Blood, and a few other highly distinguished persons. After an interval of repose, His Majesty attends mass."

"How sadly he must want his repose!"

"After mass, and a visit to the council-chamber, at one o'clock His Majesty dines. This is either *au petit couvert*, or *au grand couvert*; the *grands couverts* are rare. His Majesty commonly dines alone in his own cabinet, at a small table, three courses and a dessert being served. Monsieur de St. Quentin announces the repast, and His Majesty takes his seat. If the Grand Chamberlain be there, he waits on the Sovereign; when he is absent, this is the privilege of Monsieur de St. Quentin. Another interval of repose ensues before His Majesty drives out. He frequently condescends at this time to amuse himself with his favorite dogs. Then he changes his dress, and drives or hunts. On returning, he again changes his attire, and after a short period in his cabinet, repairs to the apartments of Madame de Maintenon, where he remains until ten, the hour of supper. At a quarter past ten His Majesty enters the supper-room, during which interval the officers have made the assay"—

"What is the assay?" asked Celia of Philip, who repeated the question.

"The assay," said Monsieur Bontems, condescending to explain, "is the testing of different matters, to see that no attempt has been made upon the most sacred life of His Majesty. There is the assay of the plates, which are rubbed with bread and salt; the knife, the fork, the spoon, and the toothpicks, which will be used by our Sovereign. All these are rubbed with bread and salt, afterwards eaten by the officers of the assay, to make sure that no deleterious matter has been applied to these articles. Every dish brought to the royal table is tested by the officers ere it may be set before His Majesty, and the dishes are brought in by the comptroller-general, an officer of the pantry, a comptroller of the buttery, and an equerry of the kitchen, preceded and followed by guards, whose duty it is to prevent all manner of tampering with the meats destined for the King."

"Poor man!" said Celia, compassionately; "I am glad to be beneath all that caution and preparation."

"This done," proceeded Monsieur Bontems, "the house-steward enters, with two ushers bearing flambeaux. Then comes His Most Christian Majesty. All the Princes and Princesses of France are already standing round the table. His Majesty most graciously desires them to be seated. Six nobles stand at each end of the table. When His Majesty condescends to drink, the cup-bearer cries aloud, 'Drink for the King!' whereupon the officers of the cellar approach with an enamelled goblet and two decanters. The cup-bearer pours out, the officers taste. The cup-bearer presents the goblet to the Sovereign, and as he raises it with his illustrious hand to his august lips, the cup-bearer cries aloud, 'The King drinks!' and the whole company bow to His Majesty."

"What a tremendous bore it must be!" was Mr. Philip's comment. "How can the poor fellow ever get his supper eaten?"

"His Majesty commonly begins supper with three or four plateful of different soups. Some light meat follows—a chicken, a pheasant, a partridge or two—then a heavier dish, such as beef or mutton. The King concludes his repast with a few little delicacies, such as salad, pastry, and sweetmeats.[11] When he wishes to wipe his hands, three Dukes and a Prince of the Blood present him with a damp napkin; the dry one which follows I have the honor to offer. His Majesty usually drinks about three times during supper."

"How much at a time?" inquired Philip, with an air of deep interest.

"Sir," replied Monsieur Bontems, gravely, "His Majesty's custom in this respect somewhat varies. The goblet holds about half-a-pint, and the King rarely empties it at a draught."

"A pint and a quarter, call it," said Philip, reflectively.

"After supper, His Majesty proceeds to his bedchamber, where he dismisses the greater number of his guests; he then passes on to his cabinet, followed by the Princes and Princesses. About midnight he feeds his dogs."

"Does he feed them himself?"

"Sir, there are occasions upon which those indescribably happy animals have the honor of receiving morsels from His Majesty's own hand. The King now returns to his bed-chamber, and the *petit coucher* commences. An arm-chair is prepared for him near the fire, and the *en-cas* is placed upon a table near the bed. This is a small repast, prepared lest it should be His Majesty's pleasure to demand food during the night. It is most frequently a bowl of soup, a cold roast fowl, bread, wine, and water."

"And how many Dukes are required to give him those?"

"Sir, my humble services are esteemed sufficient."

"He appears to be much less august at some moments than others," satirically remarked the translator.

"When our Sovereign enters his chamber, he hands to me his watch and reliquary, and delivers to Monsieur d'Aumont his waistcoat, cravat, and ribbon. Two valets and two pages assist us in the removal of the garments honored by His Majesty's wear. When the King is ready, I lift the candlestick, and deliver it to the nobleman indicated by my Sovereign for that unparalleled honor. All persons now quit the chamber save the candle-bearer, the physician, and myself. His Majesty selects the dress which he will wear the next morning, and gets into bed."

"Can he get into bed by himself? I should have thought it would have required five Dukes and ten Marquises to help him."

"After the physician has visited his august patient, he and the candle-bearer retire; I close the curtains, and, turning my back to the royal couch, with my hands behind me, await the pleasure of my Sovereign. It is to me that he delivers the wig, passing it outside the curtain with his own illustrious hand. I now extinguish the candles, light the night-lights, and take possession of the watch-bed."

"I wonder if you don't occasionally faint under such a weight of honor—and bother," observed Mr. Philip Ingram, not to Monsieur Bontems. "Well, now we have got His Most Christian Majesty in bed, let him stay there. Monsieur Bontems, I am unspeakably indebted to you for your highly-interesting account, and shall never forget it as long as I live. I beg you will not allow me to detain you further from the company, who are earnestly desirous of your enchanting conversation, though less sensible of your merits than I am."

Monsieur Bontems laid both hands upon his heart, and made three bows.

"Sir, I beg you will not depreciate your high qualities. Sir, I take the utmost delight in conversing with you."

And the head-valet of the chamber allowed himself to be absorbed among the general throng.

"Well, is he not a comical specimen?" said Philip to Celia. "He often makes me laugh till I am exhausted; and the beauty of it is that he never finds out at what one is laughing. And to think who it is that they worship with all these rites—an old man of seventy-four, with one foot in the grave, who has never been any better than he should be. Really, it reminds one of Herod Agrippa and them of Tyre and Sidon!"[12]

"'Thou shalt honor the face of the old man,'"[13] whispered Celia, softly.

"My dear," said Philip, "I don't complain of their honoring him. Let them honor him as much as they like—he is their King, and they ought to do. But what we have just heard is not honoring him, to my thinking—it is teasing and worshipping him. I assure you I pity the poor fellow with all my heart. He must have a most uncomfortable time of it. No, if I were to envy any man, it would not be Louis XIV."

"Who would it be, Philip?" asked Celia, with a smile.

"Simeon Stylites, perhaps," said Philip, drily. "I would quite as soon be the one as the other!"

"I don't know who he was," replied Celia.

"A gentleman of the olden time, who worked out his salvation for forty years on the top of a tall pillar," was the answer, accompanied by an expression of countenance which Celia had seen before in Philip, and could not understand. "Are you tired?" he added, suddenly.

"Scarcely, yet," she answered; "it is all so new to me. But what time is it, Philip?"

Philip pulled out a watch about three inches in diameter.

"Ten minutes to one."

"Do you mean to say it is one o'clock in the morning?" asked Celia, in a voice of unmitigated amazement and horror.

"It certainly is not one o'clock in the afternoon," replied Philip, with much gravity.

"I had no idea how late it was! Let me go, Philip, please do."

And Celia made her escape rather hastily. But Lady Ingram was not justified in saying that nobody would miss her, as she would have seen if she had noticed the lost and *ennuyé* look of Mr. Philip Ingram after the disappearance of Celia.

[1] Antoine Nompar de Caumont, Marquis de Peguilin and Duke de Lauzun: born about May 1633; imprisoned from 1671 to 1681; created Duke 1692; married, May 21, 1695, Geneviève Marie de Durfort, daughter of Maréchal de Lorges; died November 19, 1723, aged ninety.

[2] Pauline, daughter of François d'Adhémar, Count de Grignan, and Françoise Marguerite de Sévigné: born at Paris, 1674; married, November 29, 1695, Louis Marquis de Simiane; died July 3 or 13, 1737.

[3] Anne Marie Louise, eldest daughter of Gaston Duke of Orleans and Marie de Montpensier, in her own right Duchess de Montpensier, Princess de Dombes, and Countess d'Eu, cousin of Louis XIV., was born at the Louvre, May 29, 1627, and died at Paris, April 5, 1693; buried in the Bourbon vault at St. Denis, whence her coffin was exhumed with the rest at the Revolution, and her remains flung into a deep pit dug in the Cour des Valois, outside the Cathedral. On the Restoration, these bones were dug up from their desecrated grave, and were reverently re-buried within the sacred precincts; but as it was impossible to distinguish to whom they had belonged, they

were interred in two vaults made for the purpose. The engagement of Mademoiselle with the Duke de Lauzun is one of the saddest stories connected with the hapless Royal House of France—none the less sad because few can see its sadness, and perceive but foolish vanity in the tale of the great heart crushed to death, with no guerdon for its sacrifice.

[4] Marie Anne Louise Benedetto, daughter of Henri III., Prince of Condé, and Anna of Mantua: born November 8, 1676; married, March 19, 1692, Louis Auguste, Duke du Maine, legitimated son of Louis XIV.; died 1753.

[5] Marie Victoire Sophie de Noailles: born at Versailles, May 6, 1688; married, February 22, 1723, Louis Alexandre Count de Toulouse, brother of the Duke du Maine.

[6] Charles, Duke de Berry, was the youngest son of the *Grand Dauphin* (son of Louis XIV.) and Marie Anna of Bavaria: he was born August 31, 1686, and died at Marly, May 4, 1714, probably by poison administered by his own wife, Louise of Orleans.

[7] Nearly all the members of the Royal House of France, from Anne of Austria and her son Louis XIV. downwards, have been enormous eaters.

[8] Messrs. d'Aumont, St. Quentin, and Bontems are real persons, and this account of the private life of Louis XIV. is taken from authentic sources.

[9] *Ruelle*, the space between the bed and the wall, at the head of the bed. The *ruelle* played an important part in etiquette, only persons especially favored being admitted.

[10] Dan. vi. 7.

[11] "He was a very gifted eater. The rough old Duchess of Orleans declares, in her Memoirs, that she 'often saw him eat four platesful of different soups, a whole pheasant, a partridge, a plateful of salad, mutton hashed with garlic, two good-sized slices of ham, a dish of pastry, and afterwards fruit and sweetmeats.'"—*Dr. Doran's* "*Table Traits*," p. 421.

[12] Acts xii. 20-23.

[13] Lev. xix. 32.

VII.

THE NIGHT BOSWITH DIED.

"Thou art not weary, O sweet heart and glad!
Ye are not weary, O ye wings of light!
Ye are not weary, golden-sandalled feet
And eyes lift up in Heaven. Were we with thee,
We never should be weary any more.

So sleep, sweet love, and waken not for us.
Ah! wake not at my cry, which is of earth,
For thou these twenty years hast been of Heaven.
Still not thy harp for me: I will wail low,
That my voice reach thee not beyond the stars.
Only wait for me, O my harper! since
When thou and I have clasped hands at the gate,
We never shall be weary any more."

"O Patient! I am very sorry to have kept you up so late as this—I had no idea that you would wait for me!" exclaimed Celia, as, hastening into her bedroom, she found Patient quietly at work beside the fire.

"I should have done that, Madam, at whatever hour you had returned," was Patient's answer, as she helped Celia to unclasp her topaz and diamond ornaments, and put them away carefully in their cases. "I thought you were early; my Lady often does not quit her assemblies till day-dawn."

"You see," responded Celia, a little apologetically, awaking to the fact that Patient had not expected her for another hour or two, "I am so little accustomed to these things. I never was up at such an hour as this before."

"All the better for you, Madam," said Patient, quietly.

"You do not like these assemblies?"

"I have nothing to do with them, Madam."

"But if you had," persisted Celia, looking for Patient's opinion as a sister in the faith.

But Patient seemed scarcely willing to impart it.

"You command me to answer you, Madam?" she said.

"I want to know, Patient," replied Celia, simply.

"'What concord hath Christ with Belial?'" answered Patient. "Madam, when I was but a young maid, I looked on the world as divided into many sects—Covenanters, Independents, Prelatists, Anabaptists, and the like, and I fancied that all who were not Covenanters (as I was) must needs be more or less wrong. Methinks I am wiser now. I see the world as divided into two camps only, and the army wherein I serve hath but one rallying-cry. They that believe, and they that believe not—here are the camps, 'What think ye of Christ?'—that is the rallying-cry. I see the Church as a great school, holding many forms and classes, but only one Master. And I think less now of a fellow-scholar sitting on another form from mine, and seeing the other side of the Master's face, if I find that he heareth His voice, and followeth Him. Madam, what think you all those great ladies down-stairs would say, if you asked them that question—'What think ye of Christ?'[1] Poor souls! they never think of Him. And with them in the enemy's camp I have nought to do, so long as they remain there."

"But may we not win them over to our side?" queried Celia.

"Ah! my dear young lady!" answered Patient, rather sadly, "I have seen that question lead many a disciple astray who did run well. When a man goes over to the enemy's ground to parley, it ends at times in his staying there. Methinks that it is only when we carry the Master with us, and when we go like the preachers to the poor savages in the plantations, that we have any hope of doing well. 'Tis so easy to think, 'I go there to please God,' when really we only go to please ourselves."

Patient remained silent for a few minutes, but said presently—

"The Sabbath afore the harrying of Lauchie, Madam, which was Communion Sabbath, Mr. Grey preached a very rich discourse from that word, 'He hath made with me an everlasting covenant.'[2] After, fencing the tables, he spake from that other word of Paul, 'Ye are Christ's.'[3] And in speaking on one head—he dividing his discourse into thirty-seven points wherein believers are Christ's—he said one word which hath stuck in mine heart since then. 'We are all vastly readier,' quoth he, 'to try to follow the Master in the few matters wherein He acted as God, and therefore beyond us, than in the multitude wherein He did act as our ensample. For an hundred who would willingly follow unto the Pharisee's feasting, there is scarce one who is ready to seek out sinners, saying unto them, "Go, and sin no more."'[4] Whereupon he took occasion to reprove them among his flock that were of too light and unstable a nature, loving overmuch, gadding about and taking of pleasure. I was then a young maid, and truly was somewhat exercised with that discourse, seeing that I loved the customs yearly observed among us on the 1st day of November, which the Papistical folk called Hallowe'en."

"What customs, Patient?"

"Divers light and fantastical vanities, Madam, which you were no better to hear tell of,—such like as burning of nuts with names to them, and searching of eggs brake into glasses, for the discovering of fortunes: which did much delight me in my tender age, though now I know that they be but folly if not worse. Moreover, they would throw apples in tubs of water, and the laddies and lassies, with their hands tied behind, would strive to reach them by mouth, and many other siccan fooleries."

"It sounds rather amusing, Patient."

"So it might be, Madam, for we bairns which were of too small age for aught less foolish. But for us, who are members of Christ's body, and have heard His voice and followed Him, what have we to do with the deeds of this weary and evil world, which we cast off when we arose to follow Him? Maybe I had better not have said this unto you, Madam, seeing that (saving your presence) you are yet but a young maid, and youth is naturally desirous of vain delights. When you are a little further on in the way, the Lord will teach it you Himself, even as He hath taught me."

"To tell you the truth, Patient, while I quite see with you in the main, I think you a little severe in the particular."

"I do not doubt it, Madam. The Lord knoweth how to deaden your heart unto this world, and He can do it a deal better than I. But if you be His (the which I doubt not), it must needs be."

"I have scarce a choice now," said Celia, in a low voice, feeling doubtful how far she ought to make any remark to Patient which might seem to reflect on Lady Ingram.

"That I perceive, Madam," answered Patient, in the same tone. "Only—if you will condescend to pardon the liberty I take in saying it—take heed that the pleasing and obeying of man clash not with the pleasing and obeying of God. 'For all that is in the world—the lust of the flesh, and the lust of the eye, and the pride of life—is not of the Father, but is of the world.'"[5]

"Patient, there is one thing which I feel very much here—the want of a Protestant service."

"I used to feel that very sore, Madam. Not that I miss it not now, 'specially at times: yet scarce, me thinks, so sadly as I once did. At first I was much exercised with that word, 'Forsake not the assembling of yourselves together;'[6] and I marvelled whether I ought to remain in this place. But I began to think that it was not I that had forsaken mine own land, but the Lord which hath caused me to be cast out thence; I having, moreover, passed a solemn word to my dear Lady when she lay a-dying, that I would not leave Master Edward his lone in this strange land while he was yet a bairn. Then me thought of some words of Mr. Grey in that last sermon he ever preached. 'A soldier,' quoth he, 'hath no right to choose his position.' So now, seeing that since the Dragonnades, as they called the persecution here, there is no worship permitted to be had, and also that the Lord, and not I, hath placed me here, I am content. Every Sabbath, ay, every day, He preacheth unto me in the Word, and there is no finer discourse than His."

"What persecution, Patient?" asked Celia, as she lay down on her pillow. "This King hath never been a persecutor, hath he?"

"Ay hath he, Madam. The morn, if it please you, I will tell you some stories of the Dragonnades. My Lady hath given me further work to do for you; and if you think meet, I can bring my sewing into your closet as aforetime."

"Pray do, Patient: I like your stories. Good-night."

"Good-night, Madam, and the Lord be with you!"

"Your very obedient servant, Mrs. Celia Ingram," observed Mr. Philip, lounging into his sister's boudoir the next morning. "I hope your early rising has done you no harm."

"I rose at my usual hour, which is six."

"I rose at *my* usual hour, which is nine."

"O Philip!" cried Celia, laughing.

"Well, now, what earthly inducement have I to rise earlier? I am doomed—for my sins, I suppose—to spend four mortal hours of every day in dressing, breakfasting, dining, and supping. Moreover, I am constrained to ride a horse. *Item*, I have to talk nonsense. Fourth and lastly, I am the docile slave of my Lady-Mother. Is there anything in the list I have just given you to make a fellow turn out of bed three hours before he can't help it?"

"I should not think there was, except in the last item."

"Not in the last item, Madam, seeing that her gracious Ladyship does not shine upon the world any sooner than I do—have you not discovered that yet?"

"It seems to me, Philip, that you want something to do."

"Well, that depends," said Philip, reflectively. "It might be something I should not relish."

"Well!" said Celia, a trifle scornfully, "I never would lead such a useless life as that, Philip. 1 would either find something to do or make it."

"How very like a woman you talk!" loftily remarked Mr. Philip Ingram, putting his hands in his pockets.

Celia laughed merrily.

"I don't like it, Celia," resumed Philip, more seriously, "but what can I do? I wish exceedingly that my mother would let me go into the army, but she will not. Edward, you know—or you don't know—is a Colonel in King James's army; so that he can find something to do. I wish you would talk to my mother about it."

"*I!*" echoed Celia, in an unmistakable tone.

"You," repeated her brother.

"My dear Philip, you surely very much mistake my position with her. I have no more influence with my Lady Ingram than—than her little pug dog."

"A precious lot, then," retorted Mr. Philip, "for if anybody ruffled the tip of Miss Venus's tail, they would not be asked here again for a twelvemonth. It is you who mistake, Mrs. Celia. The only way to manage my mother is to stand up to her—to let her know that you can take your own way, and you will."

"Neither you nor I have any right to do that, Philip," replied Celia, gravely.

"I have not, that I allow," said Philip. "I don't quite see that as regards you. Her Ladyship is not *your* mother."

"I think that she takes to me the place both of father and mother, and that I have no more right to argue with or disobey her than them."

"That is your view, is it?" inquired Philip, meditatively. "Well, if you look at it in that way, of course you cannot ask her. So be it, then. I must be contented, I suppose, with my customary and highly useful mode of life."

"I find no lack of occupation," observed Celia.

"No, you are a woman," said Philip. "And as Patient's old rhyme (of which I never can remember the first line) says, 'Woman's work is never done.' Women do seem to possess a marvellous and enviable faculty of finding endless amusement in pushing a needle into a piece of linen, and pulling it out again—can't understand it. Oh! has my mother told you that we are going to St. Germains next week?"

"No," said Celia, rather surprised.

"Then there is a piece of information for you."

"She expects me to go, I suppose?"

"If you don't I won't," said Mr. Philip Ingram, dogmatically.

"Is the—the—Court"—began Celia, very hesitatingly.

"Is the Pretender there? Come out with it now—I shall not put my fingers in my ears. Yes, Madam, the Pretender is there, and his mother too, and all the rest of them."

"Oh!" sighed Celia, much relieved. "I thought you would be a Jacobite."

"You are a Whig, then, Mrs. Celia?" asked Philip in an amused tone.

"I do not know that I am a politician at all," she answered; "but I was brought up to the Whig view."

"All right!" said Mr. Philip, accommodatingly. "Don't let my mother know it—that is all."

"I think my father—Squire Passmore, I mean"—Celia explained, a little sadly, "told her so much at our first meeting."

"So much the better. And you expected to find me a red-hot Jacobite, did you? To tell the truth, I don't care two pins about it; neither does my mother, only 'tis the mode here, and she has taken it up along with her face-washes, laces, and lutestring. Of course I would not call the King anything but 'Your Majesty' to his face—it would hurt his feelings, poor gentleman, and I don't see that it would do any good. But if you ask me whether I would risk the confiscation of my property (when I have any) in aiding a second Restoration,—why, not I."

"Do you consider yourself an Englishman or a Frenchman, Philip?"

"Well, upon my word, Mrs. Celia Ingram, you are complimentary! 'Do I consider myself an Englishman or a Frenchman!' I am an Englishman, Madam, and proud of it; and I will thank you not to insult me by asking me whether I consider myself a Frenchman!"

"I beg your pardon, dear Philip," replied Celia, laughing. "But you have never been in England, have you?"

"Never—I wish I had."

"What is the Pretender like, Philip?"

"Well, Madam, the Jacobites say he would be only and wholly like his father, if he were not so very like his mother: while you Whigs are of opinion that he resembles some washerwoman at Egham, or bricklayer at Rotherhithe—don't remember which, and doesn't matter."

"But what, or whom, do you think him like?"

"Not very like his mother, in my judgment, which is very unbiased, except in his height, and the shape of his hands and mouth. Still, I should not call him unlike her. Of his likeness to his father I can say nothing, for I don't remember King James, who died when I was only eight years old. The son is a very tall man—there is over six feet of him, I should say—with a long face, nearly oval,—dark eyes, rather fine,—and a pleasant, good-natured sort of mouth."

"Is he a pleasant man to speak to? Does he talk much?"

"To the first question—yes; he is by no means without brains, and is very gracious to strangers. To the second—no, very little. If you are looking for me, Thérèse, in your wanderings up and down, here I am, at her Ladyship's service."

"It is not her Ladyship, Sir, dat want you. Dupont tell me to say you dat Monsieur Colville is in your rooms."

"Colville! that is jolly!"

And Mr. Philip Ingram took his immediate departure. Celia guessed that Mr. Colville was the solitary friend of whom he had before spoken.

"Now, Patient, I want to hear about the Dragonnades. Oh! surely you are not making up all those dresses for me?"

"Yes, Madam," answered Patient, in her passive way. "My Lady has ordered it."

"Well," sighed Celia, "I wonder when I am to wear them?"

Patient gathered up one of the multifarious dresses—a blue gauze one—and followed her mistress into the boudoir.

"You have never seen King Louis, Madam?"

"Never; I should like to have a glimpse of him some day."

"I never have, and I hope I never shall."

"Do you think so badly of him, Patient?"

"They call him The Great: methinks they might fitly give the same title to the Devil. He is a man with neither heart nor conscience. God forbid that I should judge any man: yet 'tis written, 'By their fruits ye shall know them,'[7] and the fruits of this King are truly dreadful. It doth look as if the Lord had given him 'over to a reprobate mind, to do those things which are not convenient.'[8] Privately, he is a man of very evil life; and publicly—you will hear shortly, Madam, what he is. 'Tis now, methinks, nigh upon twenty years since what they called the Edict of Nantes[9] was done away with. That decree, passed by some former King of this country,[10] did permit all the Protestants to hold their own worship, and to be visited in sickness by their chosen ministers. This, being too gentle for this King, he therefore swept away. His dragoons were sent into every place throughout France, with orders to force the the poor Protestants to go unto the wicked mass, and to harry them in all manner of ways, saving only to avoid danger of their lives. One Sabbath thereto appointed, they drave all in every place to mass at the point of their swords, goading and pricking on such as lagged, or showed ill-will thereto. I saw one crowd so driven, from a window—for my Lady being a Papist, kept safe them in her house: or else it was that I was not counted worthy of the Lord to have that great honor of suffering for His sake. Poor souls! white-headed men there were, and tender women, and little, innocent, frightened children. It was a sight to move any human heart. I heard many a tale of worse things they did. Breaking into the houses, destroying and burning the household furniture, binding and beating the men, yea, even the women; drumming with hellish noise in the chambers of the sick, until they swooned away or were like to die; burning the houses of some and the workshops of others: all this we heard, and more."

"Patient, how dreadful!" said Celia. "Why, 'tis near what they did in the days of Queen Mary."

"They only went a little further then on the same road—that was all, methinks," answered Patient, calmly. "When the Lord readeth in the Books before men and angels the stories of the persecutions in England and in Scotland, He will scarce forget the Dragonnades of France."

"I did not know that there had been any persecution in Scotland, Patient—except what King Charles did; I suppose that was a sort of persecution."

"Did you not, Madam?" asked Patient, quietly turning down a hem. "I was not thinking of King Charles, but of the earlier days, when tender women like Helen Stirk and Margaret Wilson perished in the waters, and when the bloody Cardinal brent Master George Wishart, that true servant of God and the Evangel, in his devil's-fire at St. Andrews."

"I never heard of all those people, Patient."

"Ay, perchance so, Madam. I dare say their names and their sufferings scarce went beyond their own land," replied Patient, in a constrained voice, as if her heart were a little stirred at last. "But the Lord heard of them; and Scotland heard of them, and rose and bared her arm, and drave forth the men of blood from off her soil. The Lord is their Avenger, at times, in this life—beyond this life, always."

"Tell me something more about them, Patient. Who was Master Wishart?"

"He was a Scottish gentleman of good birth, a Wishart of Pitarrow, Madam, who, giving himself up unto the service of God and the Evangel, in Dundee and other towns, and bringing the blessed Word and the blessed hope unto many a poor hungered soul, was seized by the bloody Cardinal Beaton, and brent to death as the reward of his labors, in the year of our Lord, 1546. They that did know him at that time, and Master John Knox afterward, did say unto divers persons, as I have heard, that even Master John was not fit to stand up with George Wishart. He was a true man, and one that spake so good and sweet words as did move the hearts of such as heard him. I think the Lord knew how to ease him after his sore pain, and that, now that he hath had rest in Heaven for one hundred and seventy years, he accounts not that he bare too much for the Lord's sake, that one bitter hour at St. Andrew's."

"And who was Helen—what did you say her name was?—and Margaret Wilson?"

"Helen Stirk, Madam, was a wife that was permitted to die along with her guidman for the name of the Lord, which she counted a grand mercy. I can tell you a little more concerning Margaret Wilson, for she died no so long since, and my father's sister's son, Duncan M'Intyre, saw her die. It was at Wigtown, on the 11th of May, in the year that King James became King. Duncan had business in the town, where some of his kith on his father's side dwelt; and hearing that two women were to be put to death, he, like a hare-brained callant as he was, was set on seeing it. I heard not much about Margaret Maclauchlan, who suffered at the same time, save that she was the widow of one John Millikan, a wright of Drumjargan, and a woman notable for her piety and discretion. But that of Maggie Wilson took much effect upon mine heart, seeing that she was a young maid of just eighteen years, mine own age. She and Agnes her sister, as Duncan told us, were children of one Gilbert Wilson of Glenvernoch, who with his wife were Prelatists. Maggie and Agnes, who were not able to conform unto the ill Prelatical ways wherein their father and mother were entangled, had joined many meetings of the Covenanters on the hill-sides or in the glens, for preaching or prayer."

"How old was Agnes? Was she a married woman?"

"No, Madam; she was younger than Maggie—a maid of thirteen years."

"But, Patient! I never heard of such a thing—two girls, thirteen and eighteen, setting themselves up to judge their parents' religion, and choosing a different one for themselves!" said Celia, in astonishment, for she could not help thinking of the strong expletives which would have burst from Squire Passmore, if she and Lucy had calmly declared themselves Presbyterians, and declined to accompany that gentleman to church as usual.

"Madam, their father and mother were Prelatists," said Patient, evidently of opinion that this settled the question. "They could not go with them to church and read the mass-book."

"Oh! you mean they were Papists?"

"No, Madam—Prelatists," repeated Patient, a little perversely. "Not that I see much disagreement, indeed, for methinks a Prelatist is but a Papist with a difference. Yet I do trust there be Prelatists that will be saved, and I can scarce think that of Papists."

"I don't understand you, Patient. I suppose these Prelatists are some sect that I have not heard anything about," said Celia, with much simplicity, for she never supposed that Patient's stern condemnation was levelled against her own Church, and would have been sorely grieved and bewildered had she known it. "Go on, if you please."

Patient did not explain, and proceeded with her history.

"When the late King James became King, on the death of his brother, he put forth a proclamation granting liberty of conscience unto all sects whatsoever. For a time the Puritans rejoiced in this mercy, thinking it a favor unto them, but later they became aware that 'twas but a deceit to extend ease unto the Papists. Maggie and Agnes Wilson, the which were in hiding, did shortly after this proclamation venture into the town, being wishful to speak with their kinsfolk. They never reached their kith, being betrayed by one Patrick Stewart, who came upon them with a band of men, and lodged them in the thieves' hole. Thence they were shifted to another chamber, wherein Margaret Maclauchlan already abode. Thomas Wilson, their brother, did strive to set them free, thereby but harming himself;[11] and they were had up afore the Sheriff,[12] and the Provost,[13] and some others. The indictment of them was for attending field-conventicles, and for joining in the rebellion at Bothwell Bridge and Airsmoss,—they, poor feeble souls, never having been near the same places. The jury brought the charge in proven, and the three women were doomed to be justified[14] by water. They were to be tied to stakes below the mark of the tide, in the water of Blednoch, near Wigtown, until they should be dead, the tide sweeping over them in its flow. Howbeit the Lord restrained them of having their will upon the young maid Agnes. Maybe they were nigh shamed to justify such a bairn: however, they tarried in her case. But on the day appointed, which, as I said, was May 11th, one named Windram, being in command over a band of soldiers, did hale Margaret Maclauchlan and Margaret Wilson to the place of execution. The first stake, whereto Margaret Maclauchlan was tied, was fixed much deeper in the bed of the river than the other, they hoping that Maggie Wilson should be feared at her death, being the sooner, and so brought to recant. Moreover, one of the town officers did with his halbert press and push down the poor old wife, who, having the lesser suffering of the two, was soon with the Lord. As she strave in the bitterness of death, quoth one to Maggie Wilson, 'What think ye of that?' 'Nay,' quoth she, 'what do I see but Christ in one of His members struggling there!' Then Maggie, bring tied unto the nearer stake, after singing of a Psalm,[15] did read a chapter of the Word,[16] and prayed, so that all might hear. And while she was a-praying, the water overflowed her. And to see the devilish cruelty of these men! they left her till she was nigh dead, and then, lifting her out of the water, did use all care and means to recover her, as if they meant mercy. But it was but that she might die over again. They murdered her twice over—poor, poor maid! for she was past feeling when they got her out. Then, when she could speak, this Windram did ask her if she would pray for the King. Much cause they had given her! She then answered that she wished the salvation of all men, and the damnation of none. Then a maid which stood by Duncan, and had sobbed and wept aforetime, which he thought must be of kin or friendly unto her, did cry most dolefully, 'Dear Margaret! oh say, "God save the King!" say, "God save the King!"' 'God save him if He will,' quoth she, 'for I desire his salvation.' Windram now drawing near, commanded her to take the oath unto the King, abjuring of the Solemn League and Covenant. 'I will not,' quoth she; 'I am one of Christ's children.' No sooner had she thus spoken, than one of the town's officers with his halbert thrust her back into the water, crying, 'Tak' anither drink, my hearty!' So she died."

"Patient!" said Celia, in a low, constrained voice, "did God let those men go scathless?"

"Not so, Madam. The town's officer that thrust her back was ever after that tormented with a thirst the which no draught could slake; and for many generations the children of the other, which kept down the old wife with his halbert, were all born with misshapen hands and feet."[17]

"Patient," said Celia again, in the same low reverent tone, "I wonder that He suffers such things to be!"

"I marvelled at that, Madam, years agone. It seemed very strange unto me that He suffered us to be haled down to the beach at the harrying of Lauchie, and that the storm should come on us and cut off so many lives of His servants. It exercised me very sore."

"And how did you settle it, Patient?"

"I do not know that I should have settled it, Madam, had I not met with an ancient gentleman, a minister, that used at one time to visit Mr. Francis in Paris here. He was a reverend man by the name of Colville, one of mine own country, that had fled out of Scotland of old time, and had been dwelling for many years in Switzerland and Germany."

"Was he akin to this Mr. Colville who is Philip's friend?"

"This young gentleman is his grandson, Madam; and little good he doth Mr. Philip, I fear. If he were a wee bit more like his grandsire, I would be fain. Howbeit, grace goeth not by inheritance, as I know. He was a very kindly gentleman, Madam, this old minister; and when he had sat a while ben with Mr. Francis and Miss Magdalene, he oft would say, 'Now let me go but and speak unto the Leslies.' And one day—ah! that day!—when Roswith was very ill, I asked of him the thing which did exercise me. And he said unto me, gently and kindly, holding mine hand in his quavering hand, for he was a very ancient gentleman,—'Dear child,' quoth he, 'dost thou know so little thy Father? Thou mindest me of my little son,' saith he, 'when the fire brake out in mine house. When I hasted up into his chamber, which was above the chamber a-fire, and tare the blankets from his bed, and haled him thence somewhat roughly, the bairn greet, and asked of me what made me so angry.' Well, I could not choose but smile to think of the babe's blunder; and he saith, 'I see thou canst understand that. Why, dear child,' quoth he, 'thou art about just the same blunder as my bairn. Thy Father sendeth a messenger in haste to fetch thy soul home to Him; and lo! "Father," sayest thou, "why art thou so angry?" We are all little children,' quoth he, 'and are apt to think our Father is angry when He is but short with us because of danger. And dost thou think, lassie,' he said, 'that they which saw the face of God first thing after that storm, rebuked Him because He had fetched them thither by water?' So then I saw mine error."

"Did this old gentleman teach you a great deal, Patient? I keep wondering whence you have all the things you say to me. I don't think such things as you do; and even Cicely Aggett, who is some twenty years older than you, does not seem to know half so much about God as you do. Where do you get your thoughts and your knowledge?"

"Where the Lord doth mostly teach His children, Madam—'by the rivers of Babylon, where I sat down and wept.'[18] I think he that beareth the precious seed commonly goeth forth weeping,[19] for we cannot enter into the troubles and perplexities of others which have known none ourselves. And if it behoved *Him* in all things to be made like unto His brethren, that He might be a merciful and faithful High Priest,[20] who are we that we should grudge to be made like unto our brethren likewise? That is a deep word, Madam,—'Though He were a Son, yet learned He obedience by the things which He suffered.'[21] I have not got half down to the bottom of it yet. But for the matter of that, I am but just hoeing at the top of all Scripture, and scarce delving any depth."

"Well, Patient," said Celia, with a perplexed, melancholy air, "if you think you are but hoeing on the surface, what am I doing?"

"My dear bairn—I ask your pardon, Madam," corrected Patient.

"Don't ask it, Patient," replied Celia, softly; "I like that—it sounds as if somebody loved me."

"Eh, lassie!" said Patient, suddenly losing all her conventionality, and much of her English, "did ye no think I loved Miss Magdalene's bairn? I was the first that ever fed you, that ever dressed you, that ever bare you about. I was just fon' on you when you were a bit baby." Patient's voice became suddenly tremulous, and ceased.

Celia rose from her chair, and kneeling down by Patient's side, threw her arms round her neck and kissed her. Patient held her tight for a moment.

"The Lord bless you, my ain lassie!" she faltered, "You are just that Miss Magdalene o'er again—her ain brown eyes, and her smile, and her soft bit mou'! The Lord bless you!"

Celia resumed her seat, and Patient her calm, respectful tone; but the former understood the latter a great deal better after that episode, and never forgot what a wealth of love lay hidden under that quiet manner and somewhat stiff address.

"Well, Patient, what were you going to say to me?"

"I scarce think, Madam, that you have had much dwelling by the waters of Babylon as yet. I don't mean that you have had no sorrow at all: I misdoubt if any man or maid ever grew up to your age without knowing what sorrow was. But there are griefs and griefs; and 'tis one thing to visit a town, and another to abide there. David knew what it was: 'My tears have been my meat day and night,'[22] quoth he. And though in the main I conceive that and many another word in David's Psalms to point unto Him that was greater than David, yet I dare say 'twas no pleasant dwelling in the cave with all them that were bitter of soul, neither fleeing on the mountains afore King Saul, nor yet abiding in Gath. He felt them all sore crosses, I little doubt."

"Do you think that is what our Lord means, Patient, where He says, 'Take up the cross, and follow Me'?"[23]

"I think he means whatsoever is undelightful to flesh and blood, that cometh in the way of following Him. Is the gate strait? yet 'Follow Me.' Is the way narrow? yet 'Follow Me.' Art thou faint, and cold, and an-hungered, and a-weary? Yet 'Follow Me.' 'My grace is sufficient for thee.'[24] My footsteps are plain before thee, My eye is ever over thee. 'Follow Me.'"

"But, Patient, don't you think that sometimes the footsteps are not so very plain before us?"

"We cannot see them when we don't look for them, Madam—that is certain."

"Ah! but when we do—is it not sometimes very difficult to see them?"

"Madam, blind eyes cannot see. We are all blind by nature, and even they that are God's children, I believe, cannot sin but it dims their eyes. Even of them, perchance more 'see men as trees walking.'[25] than as having the full use of their spiritual eyes. Well, it matters little how we see men, if only we have eyes to see Christ. Yet which of us, after all, ever really hath seen Him? But anent crosses, Madam, I have a word to say, if you please. There's a wonderful manufactory of crosses ever a-working among all God's saints. Whatever else we are unskilful in, we are uncommon skilled in making of rods for our own backs. And very sharp rods they are, mostly. I had a deal sooner with David, 'fall into the hand of the Lord' than into the hands of men:[26] but above all, may the Lord deliver me from falling into mine own! There is a sharp saying, Madam, which maybe you have heard,—'He that is his own lawyer hath a fool to his client:' I am sure he that ruleth his own way hath a fool to his governor. Yet every man among us would be his own God if he might. What else are all our murmurings and disputings of the will of the Lord?"

"But, Patient, you don't call grieving murmuring? You would not say that every cry of pain was a murmur? Surely when God uses His rod to us, He means us to feel it?"

"Certainly, Madam, He means us to feel it; else there were no use laying it on us. There is a point, doubtless, where grieving doth become murmuring; and where that is the Lord knoweth better than we. He makes no mistakes. He will not account that murmuring which he that crieth doth not intend to be such. I think He looks on our griefs not as they be to Him, nor perchance to others, but as they are to us; just as a kindly nurse or mother will comfort a little bairn greeting over a bit plaything that none save itself accounted the losing of worth naming."

"We are very foolish, I am afraid, sometimes," said Celia, thoughtfully.

"Foolish! ay we are so!" returned Patient. "Setting our hearts, like Jonah, on bit gourds, that grow up in a night, and are withered in a night[27]—quarrelling with the Lord when His wisdom denies us our own will—mewling and grumbling like ill bairns, as we be, at a breath of wind that crosses us—saying, all of us at our hearts, 'I am, and none else beside me'[28]—'Who is the Lord, that I should obey Him?'[29] The longer I live, Madam, the more I am ever marvelling at the wonderful grace, and patience, and love, of the Lord, that He should bear with such ne'er-do-weels as we are, even at our very best. 'I am the Lord, I change not; *therefore* ye sons of Jacob are not consumed.'"[30]

Patient was silent for a while, and Celia broke the silence.

"Patient, what became of Roswith? I never hear you name her now, but always as belonging to past time."

Patient did not answer for a moment. Then she said, her voice a little less calm than usual:

"There is no time, Madam, for her. She will never grow old, she will never suffer pain, she will never weep any more. The Master has been, and called for her."

"She is dead!" said Celia, sympathizingly.

"Dead? Nay, alive for evermore, as He is. 'Because He liveth, we shall live also.'[31] She is in the beatific vision, before the face of the Father, and shall never sin, nor suffer, nor depart any more. And we, here in this body of pain and sin, call them 'dead!' O Roswith! O my soul, my love, my darling! my wee bit bonnie bairn, sister and daughter in one, whom I loved as David Jonathan, as mine own soul! surely I am the dead, and thou art the living!"

Celia sat amazed at this sudden flow of passionate words from her usually imperturbable companion. She had seen her moved, only a short time before, but not like this. Patient bent her head low over her work, and did not look up for some minutes. When she spoke, it was to say, very softly:

"She never looked up rightly after the harrying of Lauchie. She lived, but she never laughed rightly again. The Doctor deemed that the ship wreck—the shock and the cold and the hunger—had wrought the ill. Maybe they had. But she never was a strong, likely lassie. She was ever gentle and quiet in all her ways, and could no bear much putting upon. And after that she just pined and wasted away. It was after Miss Magdalene died—after my Lady that is now was wedded—that the end came. It was one Sabbath afternoon, and I, poor fool! fancied her a wee bit better that day. She was lying on the bed in our chamber, and we had been cracking of divers things—of our Lord Christ and His resurrection, and that sweet prayer of His in John, and the like. Her voice was very low and soft—but it was ever that, I think—and her words came slowly and with pauses. And when we ended our crack, she saith, 'Patient, Sister! sing to me.' I asked her, 'What, dear heart?' and she saith, 'The Twenty-third Psalm.' So I sang:

"'The Lord's my Shepherd, I'll not want.
   He makes me down to lie
In pastures green: He leadeth me
   The quiet waters by.'

"And now and then, just for a line, I heard her weak voice joining in. I sang to the end, and she sang the last lines:

> "'And in God's house for evermore
>   My dwelling-place shall be.'

"When I had done, I thought the place felt so still, as if the angels were there. Surely they were so! for in a few minutes after I made an end of singing, she arose and went to the Father.

"I have been alone with God since that night Roswith died. I shall go some day, but it seems afar off now. Perchance it may be nearer than I deem. The Lord knoweth the time, and He will not forget me."

There was a long silence when Patient's voice ceased. Celia spoke first.

"Patient, you said once that you would tell me how my father met with my step-mother. But I want to know also why no one ever sought me out until now."

"There was no chance, Madam, so long as you were a child. The troubles in England were too great to allow of Sir Edward returning himself. I believe he charged my Lady on his deathbed to seek you out, and wherefore she tarried I know not. I had a mind once to go myself, and I named it to her, but was called a fool for my pains, and bidden to sit quiet and sew. But I was glad to see you."

"Thank you, dear Patient," said Celia, affectionately. "And now tell me about the other."

"Do you know, Madam, that my Lady was a widow when she wedded Sir Edward?"

"No!" exclaimed Celia. "I never heard of that. But Philip—he is really my brother, is he not?"

"Oh yes, Madam! Mr. Philip is your brother. I will tell you:—After my Lady Magdalene died, Sir Edward was for a time sore sick, and the doctors bade him visit and go about for the recovery of his health. I am scarce certain that it was the best thing he could do, howbeit he did as they bade him. Among the gentlemen whom he used to visit, where he whiles took his son Master Edward, and me as his nurse, was the Marquis of La Croix, and another was one Mr. Camillus De L'Orient. The Marquis was a stately old French gentleman, a kindly man to his own, I think, but one that held himself mortal high, and seemed to think that laboring men and the like were no better, if so good, as his dogs and his horses. The Marchioness, his wife, was much of the same sort, only I'm thinking she wasn't quite so stiff as he. They had no son—and very grieved they were for it—only three daughters: Madam

Claudia, Madam Sophia, and Madam Amata. The last young lady is dead; she died a maid, and to my thinking she was a hantle the best of the three. Madam Sophia you saw the other evening; she wedded the Duke of Montausier. Madam Claudia is my Lady.

"I had never any great taking for Frenchmen, but to my thinking Mr. Camillus De L'Orient was the best and pleasantest Frenchman I ever saw. There was something about him so douce and kindly to everybody; and 'tis very seldom the case with the French nobles. Sir Edward came one day into the nursery, as he often did, to play him with the bairn; and, said he, 'Patient, next week I shall go to Monsieur De La Croix's *château* in the provinces, and Mademoiselle Aimée has begged for Edward to come too; so get him and yourself ready. Mademoiselle De La Croix is to be married to Monsieur De L'Orient." Well, we went to the castle; and surely there were fine doings: Madam Claudia in white satin, and all the fine ladies and gentlemen—they were quite a picture to look at. After the wedding and the revellings were over, Madam Claudia and her husband went up to Paris for a while, and then to pay a visit to Mr. Camillus' father and mother, who lived some way off. Sir Edward meanwhile thought of going home too, but Monsieur and Madam they begged of him to stay till Mr. Camillus came back, and Madam Amata, who was mighty fond of children, and took wonderfully to little Master Ned, she begged him not to take the bairn away; so the end of it was that he stopped ever so long, and Master Ned and me, we stopped too. About two months after the wedding, Mr. Camillus and his new wife came back to the castle, and the fine doings began again. There was nought but feasting and junketing for a fortnight; and one morning, at the end of that time, Sir Edward, and Mr. Camillus, and one Mr. Leroy, and three or four gentlemen more that were staying at the castle, they went out for a stroll in the park.

"I know not rightly how it was, but there arose some words among these gentlemen, and they came to quarrelling. Sir Edward held fast by Mr. Camillus, who was a great friend of his; but Mr. Leroy, whose blood was up because of something that had been said, at last struck Mr. Camillus a blow. Everybody cried directly that he must fight him. Sir Edward ran back to the castle for pistols, for the gentlemen were not armed; and he came in all haste into the chamber where I was sewing, with little Master at his horn-book, and bade me tell Madam Claudia as gently as I could that there was to be a duel between Mr. Camillus and Mr. Leroy. I went up into the chamber where the three young ladies were together, and Madam Sophia was trying of a new gown. I told as quiet as I could what had happened. Madam Amata cried out, and ran to her sister, and clipped her round the neck. She said, 'Claude, *ma soeur, ma bonne, ma belle!* go, go to Camille, and ask him not to fight!' I looked at Madam Claudia. She went as white as a sheet the first minute; but the next she lifted her head up proudly, and she said, 'Shall I ask him not to revenge an affront to his honor? *Noblesse oblige, ma soeur.*' 'You are such a child, Aimée!' was all Madam Sophia said, as she looked round from her tiring-glass. 'You always call me so,' said Madam Amata; 'but this is dreadful—it is death, perhaps, my sisters!' Madam Sophia took no heed of her, but went on trying her new gown, and showing her woman where it did not please her. For a minute I thought that Madam Claudia was going to give way and have a good cry; but she did not. I scarce knew then that 'tis not our deepest sorrow that we weep for. She sat down, still very white, and taking no heed to her sister's new array, though she, poor thoughtless maid! kept calling to her, didn't she like this and did she no think that was too long and t'other too narrow? Madam Amata came softly up to me, and whispered '*Ma bonne*, go down and bring us the first news.' So I slipped out and down-stairs. About half an hour after a gentleman came in—a French gentleman, but I forget his name now—who I knew had been at the fighting. I called to him and asked him to pardon me for being so bold as to speak to him, but for the love of God to tell me the news. 'News?' quoth he, 'what! of the duel? Oh! they have fought, and Monsieur De L'Orient has fallen: Sir Edward Ingram is carrying him here'—and Mr. Somebody, I don't mind who it was. 'Is he dead, Sir?' I said, all of a tremble. 'I really don't know,' says he, quite careless; 'I think not quite.'

"I hadn't the heart to speak another word to such a man. I crept up again to the young ladies' chamber, and I knelt down by Madam Claudia, and told her she must make ready for the worst. She shivered all over, and then, scarce opening her white lips, she said, 'Is it all over?' I said, 'They think not quite; but Sir Edward is bringing him hither.' When she heard that, she rose and glided down the stairs to the hall, Madam Amata following her, and I likewise. Even Madam Sophia was a trifle touched, I think, for she said a bad word, as those French ladies do when they are astonished; but Madam Amata was very white and crying, for if Mr. Camillus had really been her brother born, I don't think she could have loved him much better than she did.

"Just as Madam Claudia reached the hall, Sir Edward came in, and the other gentleman, bearing poor Mr. Camillus covered with blood. There was a marble couch in the hall, with silken cushions; they laid him down there, and he just spoke twice. First he said to Sir Edward, 'Tell my mother gently, and take care of my Claude.' And then when Madam Claudia came and knelt by him, he said, '*Dieu vous garde, mamie*!' Then he laid his head back and died. But when he died, Madam Claudia threw her arms about him, and laid her head down on his breast in spite of the blood: and then suddenly springing to her feet, she flung up her arms wildly in a way that sent a shudder through me, and the next minute she would have fallen on the ground if Sir Edward had not caught her first. 'Let us carry her up, Patient, to her own chamber, poor soul!' he saith. So we took her up, I and he, and I laid her quiet on her bed. Madam Amata followed us, and, poor young maid! it was pitiful to see her.

She had never been taught to do more than make fancy-work and play the violin and such, and now she wanted to nurse her sister, and did not know how to set about it. 'Do tell me, *ma bonne*, what I can do for Claude?—my poor Claude!' she kept saying to me. 'Twas a long while ere Madam Claudia came round, and when she did, she wept and mourned every minute of the day for four days. I don't think she ever quite loved anything again as she had loved him."

Celia could hardly associate the idea of such mourning as this with her cold, fashionable, impassive step-mother.

"You think it scarce like, Madam?" asked Patience, seeing her thought in her face. "I know what you think—ay, and more than you have thought that. If you will forgive me to say it, you deem her cold and hard. So she is. Ah Madam! wherever sorrow softens and sanctifies not, it chills and hardens. I am sure, if I had known her but now, I could never have thought her that bright lassie whom I saw in her early maidenhood. You see, Madam, the Lord sends sorrow to us all; but where He has to touch one of His chosen with it, He brings it Himself. And there is a vast difference between the two. There be to whom the having been with grief is the having been with Jesus; and that always softens and tenders the heart. I think we hardly come to know the Lord's best comforts, till we come to know how sorely He can afflict whiles. But grief without Jesus—ah! that is worth calling grief!

"There is little more to tell now, Madam, for you know the end—that Sir Edward wedded Madam Claudia. I will confess I did think they might have waited a trifle longer, if it were only to the end of the year after Mr. Camillus' death. He had scarce been dead six months, and my Lady Magdalene not the year out, when they were married. Howbeit, that was their business, not mine. Madam Sophia said, in her odd way, that if her sister did not care, she saw no reason why she should: but the tears stood in Madam Amata's eyes, though she said nought. I liked Madam Amata very much. She died about two years thereafter."

"Patient, whom do you think Philip like?—his father or his mother?"

"Neither much, Madam. Sir Edward is like his father, only that he hath his mother's mouth."

"Do you know when he will be back, Patient? I do so long to see my *own* brother."

"No, Madam. He went off rather unexpected. Now, Madam Celia, if you please to try this gown?"

"Why, Patient! what have you done to that blue gauze?" inquired Lady Ingram, entering so noiselessly that neither knew of her presence until she spoke. "It is cut absurdly short in front. Turn round, my dear. *Mais c'est affreux!* Pull the rag off, I beg of you. Is that Thérèse's cutting or yours, Patient?"

"Thérèse's, Madam."

"*Incroyable!* I shall scold her right well for it. It is atrocious. *C'est une chose à déchirer de coeur!*"

Celia looked up into Lady Ingram's eyes, saw how calm and careless they were, and wondered if there were left in her anything of that early Claude De La Croix, whose sad story she had been hearing.

[1] Matt. xxii 42.

[2] 2 Sam. xxiii. 5.

[3] 1 Cor. iii. 23.

[4] John viii. 11.

[5] John ii. 16.

[6] Heb. x. 25.

[7] Matt. vii. 20.

[8] Rom. i. 28.

[9] October 22, 1685.

[10] By Henri IV. of France, April 13, 1508.

[11] "It is said that Thomas Wilson endeavored to relieve his sisters from confinement, but did not succeed. He kept himself in concealment till the Revolution, when he entered the army, and served King William in Flanders."—*Nicholson's "History of Galloway."* For a full account of these Scottish Martyrs of Wigtown, I am indebted to the kindness of a (personally unknown) correspondent.

[12] David Graham.

[13] Colbran.

[14] This word, so very odd in such a connection, is the old Scottish term for *executed*.

[15] She sang part of the 25th Psalm.

[16] Rom. viii.

[17] Nicholson's "History of Galloway."

[18] Psalm cxxxvii. 1.

[19] Psalm cxxvi. 6.

[20] Heb. ii. 17.

[21] Heb. v. 8.

[22] Psalm xlii. 3.

[23] Mark x. 21.

[24] 2 Cor. xii. 9.

[25] Mark viii. 24.

[26] 2 Sam. xxiv. 14.

[27] Jonah iv. 6-11.

[28] Isaiah xlvii. 10.

[29] Exod. v. 2.

[30] Mal. iii. 6.

[31] John xiv. 19.

VIII.

WANTED, DIOGENES' LANTERN.

"Smile, hypocrite, smile! It is no such hard labor,
While each stealthy hand stabs the heart of his neighbor:
   Faugh!—Fear not; we've no hearts in Vanity Fair."

MISS MULOCH.

We have been absent for a long time from Ashcliffe Hall. In fact, nothing has occurred there since Celia's departure of sufficient moment to be recorded. But on Easter Tuesday of 1712, Harry returned home for a short time. He brought plenty of town news, political and otherwise.

"Twelve new Tory peers were created on New Year's Day"—

The Squire swore at this piece of information.

"And the Duke of Marlborough[1] has fallen in disgrace"—

"So we heard, lad, so we heard," said his father, discontentedly. "Somebody ought to be ashamed of himself."

"And Prince Eugene[2] is come to England on a visit to Her Majesty, 'tis thought to plead for the Duke."

"O Harry! have you seen Prince Eugene?"

"Yes, Lucy, several times. Do you wish to know what he is like? Well, fancy a small, but well-made man, with a dark complexion, a large Roman nose, black eyes, lively and piercing, and black hair."

"Do you think the Queen will listen to his pleading for the Duke?"

"I doubt it. 'Tis scarce so much with the Duke as with the Duchess[3] that she is herself displeased; and Prince Eugene has already offended her by coming to court in a bag-wig instead of the peruque. She said to her ladies that next time she supposed he would come in his night-cap. Prince Eugene, you see, is a soldier, accustomed to think very little of matters of this kind; and in all points of etiquette the Queen is mighty particular."

"And what other news is there, Harry?"

"Well, Sir, the Secretary for War, a young man named Robert Walpole, has been sent to the Tower for bribery."

"Why on earth have they sent him there for *that*?" asked the Squire, sarcastically. "Does not every one of the Ministers sell all his Secretary-ships? Didn't he buy his place, to begin with?"

"Doubtless, Sir," answered Harry; "and every year the Duchess of Marlborough, whose perquisite they are, either gives or sells the Queen's old gowns; but when the blame must be laid on some one, 'tis easy to find a man to bear it."

"Any other piece of roguery?" asked his father.

"No, Sir, I remember none," said Harry. "Just before I left London, the Queen was touching for the evil.[4] 'Tis a solemn ceremony, I am told, though I was not able to see it. 'Tis stale news, I fear, that there hate been prosecutions of newspaper writers for attacks on the Ministry."

"No, Harry, I had not heard of that," said the Squire, quickly. "Likely enough! A set of beggarly printers daring to bring out lampoons on gentlemen in the Queen's service! Served 'em right!"

"There have been a good many of the lampoons, I believe."

"Is it only the Whig Ministers who suffered from these rascally newspapers?" asked his father.

"Both sides, Sir," answered Harry.

"Well, I am glad the Tories got a bit of it." chuckled Squire Passmore.

"There are gentlemen on the other side, Sir, I think," hinted Harry quietly.

"Nothing but rogues on the other side, my lad," said his father. "Why, how could they be on the other side if they weren't rogues?"

"Why, Father!" said Lucy, who could take more liberties with that gentleman than any one else, and knew it; "you don't think everybody wrong who isn't on the same side as you?"

"There can be only one right side," said the Squire, as evasively as oracularly. "I am on it because 'tis right."

"Well, my politics," said Charley, yawning, "are that 'tis right because I'm on it."

A piece of exalted egotism which provoked universal laughter.

"I met in London with a rather pleasant fellow," remarked Harry, "who told me he had been at Ashcliffe, and had the honor, quoth he, of dining with you. A man of the name of Stevens."

"Ob, aye! a painter," said the Squire.

"Well, he had been in a painter's employ," returned his son, "but is now in a newspaper office: he is employed on the *Gazette*."

"What made him change his trade in that way?"

"He told me that the painter who had employed him had been but a temporary patron, and having now done with him, he had been unable to get further employment in that line. And having some parts in the way of writing, he had offered his services to one or two of the Whig papers, and is now in the *Gazette's* office."

"He is a sensible fellow," said his father. "A right Whig, I could see, and a thorough conscientious man."

Could any person have lifted up the veil, and revealed to him the history and identity of one George Shepherd, he would have felt both amazed and humbled.

At the moment that this conversation was going on at Ashcliffe, the thoroughly conscientious man of whom they were speaking was seated in the back-parlor of a newspaper office in London. He had two companions, a man in a fair wig, and another in a black one. The wearer of the black wig, a large-limbed, long-faced, solemn-looking man, had just folded up some letters after perusal.

"Well, Mr. Mist, what say you?" asked he, laying down the letters. "If you prefer to sever our connection, rather than engage to do as I wish, of course you are at liberty to do so. But unless you will keep measures with me, and be punctual in these things, I cannot serve you further, nor be concerned any more."

"I really beg you not to name such a thing, Mr. De Foe!" replied Mist, bowing and nervously twisting a piece of paper. "I am your very humble servant in these matters—all of them; and I engage readily to conduct the *Journal*—Will you repeat your terms, Mr. De Foe?"

"The Government, Mr. Mist, have treated you with lenity and forbearance," resumed De Foe,[5] oracularly. "They permit you to seem on the same side as before, to rally the *Flying Post* as much as you please, and all the Whig writers, and even the word 'Whig;' and to admit any foolish trifling things in favor of the Tories, such as really can do them no good, nor the Government any harm."

"Well, Mr. De Foe," said Mr. Mist, with a sigh, "that is liberty enough. I am resolved that my paper shall for the future amuse the Tories, but not affront the Government."

"That, Mr. Mist," announced his dictator, "is the only way to keep yourself from a jail, and to secure the advantages which now rise to you from it; for you may be assured the complaint against you is so general that the Government can bear it no longer."[6]

"Would you mind telling me from whom you speak, Sir?" Mr. Mist meekly wished to know.

"I should mind it very much, Mr. Mist. Be satisfied that you have been spoken to—ay, and warned."

Mr. Mist was fully convinced of that.

"You will write, Mr. Mist, a declaration, full enough to satisfy the Government, of your intention to make no further attack upon them?"

Mr. Mist would do anything he was told. The poor little mouse was entirely at the mercy of the lion. He withdrew to pen his declaration, and left the arch-conspirators together.

"You see, Mr. Stevens, what difficulties we Government spies have to contend with!" sighed the author of *Robinson Crusoe*. "But you know that, of course, as well as I do."

"'Bowing in the House of Rimmon,'" responded Stevens, with a peculiar smile. "I fancy the spies on the other side have their difficulties also."

In which observation, though De Foe was completely unaware of it, Mr. Stevens was alluding to himself.

"'Bowing in the House of Rimmon!'" repeated De Foe. "I thank you, Mr. Stevens, for so apt a comparison. You see, Sir, I am for this service posted among Papists, Jacobites, and High Tories—a generation which my very soul abhors. I am obliged to hear traitorous expressions and outrageous words against Her Majesty's person and Government and her most faithful servants, and to smile at it all as if I approved of it."

"You are scarce the first person, Mr. De Foe, who has been constrained to smile at what he disapproves."

"Well, his Lordship's instructions are positive."

"You have them, I think, from himself?" asked Stevens, deferentially.

"Through Mr. Buckley. I introduced myself to Mr. Mist in the disguise of a translator of foreign news, with his Lordship's approbation, who commissioned me, in this manner, to be so far concerned in this weekly paper of Mist's, as to be able to keep it within the circle of a secret management, and also prevent the mischievous part of it; but neither Mist nor any of those concerned with him have the least guess by whose direction I do it. You, Mr. Stevens, are one of ourselves, so I speak freely to you."

"Quite so," answered Stevens, dryly.

"Some time ago," resumed De Foe, "I was concerned in the same manner with Dyer's News-Letter. Old Dyer was just dead, and Dormer, his successor, being unable by his troubles to carry on that work, I had an offer of a share both in the property and management. Well, I immediately sent to the Minister, who, by Mr. Buckley, let me know 'twould be a very acceptable piece of service, for that letter was really very prejudicial to the public, and the most difficult to come at in a judicial way in case of offence given. Upon this I took upon myself (and do still take) the entire management of the paper, so that the style still continues Tory, that the party may be amused, and not set up another, which would destroy the design."[7]

"Of course your object was not wholly political?" smilingly suggested Stevens.

"You mean, there was a matter of money betwixt us? Of course there was—money or money's worth."

"We have it on good authority that 'the laborer is worthy of his hire,'" answered Stevens, still smiling. "Ah! Mr. De Foe, 'tis in truth such as you and I that rule kingdoms—not Kings nor Ministers."

When Stevens left the office of Mist's *Journal*, which was in truth Mist's private habitation, he sauntered slowly for a while along the busy streets; turned into a (Whig) coffee-house, which he frequented every Tuesday morning, and called for a dish of coffee and the *Postboy*; wandering on, turned into another (Tory) coffee-house, which he frequented every Tuesday afternoon, and called for a glass of usquebagh and the *St. James's Chronicle*. Having made his weekly impression on the society of the two coffee-houses, he sauntered on again until he reached Gray's Inn Road. Here his proceedings suddenly changed. He walked up the Road with the air and pace of a man who had no time to spare, and entering a whitesmith's shop, inquired in a rather loud tone whether Butler (the whitesmith) could attend to a little matter of business. Mrs. Butler, who was in the shop, having informed him that her husband was at leisure to undertake anything required, Stevens sinking his voice to a low whisper, asked further—

"Is the old horse in the old stall?"

"He is, Sir," answered Mrs. Butler, in the same tone, adding, in a louder one, "Pray go up-stairs, Sir, and speak with Butler yourself."

Stevens found his way without difficulty up a dark and rickety staircase in the corner, with the intricacies of which he appeared well acquainted, and pausing at a door on the right hand, at the head of the stairs, placed his lips to the keyhole, and gave a low, soft whistle. The door opened with a spring, and Mr. Stevens was admitted to the chamber within.

In the room in question, two men were sitting at a green baize table covered with books and papers. The younger was about the age of Stevens himself, and he looked up with a nod and smile of recognition to the new-comer: the elder, a bald-headed man with a fringe of white hair, did not stir from his close examination of the papers on the table until Stevens stood before him.

"Your blessing, Father!" requested the young priest.

The old man looked up abruptly. "Peace be with thee, Brother Cuthbert," said he, in a harsh, brusque tone; and he went back immediately to his papers. The younger man pointed to a seat at his side, which Stevens took; but neither ventured to interrupt the studies of the old priest, until he at last laid down his papers and took off his spectacles.

"Well, Brother, what news?" said he, looking up at Stevens.

In answer to this query, Stevens gave him a condensed account of the information which he had just received from De Foe.

"That is awkward, Father, is it not?" asked the younger of the strangers.

"Not at all, my son," said the old Jesuit, placidly wiping his spectacles. "The Protestants are welcome to work against us as much as they please. They cannot combine; they have no organism; hence their wiles are mere shadows compared with ours. They are sure to fade and fail, sooner or later. However, we are not above learning even from enemies. It might be as well to have a friend so employed on some few Whig papers. Could you manage that?" he asked, suddenly turning to the young stranger.

The person addressed smiled, but shook his head rather hopelessly.

"I do not think I could, Father Boniface," said he.

"No," assented the old man; "your talents do not lie in that direction. Brother Cuthbert, here is employment for you—yours do."

"My talents commonly lie in any direction to which I find it convenient to turn them, Father," said Stevens, with as modest an air as if he were disclaiming praise instead of bestowing it upon himself. "And as I hold a general dispensation for anything that may be needful, I have no scruples in using it."

The old man, having finished a very careful cleansing of his glasses, put them on, and inspected Stevens through them.

"Brother Cuthbert," said he, "had you been suffered to sink into the abyss of heresy, as at one time seemed likely, it would have been a great loss to the Church."

"Well, I rather think it would," was the cool reply of Mr. Cuthbert Stevens.

"It was a blessed act of our Brother Arnold," resumed Father Boniface, "an inspired thought, which led him to steal you away, an infant untainted by heresy, from the cradle wherein your heretic mother had laid you, while she went to watch the dancing on the village-green. That was Brother Cuthbert's introduction to the Church, Jerome," observed he, turning to his companion. "Our Brother Arnold—he is among the blessed now, I trust, for I have myself offered hundreds of masses for the repose of his soul—he found, in a village in France, an infant in a cradle, by a cottage-door, with none to watch over it. Impelled by philanthropy, he inquired how this was from the next-door neighbor, and was told that a Huguenot carpenter lived in the cottage; he was out at work, and his wife had gone to see the dancers. 'This must not be,' said Arnold; 'I will myself carry the infant to his mother, and reprove her for such foolish conduct.' I should have told you that, the village being full of these misguided heretics, Arnold, in his zeal to recover some of these straying sheep to the true fold, had attired himself as a heretic teacher. 'You will do well, Master Pastor,' said the neighbor; 'for though she is kindly and well-meaning, 'tis her worst fault to love gadding about, and she is very young and needs teaching.' So Arnold took the babe, and instead of going to the green, piously brought it to us at the monastery. Thou wert a sad trouble for a long time, Brother Cuthbert; for the brethren were not wont to deal with such tender young creatures, and thou wouldst eat nothing presented to thee, and didst wail and howl ceaselessly."

And the old priest shook his head sorrowfully, as if he remembered too well the trouble which the Huguenot baby had brought upon the brotherhood. Stevens laughed, and so did Jerome; but the latter seemed to enjoy the novel idea more of the two.

"Do you know the name of the village, Father? It might be a good act to endeavor to win over some of these Huguenots."

"We thought it better, Brother Cuthbert, that you should not know the name of your birthplace. Ties of kindred are strong at times; and, as I have often observed to you, when a man becomes a priest, he ceases to have any kindred ties. The Church is your mother, her monks are your brethren, her nuns your sisters. Be satisfied."

Stevens was far too much accustomed to instant and implicit submission to offer the slightest remonstrance to this slight mandate. But this was the first time that he had ever received a detailed account of his origin. He knew that he had been brought to the monastery as an infant, but hitherto he had known nothing more, and had naturally supposed himself to be a foundling. In this idea he had grown up. He had never loved any human being, nor, so far as he knew, had any human being ever loved him. But that afternoon a vision rose before him of the poor Huguenot mother coming back from her thoughtless expedition to find her darling gone. He wished he could have found her. He would have tried to convert her to Romanism if he had done so; for he honestly believed his Church the true one. But she might perhaps have loved him; and nobody ever had done so hitherto.

"In these papers, Brother Cuthbert," resumed the old Jesuit, "you will find instructions in cipher. I need not charge you to keep them carefully."

Stevens put them safely away in a private pocket.

"And I will detain you no longer."

Stevens had reached the door, when he turned back.

"Father Boniface, if you think it not an improper request, would you tell me in what part of France I was found?"

Father Boniface looked into his young friend's face, and thought it a very improper request. But he had his own reasons for not bluntly refusing an answer.

"In Auvergne, my son," he said, shortly. "Ask no more."

Cuthbert Stevens passed out of the whitesmith's shop without stopping for his customary five minutes' chat with Mrs. Butler.

"Ah, poor gentleman!" said she to herself; "he's had a bit of bad news."

He had had something like it. He walked very rapidly up Gray's Inn Road, knowing little and caring less whither he was going, till he found himself in the fields beyond Clerkenwell. There he threw himself on the grass, and resting his head upon his hands, gave himself up for one hour to mournful and profitless visions of that Auvergne home, and of the unknown father and mother who might have loved him once.

"And I shall never see them!" he thought. "So near the Waldensian valleys:— what a stronghold of heresy they must be! Ah, well! I can say every day a mass with an intention for my parents. Who knows if God may be merciful to them, after all? The soul is worth more than the body, and eternal happiness is worth more than any amount of ease or felicity in this world. From what a fate, therefore, have I been rescued! I ought to be very thankful."

But gratitude and love are the last things into which a man can scold himself, and Stevens did not feel so thankful as he thought he ought to be. He might have been more so, had he known that Father Boniface had not troubled himself to tell him the exact truth. It was from the outermost village of the Val Martino, in the Waldensian valleys, not from Auvergne, that he had been stolen away. And in that Val Martino, though he was never to know it, every night knelt Lucetta Carmagnoli, mourning before God—less for the martyred husband, or for the two brave young sons slain in battle, than for the lost first-born, whose fate she could guess only too well. Wavering from hour to hour between the passion of hope—"Oh that Ishmael might live before Thee!"[8]—and the passion of despair—"Would God I had died for thee! O Absalom, my son, my son!"[9]

Such prayers and tears seem lost sometimes. But "are they not in Thy book?"[10] "What I do thou knowest not now; but thou shalt know hereafter."[11] It is not only Simon the son of Jonas who is asked, now in the tempest, now in the still, small voice, "Lovest thou Me more than these?"[12]

Stevens rose from his green couch, and walked back to London. His heart had been dormant all his life till now, and it went easily to sleep again. His conscience the Jesuits had crushed and twisted and trained so early that it never troubled him with a single pang. By the time that he had reached Fleet Street, and had solaced his inner man with a second dish of coffee (and something in it) at the Tory coffee-house, Mr. Cuthbert Stevens was himself again. And if he did look back on the hour spent in the fields at Clerkenwell, it was only to reflect with momentary annoyance that, as he would have phrased it, he had made a fool of himself. And it was very rarely indeed that he thought that substantive applicable in the slightest degree to the Rev. Cuthbert Stevens.

"Well, there is one comfort," he meditated, as he sat imbibing the mixture: "nobody saw me do it."

And fortified by this consideration, and the coffee, &c., Mr. Stevens walked into the residence of the Editor of the *Postboy*, and expressed his desire for an interview with that rather awful individual. There was a smile on his lips when he came out. He was engaged at a high salary to supply foreign news to the columns of the Whig paper. Mr. Buckley, the Ministerial agent, had spoken very highly of Mr. Stevens to the Editor. Mr. Stevens was rejoiced to hear it, and he told the truth for once when he said so. The Editor thought Mr. Stevens set a rather high value on his services. Mr. Stevens could assure him that he had received innumerable applications from the Tory side, and it was only his deep attachment to the Whig cause, and his respect for the *Postboy* in particular, which had led him, by asking so little, rather to underrate the importance of the information he could supply. The importance, indeed, of the information which Stevens could have supplied would not have been overrated at double the figure; but of this little fact the Editor of the *Postboy* was unconscious.

Here we part with the Rev. Cuthbert Stevens. The rest of his life was a mere repetition, with variations, of what we have seen. The Whigs continued to take him for a Whig spy, the Tories for a Tory, while he himself cared in reality for neither, and was devoted but to one thing, and ready to be either, neither, or both, in the service and at the command of that Church which supplied to him the place of home, and parents, and friends, and God. And at the close of such a life followed the priest, and the crucifix, and the unction, and the false hope which shall perish, and the death that has no bands.

Ere this Rome has employed, and destroyed, many a Cuthbert Stevens. What do the crushed devotees matter to the idol? Let the car of Juggernaut roll on! "Thou art become guilty in thy blood that thou hast shed, and hast defiled thyself in thine idols which thou hast made."[13] "In the cup which she hath filled, fill to her double."[14]

Perhaps the greatest of Lucetta Carmagnoli's mercies was what she thought the bitterest of her sorrows—that she never knew what became of her lost child.

It is time for us to return to France.

On one of these spring afternoons of 1712, Celia stood looking out of her bedroom window. They were in Lady Ingram's country-house at St. Germain-en-Laye. She was very curious, and yet almost afraid, to see the Palace—that house in which, as she knew, he dwelt whom Squire Passmore called the Pretender, and Lady Ingram the King. Celia herself had owned to no politics at all. She found it quite work enough to steer between her religious Scyllas and Charybdises, without setting up political ones. In all things not absolutely wrong, she was resolved meekly to submit to Lady Ingram, so that her step-mother might have no just cause for dissatisfaction with her in respect to those few points which to her were really matters of conscience. When Patient came quietly in with an armful of the linen which she was unpacking and putting away, Celia said—

"Patient, do you know where the *château* is?"

"The Pretender dwells over yonder, Madam," answered Patient, pointing in the direction which she wished to indicate.

"So you call him the Pretender!" observed Celia, smilingly.

"I was taught, Madam, when a wean, that the people should have nought to do with an uncovenanted King. Moreover, the reign of His Highness the Lord Protector being so much better for the faith, hath perhaps turned me a little against this one and all his."

Celia laughed softly to herself. What would Squire Passmore have said, from whose lips the gentleman so respectfully designated by Patient was, at the gentlest, "that scoundrel Oliver"? She began to wonder how many more phases of political feeling she should find.

"I ask your pardon if I have grieved you, Madam," said Patient, when Celia remained silent, "I would not willingly do that. Sir Edward, I know, was strong for King James, and would doubtless have been so for his son: and 'tis most like you will feel with your father. Only we were taught otherwise. When King James was driven out of London, I heard that, the Sabbath after, in Scotland, a certain godly minister did discourse from that word—'And death shall be chosen rather than life by all the residue of them that remain of this evil family, which remain in all the places whither I have driven them, saith the Lord of hosts.'"[15]

"I think that was rather too strong, Patient," said Celia, doubtfully.

"Perchance so, Madam. Indeed, I know there be some that do think King Charles the First safe—in Heaven, I mean. God grant it! I only know that he was a deceitful man, and an uncovenanted King."

"I have always heard him called a martyr, Patient."

"He was not *that*!" said Patient, less calmly than usual. "At least, not if a martyr be a witness for the Lord's truth. Did he not try to force Prelacy upon Scotland? Call such a man a martyr! A martyr to Prelacy, forsooth! a martyr to deceit, and broken faith, and cruel oppression! We were the martyrs, Madam." And Patient shut a drawer wrathfully, for her.

"I don't know much about it, Patient," said Celia, honestly. "I have been taught to believe that King Charles was a good and misfortunate man. But now I can hardly tell what to believe among you all. My—Squire Passmore thinks that King Charles was a good man and a martyr, yet calls this man the Pretender, and will scarce hear him named with patience. My step-mother thinks them both good; and you think them both bad. I cannot tell what to think."

Celia came from the window as Lady Ingram entered the room.

"Patient," she said, "lay out Mrs. Celia's new court-dress on the bed—you know which it is. My dear, this afternoon I will lead you to kiss the Queen's hand. Your manners are slightly improved, and I wish you to show respect to the Court."

"Very well, Madam," resignedly answered Celia.

"You will enter behind me; stop, and go forward, when I do. When I draw aside, come forward, kneel, and kiss the Queen's hand when she offers it. Should she speak to you, remain kneeling while you answer, unless she command you to rise. If she do not speak, rise, draw to one side, as I shall have done, and stand there."

"Yes, Madam."

"Do not look about you: keep your eyes on the Queen. Don't look awkward. Be self-possessed."

"I will do my best, Madam."

Lady Ingram tapped Celia's cheek with her fan, a sign, that she was unusually gracious. "Be ready in an hour," she said, and departed.

Thérèse came next to dress Celia's hair. Patient, in solemn and evidently disapproving silence, helped her to dress. She found herself, when the process was over, in a quilted pink satin petticoat, a bodice and train of white satin, trimmed with gold braid, white satin shoes, long white gloves, pearl necklace and bracelets: her hair was dressed very high, and adorned with pink roses and pearls. As Celia looked at herself in the glass, she felt much inclined to sing with the celebrated little old woman, "Sure this is none of I!" but much time was not allowed her for the indulgence of that feeling.

"Your servant, Madam!" observed Philip's voice in the corridor, accompanied by a tap at the door. "Don't keep us waiting, please,—we shall be very cross if you do. I protest! aren't you smart!"

Mr. Philip himself was scarcely less so. He wore a light blue coat embroidered in gold, a white satin waistcoat and breeches, white silk stockings, and white satin shoes with large rosettes. In the drawing-room stood Lady Ingram, attired in white and gold.

"Turn round!" was her greeting to Celia and Philip. "Nonsense, not you!" as Philip made a *pirouette* in answer. "That will do. Now, follow me; and whatever you feel, don't look awkward or afraid."

Celia meekly followed her step-mother to the carriage, which rolled away with the trio, and in a few minutes deposited them at one of the half-dozen doors of a large and stately mansion. On the terrace, before them, ladies and gentlemen were walking and chatting, most of them in rather shabby, though full, court-dress. Lady Ingram bowed to two or three, gave her hand to her son, and once more enjoining Celia to keep close behind, passed on into the Palace.

"This is English ground, Madam," observed Philip, over his shoulder.

Celia wished it were. Up lofty staircases, through suites of rooms, past groups of servants in the royal livery of England, worn and faded, she followed Lady Ingram and Philip, until in one apartment a lady dressed in black rose to meet them, and shook hands with Lady Ingram.

"You can go in to the Queen, my friend," she said; "there is only His Majesty with her."

There were only two persons in the room beyond. A gentleman stood at the window reading the *Gazette*; a lady in mourning sat writing at a very shabby little table in the middle of the room. A glance at each assured Celia that they were mother and son; and she speedily discovered who they were, by Lady Ingram's kneeling before the quiet-looking lady in mourning, who sat at the shabby little table.

"Ah, *ma chère*!" said the lady, in a soft voice, turning to her; adding, "I am very glad to see you. It is long since I had the pleasure."

Lady Ingram answered in French, and still kneeling, "I have been in Paris, Madame, and in England for a short time. I had the honor to inform your Majesty that I was going there to fetch my step-daughter."

"This is your daughter?" asked the Queen, turning with a smile to Celia.

Lady Ingram drew aside to leave room for her. "She scarcely speaks French yet," she observed.

As Celia knelt and looked up into the face before her, she was much struck with that smile. It changed the aspect of the whole face. The air of subdued sadness which had dwelt upon the classic regular features and in the quiet soft eyes, passed away, and a brighter expression lighted them brilliantly while the smile remained. She could fancy what that face might have been in the old days, when, at the close of the coronation, nearly thirty years before, the Westminster students had called up that smile by their spontaneous shout of "*Vivat Regina Maria!*" Celia forgot all about kissing the Queen's hand, until she heard Lady Ingram's voice beside her whisper, in a subdued tone, "*Cette folle!*" Then she blushed painfully and hastily performed her homage. The charm which enfolded the Jacobites had been cast around her; the spell of voice, and eyes, and smile, which she would never forget any more.

"Why so hurried, my child?" asked the soft voice, in Celia's own tongue. "Do not be frightened of me, I pray you."

Frightened of *her*? No, indeed! thought Celia, as she rose from her knees with a smile in answer to the Queen's. What fright she felt was not for Her Majesty, but for Lady Ingram. As she regained her feet, she suddenly saw that the Queen's son was standing beside his mother. The formidable mortal, whom Squire Passmore would have knocked down as his first greeting, and

Patient have sermonized as an uncovenanted King! Hardly knowing what she did, Celia knelt again and kissed the hand that was extended to her. It was a soft white hand, which did not look as if it would hold the sceptre very harshly, and on one finger glittered a large gold ring set with a balas ruby, upon which a cross was engraved. Celia would have regarded that jewel with deep interest and veneration had she known its romantic history, stranger than any romance. This was the last relic of James's fallen fortunes, the ancient coronation-ring, "the wedding-ring of England," which had gleamed from many a royal hand before, and had been employed to many a strange end. While Philip in his turn performed his homage, Celia studied the royal persons before her.

First, the King. He was tall, very tall[16]—a man whom few would pass without wondering who he was; rather thin, but with all this not ungraceful, and with an air of much distinction about him. An oval face he had, with a bright complexion; a forehead smooth and high, but not at all broad; arched eyebrows; eyes of a dark, rich brown,[17] large, and very soft; a mouth rather too large for strict proportion, but bearing an expression of mingled sadness and sweetness, which grew into fascination when he smiled. His smiles were rare, and his voice seldom heard; but very often Celia caught a momentary upward glance of the eyes, accompanied by a silent motion of the lips, and she wondered if it were possible that he was praying.[18] He wore no wig, only his own dark chestnut hair curling over his shoulders.

This was the King whom England had cast out. She would have none of him, under any pretext. Rather than be ruled by this son of her own, she had set "a stranger over her, which was not her brother."[19] Celia wondered, for the first time in her life, whether England had done well. She turned with a sigh from the son to the mother, who was conversing familiarly with Lady Ingram, seated beside her.

The Queen, Maria Beatrice, or Mary, as the English called her, Celia thought a most fascinating woman. She resembled her son in height and form, being very tall,[20] and slender.[21] Her face was oval,[22] her complexion clear and fair, but very pale;[23] her mouth rather large,[24] but her smile to Celia perfectly enchanting; her hair, eyebrows, and eyes were black. The eyes were very large, clear, and brilliant;[25] though when they smiled, as they were doing now—

"It was as if remembering they had wept,
And knowing they should some day weep again."[26]

"And now tell me all about it, my dear," the Queen was saying to Lady Ingram. "Sophia gave you my message about the Bishop?"

"Yes, Madam; and I am quite delighted to think of it. Your Majesty is aware that the Tories are in greater power than ever?"

"Dean Atterbury said so in his last note," replied the Queen, opening her desk, and apparently searching for the letter. "He has written often lately, and very kindly."

Celia listened in much surprise, to hear that an unsuspected Protestant dignitary was in constant and familiar correspondence with the Court of St. Germains.[27]

"Your Majesty has not heard from the Duke?"

"From Blenheim? no, not since I saw you: but the Duchess of Tyrconnel[28] was here not long ago, and she tells me that there seems no hope of the Duke's return to power."[29]

Celia's astonishment grew.

"Does your Majesty fear that the Princess"—suggested Lady Ingram.

"No, my dear, no," replied the Queen, rather sadly; "I do not think she can have discovered. She is not naturally suspicious, and you know that the Duchess has been her dearest friend for many years."

"I scarcely think much of that," answered Lady Ingram. "Beside, as your Majesty knows, this woman Abigail, who has crept up to power on the wreck of hers, and who is a better friend of ours than ever she was, has all the influence now over the Princess Anne; and she would doubtless willingly let her know if she discovered it, simply to spite the Duchess, and prevent her return to power. Of course the supplanter would not like to be supplanted."

"I know it, my dear Lady Ingram, I know it," responded the Queen, with a sadder air than ever.

"Also your Majesty will remember"——But here Lady Ingram bent forward and spoke low, so that Celia could hear no more. She had heard quite enough already to make her doubtful of the truth and honesty of everybody in the room but Philip.

"Is this your first visit to France?"

Celia looked up suddenly to find herself addressed by the King.

"Yes, Sir," she said, hesitating very much, coloring, and doubting whether, in saying "your Majesty," she would have been doing right or wrong. "Yes, this is my first visit."

"Do you like it?"

"Not so well as England."

"Spoken like a true Englishwoman!" said the King, with his rare smile. "Neither do I."

Remembering that he had been carried away as an infant in arms, Celia wondered what he knew about it.

"I hope you are one of my friends?" was the next question.

Celia looked up, blushed, and looked down again. "I do not know, Sir," she said.

"I compliment you on your honesty," said he. "'Tis a rare quality."

Celia was beginning to think it was.

"I beg your pardon, Sir," she replied, timidly; "I was brought up to think otherwise."

"Let us hope to convert you," he answered. "I assure you that your friends can hope for no great degree of prosperity till they become mine;[30] and I am not without hopes of changing all England on that question. Do you think it impossible?"

"I almost do, Sir," said Celia, smiling, and playing with her fan a little nervously.

"We shall see who is right," added the King, "Ingram, have you seen Colville lately?"

"And I assure your Majesty," said Lady Ingram rising, "that I shall make the fullest inquiries about it, and direct Sophie to do so."

"So be it, my dear," said the Queen, quietly. "Farewell! You will bring this little maid again? I *had* a daughter—you know. In Arcadia—once! '*Fiat voluntas Tua.*'"

The last words were spoken very low and falteringly. The beloved Princess Louise, surnamed by her father *La Consolatrice*, had been taken away from her mother's eyes as with a stroke, only six weeks before.[31]

And for one minute Celia forgot dishonesty and Popery and everything else on the part of the exiled House, as she looked pityingly into the tear-dimmed eyes of the almost desolate mother. There were four graves at Westminster[32] beside the one at Chaillot, and the young man who stood beside the Queen was the last of her children: "the only son of his mother, and she was a widow!"[33]

And the verdict Celia whispered to her own heart at the close was—"Yes, England has done well—has done right. But oh, if it had not been necessary!"

"Chocolate!" announced Mr. Philip Ingram to himself, simultaneously with the presentation of himself at his sister's boudoir-door. "Patient, bring me a cup—there's a good soul. Why, how long is it before supper?"

"Scarcely two hours, I know," said Celia; "but I had very little dinner, and I am hungry."

"You dined on your coming interview with the Queen, did you? Well, how do you like her?"

"I like her face very much, and feel very sorry for her."

"You like her face!" repeated Philip, putting his hands in his pockets. "What a droll answer! Do you mean that you dislike her voice, or what part of her?"

"Nothing in that way. Philip, I wonder if there is a scrap of honesty left in the world!"

"Precious little, my dear—I can tell you that. Patient, you are a diamond of the first water!" The last remark by way of receipt for the chocolate.

"Well, I think so! I never could have imagined that such men as the Duke of Marlborough and Dean Atterbury were eating the Queen's bread, and deceiving her every day by writing to these people and offering help."

Philip laughed. "So that is what has angered and astonished you? Why, any man in Paris could have told you that months ago. 'Tis no secret, my innocence—from any but the Princess Anne."

"'Tis rank dishonesty!" exclaimed Celia, warmly. "I don't complain of their helping this Court, but of their want of truth. If they are Jacobites, let them have the manliness to say so."

"You are such an innocent!" responded Philip, still laughing. "Why, my simple little sister, all is fair in politics, as in love and war."

"I don't see that 'all is fair' in any of the three. What is right is right, and what is wrong is wrong."

"Excellent, my logical damsel! But what are right and wrong? That is the first question. Is there a certain abstract thing called right or virtue? or does right differ according to the views or circumstances of the actor?"

"I do not understand you, Philip. To do right is to obey God, and to do wrong is to disobey God. There was no wrong in Adam's and Eve's eating fruit: what made it wrong was God's having forbidden them to touch that one tree. St. Paul says, 'Where no law is there is no transgression.'"[34]

"Upon my word, you are a regular divine! But—leaving St. Paul on one side for the present—how, according to your theory, shall we discover what is wrong?"

"Just by not leaving St. Paul on one side," answered Celia, smiling; "for the Bible is given us for that purpose."

"Very few definite rules are to be found in the Bible, my doctor of divinity."

"Quite enough for all of us, Philip."

"Pardon me! The very thing, I think, is, that there are not enough. A few more 'thou shalts' and 'thou shalt nots' would be of infinite service. Your view, if I understand it, is to bring the Bible to bear upon every act of life; but how you contrive to do so I can't imagine. Now, look here! I will give you a case, my fair casuist. Would it be right or wrong for me, at this moment, sitting on this sofa, to take a pinch of snuff?"

"I must ask you a few questions before I can answer."

"Catechize, by all means. 'What is my name?' Philip Eugene. 'Who gave me this name?' Don't recollect in the least. 'What did they do for me?' Why, one of them gave me a gold goblet, and another a set of silver Apostle-spoons:[35] and I am not aware that they did anything else for me."

"Philip, Philip!" remonstrated Celia, laughing in spite of herself. "Please don't let us jest upon these serious subjects. I don't want to ask those questions."

"Well, I won't jest, my dear. I will be very quiet and grave."

"Does your mother object to your taking snuff?"

"Not exactly. I don't think she much likes it."

"Then your question is answered. If she does not like it, it is—for you—wrong."

"Oh! you arrive at your conclusions in that roundabout sort of way? That is rather clever but I will see if I cannot puzzle you yet."

"I have no doubt you can, very easily," said Celia. "You may readily propound fifty such cases which I could not answer. You see, those are not my circumstances: and we can scarce expect that God will give us grace to see what is right in difficulties which He does not lay upon us. Do you not think so, Patient?"

"I do so, Madam. I have ever found it harder to see the way out when I had hedged up mine own way, than when the Lord, as with Noah, had shut me in."

"Ah! there you come round to your divinity," said Philip, lightly. "Whatever I ask you, you always centre there; and Patient will say Amen to all your propositions, I have no doubt. But to return to our point of departure: I hardly see your 'rank dishonesty' in the acts of the Court. I believe this—that if the Queen thought it dishonest, she would not do it. She is considered here a very religious woman: not in your way, I dare say. But we freethinkers, you know, do not set much value on small differences. If a man be sincere, that is the chief thing; even some of the more enlightened of the Catholic Fathers allow that. Does not the Bible say that there are twelve gates to Heaven?[36] There is a reference for you."

"A reference that'll no hold water, Mr. Philip," said Patient, looking up. "For though there be twelve gates into the City, there's only door into the Fold:[37] and I'll be fain to know how you are shaping, without passing the one door, to get in at any of the twelve gates. For whoso 'entereth not in by the door into the sheepfold, but climbeth up some other way, the same is a thief and a robber.'"[38]

"Philip," added Celia, softly, "there is but one gate and one way to life, which is Jesus Christ."

"Ah! at it again!" said Philip, lifting his eyebrows, and finishing his chocolate.

"Always at it," answered Celia, in the same tone. "'Out of the abundance of the heart the mouth' must speak.[39] Philip, your idea about sincerity will lead you terribly astray—I am sure it will. There is but one truth; and if a man believe falsehood, will his thinking it truth make it so? Sincerity is not the chief thing. The chief things are faith and love in us, and the Lord Jesus Christ out of us. 'He that hath the Son hath life: and he that hath not the Son of God hath not life.'[40] O Philip! listen to me this once! 'It is not a vain thing for thee, because it is thy life!'"[41]

Philip looked into his sister's earnest eyes, rose and kissed her, and sat down again.

"You are a capital little sister," he said, "and admirably cut out for a *réligieuse*. I am quite glad the Protestants don't take to that amusement, or I should certainly lose you, and I like you too well to afford it."

Celia sighed. Her words did not appear to have made the faintest impression.

"What a sigh!" said Philip. "My dear little Celia! do you take me for an utter reprobate, that you think it necessary to mourn over me in that way?"

"Philip," said Celia, very solemnly, "a man must be either inside the sheepfold of Jesus, or outside it. Without is without, whether the door which he refuses to enter be a yard from him or a thousand miles. Without the Fold now, without the City hereafter. And 'without are dogs, and sorcerers, and whoremongers, and murderers, and idolaters, and whosoever loveth and maketh a lie.'"[42]

"I know mighty few people who are in, then," said Philip, whistling, and considering the carpet.

"I am afraid so," answered Celia, shortly. "But the one question for us, Philip, is—Are *we* in?"

A question to which Mr. Philip Ingram made no reply.

[1] John Churchill, Duke of Marlborough, second son of Winston Churchill and Elizabeth Drake his wife: born at Musbury, 1650; died at Windsor Lodge, June 16, 1722; buried in Westminster Abbey, August 9, 1722.

[2] Eugenio Francesco, fifth and youngest son of Eugenio Maurizio, Prince of Carignano, and Olympia Mancini his wife: born at Paris, October 18, 1603; died at Vienna, April 10, 1736.

[3] Sarah, daughter and co-heir of Richard Jennings: born at Holywell, St. Albans, May 29, 1660; married, in the spring of 1678, John Churchill; died at Marlborough House, October 18, 1744; buried at Blenheim.

[4] Queen Anne was the last Sovereign who performed this ceremony.

[5] Daniel De Foe, author of "Robinson Crusoe:" born 1663; died in London, April 24, 1731.

[6] The account of his dealings with Mist, which are little to De Foe's credit, has lately been brought to light. It is contained in a series of letters from himself, recently discovered in the State-Paper Office. They have been printed in the *London Review*, June 4-11, 1864, and in *Notes and Queries*, 3d S., vi. 527. These letters show painfully the utter demoralization of parties at the time in question. The account given above of De Foe's interview with Mist is taken almost verbatim from his own letters, and has received no further change than was necessary to throw it into the form of dialogue; but the event has been ante-dated by six years. It really took place in 1718, and Lords Townshend and Sunderland were De Foe's employers.

[7] See De Foe's Letters, quoted above.

[8] Gen. xvii. 18.

[9] 2 Sam. xviii. 33.

[10] Ps. lvi. 8.

[11] John xiii. 7.

[12] John xxi. 15.

[13] Ezek. xxii. 4.

[14] Rev. xviii. 6.

[15] Jer. viii. 3.

[16] Gray, the poet, who gives a very spiteful portrait of James, as if he had some personal pique against him, speaks of his "rueful length of person," and "extreme tallness and awkwardness." Spence describes him as "a tall, well-limbed man, of a pleasing countenance. He has an air of great distinction."

[17] His Stonyhurst portrait gives him gray-blue eyes, and some others dark blue, but the majority have brown.

[18] Gray cynically remarks that "he has extremely the air and look of an idiot, particularly when he laughs or prays; the first he does not often, the latter continually."

[19] Deut. xvii. 15. This passage was very frequently cited by the Jacobites as barring the accession of William of Orange, though his mother was the eldest daughter of Charles the I., and he stood next in succession to the children of James II. It was much more applicable to the House of Hanover, which was further from the original English stock.

[20] "Tall and admirably shaped," said Lord Peterborough, in describing her to his royal master when negotiating the marriage in 1673. She was then fourteen. In 1688 Mademoiselle Do Montpensier thought her "*une grande créature mélancolique.*" Lady Cavendish (*née* Rachel Russell), writing to a friend, describes Mary II. as "tall, but not so tall as the last Queen" (Maria Beatrice).

[21] "*Fort maigre*"—Mdlle. De Montpensier.

[22] "Face the most graceful oval."—Lord Peterborough.

[23] "Complexion of the last degree of fairness."—Lord Peterborough. "Complexion clear, but somewhat pale."—Mad. De Sévigné. "*Assez jaune.*"—Mdlle. De Montpensier.

[24] "Mouth too large for perfect beauty, but her lips pouting, and teeth lovely."—Mad. De Sévigné.

[25] "Hair black as jet; eyebrows and eyes black, but the latter so full of light and sweetness, that they did dazzle and charm too."—Lord Peterborough. "Her eyes are always tearful, but large, and very dark and beautiful."—Mad. De Sévigné. Some of her portraits give her very dark brown hair and eyes.

[26] Mrs. Barrett Browning's "Aurora Leigh."

[27] Francis Atterbury, second son of the Rev. Lewis Atterbury and Elizabeth Giffard his wife: born 1662; consecrated Bishop of Rochester, July 5, 1713; was deprived for treason, May 16, 1723, and died in exile at Paris, February 15, 1732. At this period he was Dean of Carlisle.

[28] Frances, eldest daughter of Richard Jennings, and sister of Sarah Duchess of Marlborough, celebrated at the Court of Charles II. as La Belle Jennings: married Richard Talbot, Duke of Tyrconnel; died at Dublin, March 7, 1730.

[29] The Duke of Maryborough corresponded with the royal exiles, especially towards the close of Queen Anne's reign, and appears sometimes to have held out hopes to them which it is doubtful whether he ever intended to fulfil.

[30] James said this to Mr. Spence about a dozen years later.

[31] Louise Marie Thérèse, born at St. Germains, June 28, 1692; died at the same place, after a few days' illness, of small-pox, a disease very fatal to the House of Stuart, April 18, 1712.

[32] Katherine Laura, buried October 5, 1675; Isabella, buried March 1681; Charles, buried December 1677; and Charlotte Maria, buried October 1682.

[33] Luke vii. 12.

[34] Rom. iv. 15.

[35] Apostle-spoons were spoons whose handles were carved into figures of the Apostles. Twelve went to a set.

[36] Rev. xxi. 12.

[37] John x. 7.

[38] Ibid. 1.

[39] Matt. xii. 34.

[40] 1 John v. 12

[41] Deut. xxxii. 47.

[42] Rev. xxii. 12.

IX.

INSIDE AND OUTSIDE.

"But sure he is the Prince of the world; let his nobility remain in his Court. I am for the house with the narrow gate, which I take to be too little for pomp to enter: some, that humble themselves, may; but the many will be too chill and tender; and they'll be for the flowery way, that leads to the broad gate and the great fire."

—SHAKSPEARE, "*All's Well that Ends Well*," Act iv. Scene 5.

"My Dearest Mother,—(For I cannot bear to call you anything else)—I have so much to tell you that I know not where to begin. I am now, as you will see by my date, at St. Germains, which is a rather pretty place. My stepmother is kind to me, in her way, which is not exactly your way; but I am quite comfortable, so pray be not troubled about me. I like Philip, my younger brother, very much; he oft reminds me of Charley. My elder brother, Edward, I have not yet seen, he being now absent from home. I have seen the Pretender and the late Queen Mary,[1] both of whom are very tall persons, having dark hair and eyes. I have made no friends here but one; you shall hear about her shortly. So much for my news.

"And now I wish very much to hear yours. Are you all well? And pray tell me anything of note concerning any person whom I know. All news from England has great interest for me now.

"Pray give all manner of loving messages for me. Tell my dear father that the people here hunt a great deal, but always stags. There is no cock-fighting, at which I am glad, for 'tis but a cruel sport to my thinking; nor no baiting nor wrestling, but a great deal of duelling. I like the French gentlemen ill, and the ladies worse. Bell should come here to see the modes; 'twould give her infinite pleasure. I can speak French tolerable well now, and if my father and you choose, could teach Lucy on my return. For I am looking forward to that, Mother dear—sometimes very much indeed. To think that 'tis six months, nearly, since I saw one of you! and if you have writ I have not had your letters. If aught should bring Harry to Paris, do pray bid him visit me; I should be so infinitely glad. Pray give my love to Cicely, and tell her I would she knew my woman here, whom I like mightily, and so would she. I hope Charley is a good boy, and that Lucy tries to fill my place with you. At the end of this month, if my Lady Ingram say nought, I shall ask her when she will part with me. I beg that you will write to me, if 'twere but a line. Indeed

I should like dearly to hear from every one of you. Anything you like to write will be infinitely welcome to—

"Madam,
"Your dutiful child and faithful servant,
"CELIA INGRAM.[2]
"ST. GERMAIN-EN-LAYE,
May 15, 1712."

Celia folded her letter, addressed it, and sat thinking. How would they receive it? She pictured Lucy rushing into the parlor, waving it above her head, and Isabella languidly rebuking her for her rough entrance. She could guess the Squire's comments on many things she had said, and she knew that the very mention of the Pretender would call forth some strong participles. Madam Passmore would fold up the letter with "Dear child!" and drop it into her ample pocket. Cicely would courtesy and ask if Mrs. Celia was a-coming. One month more, and then surely Lady Ingram must be satisfied. But then came another thought. She would be very sorry to leave Philip and Patient, even to return to Ashcliffe. Would Lady Ingram be induced to let her take Patient with her? As to Philip, surely he could visit her if he chose.

"Mademoiselle!" said the voice of Thérèse beside her.

Celia turned, and saw that Thérèse was holding a little pink note, which having delivered, the French maid departed. She broke the seal, and discovered to her surprise that the note was from Lady Ingram herself. It ran thus:

"MY DAUGHTER,—I shall not be able to receive you this afternoon, as I am suffering from megrims.[3] I will send Philip to keep you company. I wish you to know that when I return to Paris, which will be in four days, I will lead you to kiss the hand of the King of France. After this you will be able to enter into company.

"CLAUDE INGRAM."

Celia dropped the note in the trepidation which it caused her. She had no desire to be presented to the originator of the Dragonnades. And what was "entering into company?" She was sure it meant what she would not like, and might think actually wrong.

"Do you drive out this afternoon, Madam?" asked Patient, appearing at the door.

"No, Patient," said Celia, hesitatingly, for she was still thinking of the note. "Mr. Philip will drink a dish of chocolate with me here."

"Yes, Madam," replied Patient, and disappeared.

Celia changed her dress with a heavy heart, and came back into her boudoir, where preparations for the chocolate were made. She found Mr. Philip Ingram very comfortably established on her sofa.

"Good evening, Madam," observed that gentleman, without any alteration in his attitude of repose.

"Philip, what is it to go into company?"

"To dress fine and tell lies. Why?"

Celia gave him the note in answer.

"Ah!" remarked he. "Megrims, has she? Let me see now—the megrims are Père Letellier; yes, Père Dumain is a cold on the chest."

"What do you mean, Philip?" asked Celia, in bewilderment.

"Only my Lady-Mother's style of cipher correspondence, my dear. She gives an occasional *séance* to her spiritual advisers, on which occasion she tells the world—fibs."

"You do not really mean it?"

"Of course I do."

"But what does she do?"

"In her *séance*? Confesses her sins—that is, so far as I can judge from my recollection of one such occurrence at which I was present when a small kitten, she regales her spiritual pastor with some very spicy tales of all her friends and acquaintances."

"I am sure you are joking, Philip. But please tell me what it is that she wants me to do? Is it to go to all her assemblies?"

"Precisely, my Grey Sister—and to a few Court balls, and a play or two."

"O dear!" sighed poor Celia. "I never can do *that*,"

"Don't sigh in that heart-rending style," said Philip. "As to assemblies, there will not be above three more this summer, and we may be in China by next year. What is your special grief?"

"It looks like conformity to the world," answered Celia, in a low tone, for she did not expect Philip to understand her.

"Where is the world?" laughed that irreverent young gentleman. "That superb satin gown of yours, or the chocolate, or the talk? Eh, Patient? What do you say, my veteran prioress?"

"In your heart, Mr. Philip," answered Patient, setting down the chocolate-pot which she had just brought in. "The world outside, and an evil worldly human heart within, will work no little mischief. I'll warrant it did *Him* no harm dining with the Pharisee[4]—not that Simon was an over-pleasant man to do with, I should say: and when your heart is as pure and holy as His, why, Sir, I'm thinking you may go, and welcome. But I've work enough cut out for me in keeping the devil without mine own door, without calling at his to ask how he fareth."

"Thank you, Dr. Patient. Rather a short sermon. Celia, my dear, I have a scrap of information for you which will make you open your eyes."

"The shortest sermon I ever heard of was one of the most salutary, Sir,—to wit, when Nathan said to poor sinful David, 'Thou art the man!'"[5]

"You are very disrespectful to His Israelitish Majesty," said Philip, lightly. "Well, Mrs. Celia, know that I have succeeded at last in obtaining her Ladyship's leave, and the King's commission, to go into the army. Lieutenant Ingram, Madam, at your service!" and Philip rose and made a bow which would not have disgraced Monsieur Bontems.

"Philip! Are you really a lieutenant?"

"Really. And the best half of the battle is the battle. There is a prospect of the troops being called to active service."

Celia turned pale.

"Does your mother know that?"

"No."

"O Philip! you have not been deceiving her, have you?"

"Smooth your ruffled brow, my fair reprover. I did not know it myself until after His Majesty had promised me a commission. Of course, after this I must be a fervent Jacobite. So don't you talk any politics in my hearing, Mrs. Patient Irvine, unless you wish me to fight you."

"I shall scarce be like to do that, Sir, unless you give me the starting," quietly responded Patient.

"Thank you, no! I will keep my hands off that gunpowder-magazine. I know how you can go off sometimes when touched by a few odd matches. So, my charmer, your interview with me on the 18th of next month will be the last for a while."

"Where are you going, Philip?"

"We march to the Netherlands Border, and meet Prince Eugene. We are to be at Landrécies by the 10th of July."[6]

"Mr. Philip, you shall not go hence without a Bible in your knapsack."

"Thank you very much. Am I to read it when I am not firing?"

"If I could help it, Sir, you would not go without one other thing, but that I cannot give you."

"What thing may that be?"

"The grace of God in your heart, Sir."

"You think me entirely devoid of it?" asked Philip, gravely.

"I do so, Mr. Philip," said Patient, looking him full in the face.

"Well, you are candid, if not complimentary," said he. "'Tis fortunate for me that my conscience gives a rather fairer report than you do. I wish Edward were back. I should like to have gone into battle under dear old Ned's wing, and I'm in his own regiment, too. He must have got an awful furlough."

"Your conscience, Sir!" exclaimed Patient, in a peculiar voice. "Do you think that when Adam fell he left his conscience out?"

"My dear Patient, I wonder what you mean? God has given to every man his conscience as his ruler, counsellor, and guide. He who hearkens to his conscience is hearkening to God."

Patient did not answer at once. Then she said:

"Sir, I desire to speak with due reverence of the Lord's dealings. But 'tis my true belief that he did nothing of the kind you say. He gave, 'tis true, a guide to every man; but that guide was His own blessed Word and His own Holy Spirit, not the man's poor, miserable, fallen conscience. Truly, I would not take my conscience, which is myself, to be my 'ruler, counsellor and guide.' One is my Ruler, which is in heaven. One is my Counsellor—the Wonderful Counsellor.[7] And one is my Guide—the Spirit, in the Word which He hath written. Conscience given us for a guide, Mr. Philip! Why, Paul went according to his conscience when he kept the clothes of them that stoned Stephen.[8] Peter went according to his conscience when he withdrew himself from them that were not of the circumcision, and refused to eat with them.[9] Alexander the coppersmith very like went according to his conscience when he did the Church much evil.[10] To come to our own day, I dare be bold to guess that King Charles went according to his conscience,—Charles the First, I mean; I doubt his son had none. And Claverhouse, and this King Lewis, and the Pretender—ay, the Pope himself, poor old sinner!—I'll be bound they go according to their consciences. Nay, nay, Mr. Philip! When Adam fell in Eden, surely his conscience fell with him. And just as there can be nothing more sweet and gracious than an enlightened conscience and a sanctified will, so there is little worse than a blind conscience and a carnal will."

"You have such a curious set of arguments as I never heard. You are for ever talking about the fall of Adam, which you seem to fancy accounts for the falls and slips of you and me. I never knew Adam, I am sure, and I don't hold myself responsible for his taste in apples. How do you know that Adam 'fell,' as you are pleased to call it? And supposing that he did, what in the name of common sense has that to do with me?"

"It has more to do with you than you think for, Mr. Philip. As Christ is the Head of His saved Church, so is Adam the head of the whole family of man. 'In Adam all die.'[11] And as to knowing that Adam fell, to say nought of the Lord's record of it, I scarce think I need more evidence of that than your doubting it, Sir. If you can look upon this world, as it is at this moment, and doubt that man is a fallen, lost, ruined, miserable creature, there must be something sore wrong with the eyes of your understanding."

"Or of yours," suggested Philip. "Oh, I see evil enough in the world, I warrant you: but I see good along with it. Now the principle you are fond of laying down is according to a text which I think you have quoted to me twenty times—'In us dwelleth no good thing.'"[12]

"I wish you thought so, Mr. Philip."

"Thank you for wishing me such an agreeable view of myself. But while you are fixing your eyes intently on all the evil in the world, you leave the good unseen."

"Would you kindly point it out to me, Sir?"

"Willingly. Take only one point. There are hosts of people in the world—Catholics and others, even Mahometans and idolaters, I dare say—whom you would consign kindly and certainly to everlasting perdition"—

"I consign no man to perdition, Sir. The keys of hell and of death are not in my hands, thank God! But I read of 'the son of perdition,'[13] who went to his own place.'"[14]

"Well, among all these very wicked people, there is a vast deal of charity. Is that good or bad?"

"Charity is good, Sir," said Patient, cautiously. "Paul would have counted himself nothing worth if he had not charity.[15] But"—

"Then they are good for indulging it?" interrupted Philip.

"Sir, 'charity' is a much misused word. You are speaking of mere alms, the which are good for them that receive them, if they use them rightly; and good for them that give them, when given in a right spirit. But these are no more evidence of a man's standing before God"—

"Patient Irvine, have you read the Twenty-fifth chapter of Saint Matthew?"

"I have read the Twenty-fifth of Matthew, Sir," answered Patient, dryly, leaving out the "Saint."

"And are not the good people commended in that chapter, and do they not obtain everlasting life, simply and solely for their charity to the poor?"

"No, Sir," said Patient, placidly.

"Well, upon my word!" exclaimed Philip.

"Sir," resumed Patient, gravely, "it takes but a kindly heart to give alms for its own sake, or for the receiver's sake. But it takes a renewed heart to give alms for Christ's sake. Not the giving of alms was the title to life everlasting, but the giving them 'unto Him'[16] was the seal and evidence of their grace. They that know Christ will look for a savor of Him in all things, and such as have it not are bitter unto them. And I would call to your mind, Sir, that 'tis 'he that believeth'[17] which shall be saved: not he which giveth alms. At least, there is no such passage in *my* Bible."

"You always run off to something else," said Philip, discontentedly. "However, to come back to our first point—as to my conscience, begging your pardon, and with your gracious leave, I think that God has given it to me as a guide, and that I am bound to follow it."

Patient laid down her work, and looked Philip in the face.

"I read in the Word, Mr. Philip, of different sorts of consciences. There is a defiled conscience. 'Unto them that are defiled and unbelieving is nothing pure; but even their mind and conscience is defiled.'[18] There is an evil conscience. 'Having our hearts sprinkled from an evil conscience;'[19] and nought in earth or heaven will sprinkle them to this end save the blood of Christ. There is a conscience lost and smothered in dead works. 'How much more shall the blood of Christ ... purge your conscience from dead works?'[20] Now, Mr. Philip, see your 'good' and charity to the poor. *Works*, you see: but, coming from dead hearts and souls—*dead* works. And lastly, deepest and deadliest of all, I read of a conscience 'seared with a hot iron.'[21] Ay, there have been some of those in our day. The Lord protect us from it! The devil hath such a grip of them that they cannot free themselves; and, poor blind souls! they never know it, but think they are doing God's service. Are these consciences given as guides, Mr. Philip?"

"Well, you see, all that is Saint Peter's opinion."

"I ask you pardon, 'tis Paul, not Peter.'

"Oh, St. Paul? Well, 'tis all the same."

"Ay, Mr. Philip, it is all the same, for it was the Holy Ghost that spake through both of them. And *His* opinion is scarce to be dealt with so lightly, methinks, seeing that by His word we shall be judged at the last day."

Patient took up her work again, and said no more. Philip was silent for a time: when he next spoke it was on a different subject.

"Celia, I want you to come down at my mother's next assembly. I should like to present my friend Colville to you."

"I am rather curious to see him," she admitted.

"Mr. Philip, if I might presume to say a word"—

"'Presume to say a word!' you may presume to say a thousand, my dear old Covenanter. What's in the wind now?"

"I wish you went less about with that Mr. Colville."

"Why? Does he wear his cravats without starch?" asked Philip, stretching himself out lazily.

"I am afraid, Mr. Philip, that he wears his soul without grace," said Patient, determinately. "If he were such another as his grandsire, I would wish no better than to see you in his company. But I am sore afraid that he draws you off, Sir, to places where you should not go."

"He never draws me off, Reverend Mother, to any place where I don't choose to go, I assure you. He would find that a hard matter."

"The case is scarce bettered by that, Mr. Philip," replied Patient, mournfully. "Nay, rather worsened, I'm thinking. O Mr. Philip! bear with me, Sir, for I have sobbed many a prayer over your cradle, and many a wrestle have I had with the Lord for a blessing on your soul. You little ken, Sir, how even now, whenever I see you go out with that Mr. Colville, I lay the case before the Lord at once. I could not rest else."

"My dear old darling!" said Philip, smiling, and very affectionately, "I wish you did not look at me through such very black spectacles. There are better men than I am—many a one; but I hope there are a few worse."

"That won't satisfy me, Sir," answered Patient. "I would have Sir Edward and you the two best men in the world."

"And we are not!—at least I am not; I am not sure that Ned is not. What a pity!"

"Ay, Mr. Philip, a bitterer pity than you'll ken till you come to stand before God. I have watched you for years, Sir, like a mother her babe, trusting to see you quieted and calmed by grace: and to-night you seem to me lighter and gayer than ever. 'Tis no manner of use—no manner of use. 'I have labored in vain; I have spent my strength for nought.'"[22]

"Dear Patient," said Celia, as the door closed on Philip, "have you forgotten that verse we read last Sunday—'Though Israel be not gathered, yet shall I be glorious in the eyes of the Lord, and my God shall be my strength.'[23] It comes, you know, just after the text you repeated."

"Ou ay, Mrs. Celia," answered Patient, dropping into Scotch, as was usual with her when deeply stirred,—"ou ay, I mind that word. But it was the gathering I wanted, Madam—it was the gathering!"

Back in Paris, and once more attired in full court costume, Celia somewhat sadly joined her step-mother. This visit to the Tuileries was even more distasteful to her than that she had paid at St. Germains. The idea of kneeling to kiss the hand of the man who had ordered the Dragonnades, came, she thought, very near the border of absolute wrong; at the same time, she did not feel so certain of the wrong as to make her resist Lady Ingram's order. Her position was exceedingly disagreeable, since, while she could not be sure that she was doing wrong, she felt very doubtful whether she was doing right. Philip tried to rally her upon her sorrowful face, but his banter fell flat, and he looked puzzled and compassionate.

"I am ready, my dear," said Lady Ingram as she came in. "But what a face! Do you think that I am taking you to see an execution?"

"Madam," said Celia, summoning all her courage, "I wish your Ladyship would allow me to remain at home."

"Is this wicked, my votaress?" asked Lady Ingram, with the scornful smile which by this time her step-daughter knew so well.

"I cannot say that, Madam; but I am not quite sure that it is right. Does your Ladyship wish me particularly to accompany you?"

"Of course I do, my dear. 'Tis an opportunity which it would be a sin to lose. You consider it a venial sin, I suppose. Well, you can say another prayer or two."

"I know nothing about venial sins, Madam. Sin is sin to me; but as I am not sure that this is a sin, if your Ladyship absolutely commands me, I will go: at the same time, I would much rather remain."

"Ah! I know what that means, my *réligieuse*," said Lady Ingram, laughing; "you want an excuse for your conscience. Very well, then, I command you. The coach is here. Come!"

Celia followed slowly. Lady Ingram had entirely misunderstood her—in all probability was incapable of understanding her. Any further explanation, she felt, would merely plunge her deeper into the mire; so she sat grave and silent until the carriage drew up on one side of the Place du Carrousel. Lady Ingram gave her hand as usual to Philip, and Celia followed them in silence. After the customary passage through suites of rooms, they paused at a door; and on giving a gentle tap, a gentleman in black came out and bowed low before them.

"Madam," said he, "my duty is my duty. I regret unspeakably to be constrained to inform you that His Most Christian Majesty can receive no person to-day."

"I regret it exceedingly also," answered Lady Ingram. "I can proceed, I suppose, to visit the ladies?"

"Certainly, Madam."

Lady Ingram turned off through further suites of apartments, and the gentleman in black, straightening himself up, disappeared again behind the door. Celia felt relieved. There could be nothing wrong, she thought, in paying respect to the Queen and Princesses, to whom she supposed Lady Ingram to refer; and she followed with a lighter step and heart than before. Her ignorance of the state of the Royal Family of France was very great indeed. That state, in the summer of 1712, was a strange and lamentable one. There was no Queen, yet the King was married; there were no Princesses save one, the Duchess de Berry, yet three of the King's daughters sat round his table every evening.

"Now, Celia!" said Lady Ingram, looking back, "we will pay our respects first to the Duchess de Berry."

"Who is the Duchess de Berry?" Celia inquired softly of Philip.

"The wife of the King's grandson," he whispered in reply.

The Duchess de Berry could receive them, they were told, on asking; and the gentleman usher opened the inner door, and gave access to a large and handsome room, wherein about two dozen ladies and gentlemen were seated at a table, playing cards. A much larger number stood round the room, close to the walls, watching the players. Lady Ingram made her way to a very young girl who sat at one end of the lansquenet-table, and who, Celia thought, was scarcely seventeen. This surely could be the wife of nobody, she mentally decided.

The girl certainly looked very young. Celia, on consideration, doubted if she were seventeen. A soft, bright, innocent face she had, laughing eyes, and a blooming complexion. She looked up with a smile as Lady Ingram approached her, and said a few words in a low tone. Lady Ingram took off her gloves, and sat down quietly at the lansquenet-table, having apparently forgotten her companions.

"Are we to remain here?" asked Celia of Philip, in a tone inaudible to any one but himself.

"Wait a minute, till I see the result of her first venture," answered Philip, biting his lip.

Celia looked back at the card-table. She was accustomed to see Squire Passmore play cards, but never for money, except when he received or went into company; and even then, a few half-crowns were all that changed hands. She gazed with surprise on the piles and rouleaux of gold which lay upon this table, and the quantity of loose pieces scattered about. Hands were constantly extended with a dozen or two of louis in them, and one lady in particular Celia noticed, who piled up her gold until the tower would go no higher, and each time staked the heap on a single card.

"Who is that girl next my Lady Ingram, at the end of the table?" Celia next inquired of her brother.

"That is the Duchess de Berry," said he.

"That the Duchess! Why, Philip! she is scarce more than a child!"

"She is the mother of two children herself," replied Philip. "Perhaps you guess her younger than she is—eighteen."

"She looks so young and innocent," said Celia.

"Young, yes—but innocent! My dear, this girl of eighteen is already one of the worst women in France. Deuce-ace—ah! She will go on. We may go."

Philip slipped round the table to his mother's side, and whispered a few words to her, to which she responded without turning her head. Coming back to Celia, he gave her his hand and led her out of the room.

"Is my Lady not coming?" she asked, glancing back.

"Not when she has thrown deuce-ace," said Philip, dryly. "She considers that her lucky number, and always goes on playing when it comes at the first throw. Now come with me for half-an-hour. You will see a little of Court-life, and you shall go home when you are tired. We will visit the great drawing-room."

He led her into a large, handsome room, hung with crimson. Round the apartment lines of spectators, three or four deep, were standing, and at a very large table in the midst about forty more were seated. The game played here also was lansquenet, for such immense losses had occurred at basset that the King had forbidden the latter game in all rooms but the private boudoirs of the Princesses.

"Have we any right here, Philip?" whispered Celia, doubtfully.

"Yes," said Philip, coolly. "Any person known to the gentlemen-ushers can enter. Come round a little to the right—there is more room, and you will see better. I will be your directory. That gentleman with the blue coat and the orders on his breast, at the top of the table, is the Duke of Orleans.[24] If the King die while his heir is under age, as is most likely, that man will be Regent of France. He is considered a clever fellow."

Celia looked, and saw a man of middle height, and about forty years of age. He had bright eyes, a laughing mouth, a florid complexion, and a thick, flat nose. The hand which held his cards was as small, white, and delicate as that of a woman.

"And who are the ladies beside him?" Celia wished to know.

"On the right, his cousin, the Grand Duchess of Tuscany,[25] and on the left another cousin,[26] the Princess of Conti. Next to her is her half-sister, the Duke's wife."[27]

"I do not quite like the Grand Duchess's face."

"She is not considered particularly amiable. One of her sisters[28] was married to the Duke de Guise, which was so marvellous a condescension that the poor man might never eat his dinner without his wife's leave. Every day he stood beside her chair, and presented her dinner-napkin: the cover was laid for her only; and he might not presume to help himself even to a biscuit until Her Royal Highness was graciously pleased to command a plate and chair to be brought for Monsieur de Guise. Then he made a low, grateful bow to his very superior wife, and might sit down and dine."

"Is that really true, Philip?" asked Celia, laughing softly.

"Perfectly true."

Celia turned her attention to the Princess of Conti. She liked to look at her fair, quiet face, with its large, soft brown eyes; and she was wondering what her character was, when suddenly a lady, who had been staking extremely high, rose from her seat, flinging down her cards, cursing and swearing in most voluble French. This was the first time that Celia had heard a woman use such language, and she hid her face, shuddering.

"Ruined!" said Philip, coolly. "You had better come away."

The ladies and gentlemen at the card-table set up a shrill chorus of laughter.

"O Philip, take me home!" sobbed Celia. "I cannot bear this!"

She had heard Squire Passmore swear before now, but it was generally when he was excited or angry, and was commonly accompanied by a gentle "Hush, John!" from his wife. Philip led his sister out of the room to the seats in the recess of the corridor window.

"Sit down here a minute," he said, "and recover yourself, before I take you up-stairs. That was an unfortunate accident. If I had known I should not have brought you here."

"O Philip, let me go home! No more visits like this, please!"

"You shall do as you like, my dear," said Philip, kindly; "but the next visit will be very different from this."

Celia rose, trying to compose herself; and, afraid of disappointing her brother, she consented to be taken where he wished.

"Does Madame de Maintenon receive this afternoon?" was Philip's question to the usher upstairs.

"She does, Sir; and His Royal Highness the Duke of Bretagne is with her."

"Oh, I don't want to see anybody who will swear!" said Celia, drawing back.

"If the Duke of Bretagne have learned to swear," answered Philip, gravely, "he must be a marvel of juvenile depravity; for he will not be three years old until next February."

"A child!" said Celia. "I beg the little thing's pardon; I have no objection to that."

"The future King of France, my dear," said Philip. "He will be Louis XV. (if he live) in a few years, at the utmost. Now, three low courtesies for Madame de Maintenon."

In a quiet, pleasant chamber, hung with dark blue, an old lady sat showing a picture-book to a very little boy who stood leaning against her knee. She did not look her age, which was seventy-eight. Her figure was rather inclining to be tall, and she preserved the taste, the grace, and the dignity which had always characterized her. A complexion of extreme fairness was relieved by black eyes, very large and radiant, but the once chestnut hair now required no powder to make it white.

"Mr. Philip Ingram?" she said, with a peculiarly pleasant smile; "I am very much pleased to see you."

"My sister, Madame," said Philip, as he presented Celia.

"I did not know that you had a sister," she answered, receiving Celia very kindly. "Louis, will you give your hand to this lady?"

The pretty little child[29] addressed trotted forward, and looking straight in Celia's face with his great brown eyes, presented his baby hand to be kissed. Resisting a strong inclination to take him on her knee and kiss him, Celia performed her homage to the future Sovereign. With much gravity the little Duke offered the same privilege to Philip, and trotted back to his picture-book.

"My Lady Ingram is not with you?" asked the old lady.

"In the Duchess de Berry's saloon at lansquenet, Madame."

"Ah! Do you play, Mademoiselle?"

"No, Madame," said Celia.

"I am glad to hear it," replied Madame de Maintenon.[30] "It is a great waste of time and temper, which were not given us for such uses."

"Turn over!" required the little Prince, authoritatively.

Madame de Maintenon smiled and obeyed.

"I hope His Majesty is not ill?" asked Philip. "I hear he does not receive."

"Not ill, but not well. One of his troublesome headaches. Neither men nor women live forever, Mr. Ingram—not even Kings."

"True, but unfortunate, Madame," was the civil answer with which Philip took his leave.

"Now we will go home," said he. "A short visit, but I thought we had better not interrupt the Duke's reading-lesson. Did you like this scene better than the other?"

"O Philip, how different! Is that lady his nurse?"

"Well, not precisely, my dear. She is—only that she is not called so—the Queen."

"The Queen of France?" asked Celia, opening her eyes.

"The King of France's wife, which I suppose is the same thing; only that in Madame de Maintenon's case it is not the same thing. There is a paradox! A strange life that woman has led. She was born in a prison, the daughter of a Huguenot father and a Catholic mother; imbibed her father's teaching, and when young was a determined little Huguenot. Her father died early. Her mother took her to church, and she turned her back on the altar. Madam d'Aubigné slapped Miss Fanny and turned her round; but Fanny only presented the other cheek. 'Strike away!' said she; "tis a blessed thing to suffer for one's religion!' Her mother now thought there was nothing to be done with the obstinate little heretic, and gave her up. Next, the house was burnt—fortunately while they were out of it; but for days Fanny cried inconsolably. Her mother, who appears to have been a practical, matter-of-fact woman, when this sort of thing had gone on for several days, thought it desirable to treat Miss Fanny to a slight scolding. 'What a little goose you are!' she said, 'crying everlastingly for a house!' 'Oh! it isn't the house!' sobbed Fanny; 'it isn't the house—it is dolly!' Well, Madame d'Aubigné died while Fanny was still a girl, and she was left entirely destitute. In these circumstances she married, for a home, the ugliest man in France. He was a comic poet, a poor deformed fellow, of the name of Scarron. Fanny did not gain much by her marriage, for they were very poor; but her taste in dress was so exquisite that I have heard ladies say she looked better in a common gown of lavender cotton than half the Court ladies in their silks and satins: and her conversation was so fascinating that clever men used to dine with Scarron just for the sake of hearing her talk.

"There is a story told of one such dinner, at which the servant whispered in Madame's ear, 'Please to tell another story; there is not enough roast beef.' I have heard these and many other anecdotes about her from Aunt Sophie, whose mother-in-law knew her well for many years. When her husband died, she was again thrown on the world; and for some time she petitioned the King in vain for some little property or pension to which she was entitled us Scarron's widow. At last he became perfectly tired of her petitions; but he had never seen her. 'Widow Scarron!' His Majesty used to say, as he took up another petition: 'am I always to be pestered with Widow Scarron?' A short time afterwards he met her somewhere; and her grace, beauty, and wit made such an impression upon him that he gave her the appointment of governess to a *posse* of his children. When he came to see them, he saw her; and 'Widow Scarron' so grew in his esteem, that it is supposed about two years after the death of his Queen, he married her."[31]

"And why do they call her Madame de Maintenon?"

"His Majesty gave her the estate of Maintenon, and wished her to bear the name."

"And what will become of her when he dies?"

"Ah, that is just the point! I should think she will go into a convent."

"I thought you said she was a Huguenot?"

"So she was, but she is generally supposed to be a Catholic now."

"What a pity!" said Celia, thoughtfully. "How much good she might have done in turning the King's heart towards the Huguenots, if God had permitted her!"

"On the contrary, she is thought to have turned him from them. Many persons say that we may thank her for the revocation of the Edict of Nantes."

"I can scarce believe that, Philip!"

"I hardly do myself."

"Do you think, Philip," asked Celia, slowly, after a pause, "that there is one really good man or woman among all your acquaintance?"

"My dear," replied Philip, in his gravest manner, "I have met with so many good men and women that I have lost all faith in the article. I have seen excellent mothers whose children have died from neglect, excellent husbands who have run away with other people's wives, excellent sons and daughters who have left a kind mother alone in her old age, and excellent friends who have ruined their friends' reputations by backbiting. Never a one of your good men and women for me, if you please. We are all a bad lot together—that is the truth; and the best of us is only a trifle less bad than the others."

"But, Philip, do you really know none who has the fear of God in his heart?"

"Yes, I know three people who have it—you, and Ned, and Patient. I cannot name a fourth."

"O Philip! I wish you were the fourth yourself!" sighed Celia.

"So do I, my dear," said Philip, so gravely that Celia looked up into his face to see what he meant. She was perplexed, and scarcely satisfied with what she read there.

"Philip," she asked, dropping her eyes again, "do *you* play at these card-tables?"

"Never. I believe Patient thinks I do, but she is mistaken. I threw at basset once, and I shall never do it again."

"Did you lose?"

"No, I won."

"Then what made you determine not to do it again?"

"A remark of Leroy, who was standing near. He said, 'No man ever loses at the first throw. I never saw one lose. The Devil is too cunning for that.' I thought that if the habitual frequenters of the basset-table acknowledged that gentleman for their president, the less I saw of it the better."

"I think you were very wise, Philip," said Celia. "Monsieur Leroy! The man who"—she stopped suddenly, wondering whether Philip were acquainted with the facts of which she was thinking.

"'The man who'—precisely: Savarie Leroy. I see Patient has told you that sad story."

"Philip," said Celia, very seriously, "I wish I could do something to help you. If you do *really* wish to fear God"—

"My dear little sister," replied Philip, putting his arm round her, "have you any idea how much you have helped me already? I am not quite the Gallio you and Patient think me—caring for none of these things. Now I will just give you a glimpse into my heart. I always knew what Patient was—she never concealed her thoughts on the matter; but there are thirty years between her and me, and I fancied—perhaps foolishly—that the religion which might be very good for her would not do for me. I thought many a time, 'If I could find some one in my own rank, and near my own age, who had not been brought up with Patient as Ned and I have, and therefore had not taken the tone of his feelings from her; if this person should think, feel, and talk in the same way that she does, having derived it from a different locality and breeding, and all that,—why, then, I should feel that, whatever else this religion of hers were, at least it was a reality.' Now this I never could have found in Ned, for two reasons: as to religious breeding, Patient has brought him up; the tone and color of his religion he derives from her. And, secondly, Ned is rather close. Not in the least sternly or unkindly so—nothing of the sort; but he is not such an open, foolish, off-handed fellow as I am. It is not natural to him, as it is to me, to say everything he thinks, to everybody who comes in his way; and in religious matters particularly, what he thinks and feels he keeps to himself. Well, then you came. For the first few weeks that you were here, I watched you like a cat watches a mouse. If you had made one slip—if I had once seen your profession and practice at variance—if you had been less gentle and obedient to my mother, when I could see that she was making you do things which you would much rather not do: or if, on the other hand, you had allowed her to lead you into something which I knew that you considered positively forbidden—if I had seen anything of this,

Celia, I should have gone away more irretrievably disgusted than ever with religion and all who professed it.

"Now, my dear, I don't want to make you proud and puff you up, but as I am telling you all this, I must add that I found not one slip in you. I cannot understand how you have done it. It seems to me that you must have a very large amount of what Patient calls 'grace,' that I, who have been watching you so narrowly, could detect nothing in you which I thought wrong. Now will you forgive me for the ordeal through which, unknown to you, I have been putting you? The conclusion to which it has led me is this:—This thing—this religion of yours and Patient's—call it fear of God, or what you will—is a real thing. It is not the disordered fancy of one good woman, as I for a time imagined that it might be. It is a genuine compact and converse between God and your souls, and I only wish I were one of you."

Rather to Philip's surprise, Celia, who while he spoke had been earnestly regarding him, with brilliant eyes and smiling lips, put her head down and burst into tears.

"My dear!" he said.

"O Philip, I am so glad!" she said,—"so glad, so thankful—so very, very glad!" And she sobbed for pure joy.

"Then I am very glad that I have told you, my dear. And if it gives you any satisfaction, I will say again what I have said:—from my soul I wish I were one of you!"

[1] The ugly word "ex-queen" had not yet come into use, and the English spoke of Maria Beatrice as they would have done if she had died.

[2] I must own to having left my heroine's letter defective in one point. In her day ladies' orthography was in a dreadful state. Queen Anne usually signed herself the "affectionat freind" of her correspondents; and it had only just ceased to be the fashion for ladies to employ the longest words they could pick up, using them in an incorrect sense, and with a wrong pronunciation. Addison gives an account of one French lady who having unfortunately pronounced a hard word correctly, and employed it in the proper sense, "all the ladies in the Court were out of countenance for her."

[3] Headache.

[4] Luke vii. 36.

[5] Sam. xii. 7.

[6] Prince Eugene was now besieging Landrécies, a town on the border between France and Flanders.

[7] Isaiah ix. 6.

[8] Acts vii. 58; viii. 1.

[9] Gal. ii. 12.

[10] 3 Tim. iv. 14.

[11] 1 Cor. xv. 22.

[12] Rom. vii. 18.

[13] John xvii. 12.

[14] Acts i. 25.

[15] 1 Cor. xiii. 1, 2.

[16] Matt. xxv. 40.

[17] Mark xvi. 16.

[18] Titus i. 15.

[19] Heb. x. 22.

[20] Heb. ix. 14,

[21] 1 Tim.

[22] Isaiah xlix. 4.

[23] Ibid. 5.

[24] Philippe, younger son of Louis XIII. and Anne of Austria: born August 2, 1674; died December 2, 1723.

[25] Marguerite Louise, daughter of Gaston Duke of Orleans and Marguerite of Lorraine: born July 28, 1645; married at the Louvre, April 19, 1661; died in France, September 17, 1721.

[26] Marie Anne, natural daughter of Louis XIV. and Louise de La Vallière: born at Vincennes, October 2, 1666; married, January 16, 1680, Louis Prince of Conti; died May 3, 1739.

[27] Françoise Marie, natural daughter of Louis XIV. and Athenaïs de Montespan; born May 4, 1677; married February 18, 1692; died 1749.

[28] Isabelle, daughter of Gaston Duke of Orleans and Marguerite of Lorraine: born December 20, 1646; married 1667; died March 17, 1696.

[29] Louis XV.: born February 15, 1710; died at Versailles, of small-pox, May 10, 1774.

[30] Françoise, daughter of Constant d'Aubigné and Jeanne de Cardillac; born at Niort, November 27, 1635; married at Versailles 1685; died at St. Cyr, April 15, 1719.

[31] All these little anecdotes concerning Madame de Maintenon are authentic.

X.

ANENT JOHN PATTERSON.

"One Faithful, meek fool, who is led to the burning,
  He cumbered us sorely in Vanity Fair."
—MISS MULOCH.

"Look out for rocks, Madam Celia," was Patient's enigmatical comment when she heard what Philip had said.

"I do not understand you, Patient."

"Madam, there is nothing harder in this world than humility, because there is nothing so near to the Lord. There are but two places wherein He dwelleth—the high and holy Heaven, and the humble and contrite heart. Paul, you mind, was sent a thorn in the flesh because of the abundance of the revelations. I have near always found that when I have had some work to do for the Lord which was like to make me think well of myself, there has either been a thorn in the flesh or a thorn in the spirit sent to me, either just before or just after. Most commonly just before. And it does not need abundance of revelations, neither, to set up poor fools like us. Anything can do that. If we are trying to walk close to the Lord, and give no occasion for stumbling, the Devil can make pedestals of our very graces whereon to stick us up and cause us to fall down and worship ourselves. Ay, of our very sins he can! Many's the time when I have been set up in the forenoon on account of some very thing which, when I was calmer, had to be laid open and repented of before the Lord at night. Depend upon it, Jonah was no feeling over lowly when he thought he did well to be angry.[1] And then, when a little breeze of repentance does stir the heavy waves of the soul, the Devil whispers, 'How good, how humble, how godly you are!' Ah, 'his devices!' Thank God 'we are not ignorant' of them.[2] Look out for rocks, Madam. I am no true prophet if you find not a keen wind soon after this."

"Tell me, Patient, does my brother Edward fear God?"

"Yes, Madam."

"You know he does?"

"I have no anxiety about Sir Edward, Madam. I only wish I were half as sure of Mr. Philip."

"Do you think?"—

"Madam, the way is rough and the gate strait, and 'few there be that find it.'[3] And I don't think Mr. Philip likes rough walking. But the Lord kens that too. If he have been given to Christ of the Father, he'll have to come—'shall come to Me'[4]—and he'll find no more to greet over than the rest of the children when we all get Home to the Father's House. 'Neither shall any man pluck them out of My hand.'"[5]

Lady Ingram did not return from the Palace before eight o'clock in the evening, and then in an exceedingly bad temper. Fashionably so, only; she was much too accomplished and polished to go into a vulgar passion. Thérèse discovered the state of her mistress's mind when she found that she could do nothing to please her. The new dress, of which Lady Ingram had expressed her full approbation in the morning, was declared "*effroyante*" at night; and Thérèse had to alter the style of her lady's hair five times before she condescended to acknowledge herself satisfied. At length she appeared in her boudoir, and after breakfast, instead of paying her usual visit to Celia's room, sent a message desiring Celia to come to her.

"Are you not well, Madam?" was Celia's natural query, when she saw how pale and heavy-eyed Lady Ingram looked.

"Well! yes, my dear; but I have scarcely slept. I left fifteen hundred pounds behind me at that horrible lansquenet."

Celia's eyes opened rather wide. The sum indicated was almost incredible to her simple apprehension.

"My dear," said Lady Ingram, pettishly, "you are still only half-formed. Do not open your eyes in that way—it makes you look astonished. A woman of the world never wonders."

"I am not a woman of the world, Madam."

"Then my lessons have been of very little use to you. I am afraid you are not, really, and never will be. That reminds me of what I wished to say to you. I am informed by some one who saw you, that after you and Philip left me in the saloon of the Duchess, he took you into the great drawing-room, and that at something you saw there you burst into tears. Now really, my dear, this is totally inadmissible. You scandalized those who saw you. Had you heard some dreadful news, or some such thing, it might have been proper and even laudable to shed a few tears; but actually to sob, in the sight of all the world, just as any laundress or orange-girl might have done,—really, Celia, you must get over this weakness!"

"I beg your pardon, Madam," replied Celia, timidly, "but really I could not help it. There was a lady at the card-table who had lost a great deal—at least

Philip thought so—and she began speaking such horrible words that it terrified me; I could not help it."

"'Could not help it!'" repeated Lady Ingram, contemptuously. "Cannot you help anything you choose? Oh, yes! it was the Countess des Ferrières,—she had lost £30,000 and her estates, every livre she had, even to the earrings which she wore, so of course she was ruined. But you quite mistake, my dear—you need not have felt terrified. You are in error if you suppose that swearing is interdicted to men, and even women, of quality.[6] Quite the contrary, it is rather modish than otherwise. A few gentle oaths, such as"— (and Lady Ingram gave a short list)—"are quite admissible in such circumstances. You would hear them from the lips of the best families in France. If it were not modish, of course it would be highly improper; but you are entirely mistaken if you suppose it so. Any of those I have mentioned would be quite proper—for you, even. I have heard much stronger words than those from the Duchess de Berry, and she is younger than you are. But mercy on us, child! what eyes you make!"

They were gleaming like stars. Lady Ingram a words had lighted up a fire behind them, and every feeling of timidity was burnt up in the blaze of its indignation.

"My Lady Ingram!" said Celia, with a dignity in her voice and manner which her step-mother had never seen her assume, and believed to be quite foreign to her nature, "I did not come to Paris either to deny my religion or to outrage my God. In all matters which concern Him not, you have moulded me at your will. I thought that you took to me the place of my dead father and mother, and I have obeyed you as I would have obeyed them. But into the sanctuary of my soul you cannot penetrate; on the threshold of the temple even you must pause. God is more to me than father or mother, and at the risk of your displeasure—at the risk of my life if needs be—I must obey Him. 'The Lord sitteth upon the flood, yea, the Lord sitteth King forever;'[7] and 'He will not hold him guiltless that taketh His Name in vain!'"[8]

Notwithstanding all Lady Ingram's condemnation of feelings, she was just now overpowered by her own. In the foreground was amazement. Had her little pug Venus opened its mouth and emitted a moral axiom, she could hardly have been more astonished. Behind her surprise came annoyance, amusement, and respect for the strange, new bravery of Celia; but in the background, beyond all those, was a very unpleasant and unusual sensation, which she did not attempt to analyze. It was, really, the discovery of a character which she could not fathom, of a strength which she could not weaken, of a temple into which she could not enter. She had always prided herself upon her ability to read every person's character at a glance: and here was the especial character which she had set down as simple, and almost beneath notice, presenting itself in an aspect which it was beyond her skill to comprehend. She had not, indeed, forgotten Celia's confession at the outset of their acquaintance; but she had set it down to her English education, as a past phase of thought which she had succeeded in dispelling. A little more banter on the one hand, and firmness on the other, would, she thought, rid Celia of her absurd and obsolete notions. She had threaded all the mazes, and she meant her speech just uttered to be the last turn in the path, the last struggle between herself and her step-daughter. And lo! here, at that last turn, stood a guarded sanctuary, too strong for her weapons to attack, into which she knew not the way, of whose services she had never learned the language. A strange and sudden darkness fell over her spirit. There was a Power here in opposition to her stronger than her own. This simple, docile, untaught girl knew some strange thing which she did not know. And with this conviction came another and a disagreeable idea. Might it not be something which it immediately concerned her to know? What if Celia were right—if all things were not bounded by this life; if there were another, unknown world beyond this world, guided by different laws? What if God were real, and Heaven were real, and Hell were real? if there were a point beyond which prayers were mockery, and penances were vain? A veil was lifted up for a moment which had covered all this from her; a dark, thick, heavy veil, which all her life she had been at work to weave. A voice from Heaven whispered to her, and it said, "Thou fool!" When moments such as these do not soften and convict, they harden and deaden. The veil dropped, and Lady Ingram was herself again—her heart more rock than ever. It was in a particularly cold, hard voice that she spoke again.

"Celia, if you do not take care, I shall wash my hands of you. I will not be braved in this manner by a mere girl—a girl whose character is wholly unformed, and whose breeding is infinitely below her quality. Go to your chamber, and remain there until you are sufficiently humbled to request my pardon for treating me with so little respect."

"Madam," was the soft answer, "if I have shown you any disrespect, I will ask your pardon now. It was not my wish to do so."

Ah! the thing which Celia had shown Claude Ingram, and at which she could not bear to look, was her own heart.

"Will you then retract what you have said?"

"If I have said anything personally offensive to your Ladyship, I will retract it and ask your forgiveness. What I have said of my own relation to God I never can retract, Madam, for it is real and eternal."

Lady Ingram was silent for a moment. Then she said, in her hardest voice and coldest manner, "Go to your chamber." Celia, courtesying to her step-mother, retired without another word. Left alone in her own boudoir, again that cloud of dread darkness rolled over Claude Ingram. The presence of the accusing angel was withdrawn, but the accusations rankled yet. She sat for some time in silence, and at length rose with a sudden shiver and a heavy sigh. Opening with a little silver key a private closet, richly ornamented, a shrine was disclosed, where a silver lamp burned before an image of the Virgin. Here Lady Ingram knelt, and made an "Act of Contrition" and an "Act of Faith."[9] The repetition of vain words put no more contrition nor faith into her heart than before she uttered them. Only the soul was lulled to sleep: and she rose satisfied with herself and her interview.

"Do you think I did wrong, Patient?" asked Celia, sadly, of her sole *confidante*, at the moment when, at the other end of the house, Lady Ingram was finishing her devotions.

Patient replied in a measured and constrained voice, "'He that loveth father or mother more than Me is not worthy of Me.'"[10]

"Yes, I know; but I am so very anxious not to be wanting in respect to her—not to put any obstacles in her way."

"The more obstacles in her way the better, Madam; for it is the broad road that leadeth to destruction, and many there be which go in thereat."[11]

Celia sighed heavily, but made no answer.

"Ah, poor blind soul!" continued Patient. "If only we would look more at all men and women in one light, and measure them by one test—friends of Christ, or enemies of Christ—I think we would behave different from that we do."

Patient stitched away without saying more, and Celia sat looking thoughtfully out of the open window. From some cause unknown to herself, there suddenly rose before her a vision of the great laurel at Ashcliffe, and the stranger blessing her in the name of the Virgin. She exclaimed, "Patient!" in a tone which would have startled any one less unimpressionable than the placid woman who sat opposite her.

"Madam!" replied Patient, without any change of manner.

Celia told her the circumstance of which she was thinking, and added, "Can you guess who it was, Patient?"

"What manner of man was he, Madam?"

Celia closed her eyes and tried to recall him.

"A tall, thin, comely man, with a brown skin, and no color on cheeks or lips: dark hair somewhat unkempt, bright dark eyes, and a very soft, persuasive tone of voice. His clothes had been good, but were then ragged, and he looked as if he had been ill, or might become so. I always wondered if it could be my father; but as he died when I was but a child, that is not possible."

"And what was the day, Madam?"

"Some day in November, 1710."

"I think I can guess who it was, Madam Celia. No, it could not have been your father; and I know but one who answers to that description, yet I knew not that he had been in England so late as that. It was my husband, Gilbert Irvine."

"Patient!" exclaimed Celia, interested at once. "Had he been ill?"

"Nay, Madam, 'twas the other way: he fell ill afterward. He died about twelve months thereafter."

"Poor Patient!"

"Do not pity me, Madam. I had nought but what I deserved."

"I am afraid I should not like to have all I deserve, Patient. But what do you mean?"

"Madam, do you mind the Israelites under Joshua, which accepted the Gibeonites because of their spoiled victuals and clouted shoon, and asked not counsel at the mouth of the Lord? That was what I did. I was a plain, portionless maid, having nought but my labor, and he was my Lady's gentleman-usher, in a better place than I, and a rare hand at talking any one over to what he had a mind to—ay, he was that! And so I took him because of his comely face and his flattering tongue, and such like, and asked not counsel at the mouth of the Lord. And 'tis mine experience, Madam, that while the Lord never faileth to bring good out of evil for His people in the end, yet that oft for a time, when they be obstinately bent on taking their own way, He leaveth them to eat of the fruit of it. I say not how 'tis with other believers; but this I know, that my worst troubles have ever been them I have pulled on mine own head. There is a sort of comfort in a trouble by Divine ordinance, which it lacks when 'tis only by Divine permission, and you know you are yourself to blame for it. And little comfort I had with Gilbert Irvine. I've envied Isabel Paterson in the cave with her guidman—ay, many and many a time! And I have asked the Lord to do more than a miracle for me—for to turn Gilbert's heart would have been on the thither side of a miracle, I'm thinking,—more wonderful yet. You mind, Madam," added Patient, suddenly, as if afraid of being misunderstood on this point,

"Gilbert was no a Papist when I and he were wed. I should have seen my way through *that*, I think, for all the blind fool that I was; but it was no for five years thence. He professed the Evangel then, and went to the preaching like any Christian. The Lord forgive him—if it be no Papistry to say it: anyhow, the Lord forgive *me*!"

"There are no miracles, now, certainly," said Celia, reflectively. "I can quite fancy what a comfort it must have been to live in the days of miracles. But who was Isabel Paterson, and what cave did she live in?"

"Are there no miracles now, Madam?" asked Patient. "Ah, but I'll be long ere I say that! If the Lord wrought no miracle for John Paterson—ay, and twice over too—I little ken what a miracle is. But truly he was a godly man above many. 'Tis mostly Elijahs that be fed by angels and ravens, though I'm no saying that, if it pleased the Lord, He might not work wonders for you and me. 'Tis ill work setting limits to the Lord."

"But who was Isabel Paterson, and who was John Paterson?" urged Celia again.

"I'll tell you, Madam. John Paterson—he was Isabel's guidman—was a small farming-man at Pennyvenie, but at one time he dwelt for a season no so far from Lauchie. 'Twas when I was a young maid that these things happened. I knew Isabel Paterson, and many a crack I've had with her when I was a lassie, and she a thriving young wife with wee weans about her. Well, John, her guidman, was a marked man to King Charles's troopers, and many a time they set out to hunt him down. He could no dwell in his own house, but was forced to seek sleeping-room on the Crag of Benbeoch, between two great rocks, only visiting his own home by stealth. The first of these times the dragoons came on him as he was coming down from Benbeoch to the little white farmhouse below, and Isabel was watching his coming from the window. As he was crossing the moor they saw him, and he saw them. John, he turned and ran, and they galloped after. He heard them coming over the moor, and leaping the stone wall that girdled Benbeoch Crags, and he thought, 'Ah! sure 'tis all over with me now!' For only that week had Claverhouse hanged Davie Keith at his own door, and he was sib to Paterson. John he ran, and the troops they galloped: he crying mightily unto the Lord to save him for His Name's sake. And while the words were yet in his mouth, and the dragoons were so near him that he could hear their speech to one another, all at once his feet caught at a stone, and down he fell. He gave himself up for lost then, for the horses were right on him. 'But where am I going?' thinks he. Through the heather he fell, through the grass, through the very solid earth aneath him. Madam, the Lord made a new thing, and the earth opened her mouth and swallowed him up, rather than he should fall into the hands of his enemies. When he came to himself—for he was a bit bruised and stunned by the fall—he felt that he was in some wide dry cavern, many a foot across, and he heard overhead the troopers cursing and swearing that they could not find the hole where, quoth they, the fox had run to earth. And John down aneath was kneeling and giving thanks to the Lord, enjoying, as he told afterwards, the blessedest hour of communion with Him that ever he had. After a while the troopers gave it up as a bad job, and off they went. And when John dared to climb up out of the hole, and pop up his head through the long grass and heather, there was nought but the green grass and the purple heather, and God's blue sky over all. After a time he ventured forth, and hearing a wail of a woman's voice, found Isabel mourning on the hill-side, seeking his dead body, never doubting that the troopers had slain him. He helped her into the cave, and there they knelt down together and praised the Lord again. And by degrees, after a while, they carried bedding and household goods such as could be spared to this safe shelter which the Lord had provided for them, and not only John, but others of the brethren, hid there for many a day after, when Claverhouse was known to be in the country."

"Patient, is that really true?"

"True as Gospel, Madam. I had it from Isabel her ain sel'."

"But the cave must have been there before, surely."

"Maybe, Madam, or maybe not," said Patient, a little obstinately. "We ken little of what goes on in the heart of the earth. Anyhow, it had never been found before, though there were shepherds who knew every inch of Benbeoch Crags: and there it was ready when John Paterson fell in need of it."

"And what was his second escape, Patient?"

"That, Madam, was well-nigh as strange, for the Lord made choice of a poor silly beast as his deliverer. 'Twas indeed the earlier deliverance of the two. It began just like to the other:—John was running over the moor afore Claverhouse's troops, a meeting in the Black Glen having been broke up on the rumor of their coming. But this time the men had dogs with them. John, he ran as long as he could over Longstone Moss, calling on the Lord for deliverance as he ran. All the way across the bog he kept pace with them, for the horses being heavier, and the troopers armed, they had ill work to get on through the bog. But he, knowing that the Moss once passed, they would be far swifter than he on the hard ground, looked around earnestly for some safe hiding-place. Coming upon a deep furrow of moss and long grass running across the bog, he lay down in it, scarce hoping that it could be enough to hide him, but for just what men call a chance. Hitherto he had seen only the troopers, and had not noticed the dogs; but all at once, as he lay in this long grass, he heard their deep bay come across the moor. 'That sound,' quoth he, 'struck upon my heart like a death-knell. That sense of smell which God had given them was sure and unerring; and these men were now using it to hunt God's children to the death.' Straight and sure came the hounds rushing upon him. He cried once more unto the Lord, and then was about to rise lest the dogs should tear him. When, all at once, he heard among the long grass at his head a whirring sound, and a fox dashed close past him. Ay, but that was a scurry! Horses, dogs, and men, away they set after the fox, and they never came back that day.[12] So again the Lord delivered him."

"But you don't think, Patient, that He made the fox on purpose?"

"Madam," said Patient, a little dryly, "I am not in the Lord's counsels. I should fancy that He guided a common fox to do the thing; but I cannot presume to say that the bit beastie was not created there and then. We are too apt to limit the Lord, Madam."

"But God has given over creating, Patient."

"Has He so, Madam?" asked Patient, dubiously. "Is it no new creation when the buds spring forth, when the grass groweth up, and 'He reneweth the face of the earth'?[13] 'God did rest the seventh day from all His works;'[14] but the Scripture doth not tell us what He did on the eighth. Moreover, saith our Lord that 'the Father worketh.'[15] This I know—that if the purpose of the Lord were to preserve John Paterson by means of a fox, that fox should sooner have been brought from the Indies as on dry land than that His purpose should fail. 'He will work, and who shall let it?'"[16]

"I say!" observed Mr. Philip Ingram at the door, "what have you been doing, or saying, or something, to my mother? I have not seen her in such a state I don't know when."

"I am afraid I have displeased her," said Celia, "but I could not help it. If I had it to do over again, I must say just the same thing in substance."

"Have you been running a tilt with her, my pugnacious warrior?" asked Philip, glancing at his reflection in the mirror.

"Something like it, I am afraid."

"Ah! I thought as much when I was desired, just now, to talk upon some subject more agreeable than you. I said I did not know any, and departed; doubly willing to do so as I found that she had the megrims."

"I thought she looked poorly," said Celia, compassionately.

Philip indulged in a peal of laughter.

"My sweet rustic innocence! I thought I told you that megrims stood for Père Letellier. He is closeted with her Ladyship, assisting her to mourn over your lamentable departure from the faith and the mode. I should not very much wonder if you were treated to a visit from his reverence."

"Oh dear!" said Celia, involuntarily.

"He isn't such a formidable being," said Philip. "He used to confess me when I was about the height of that table, and order me a certain quantity of sugar-plums for penance—I know it was two for squalling, and four for stamping and kicking. I lost my temper with tolerable frequency under that discipline."

Patient sighed and shook her head slowly.

"Now how much wisdom lies in a shake of some people's heads! Patient, my dear creature, you could not have conveyed your meaning half so well in words."

"I am doubtful if you know my meaning, Mr. Philip."

"Know your meaning! Why, it was written on your head in that shake! Did it not say, 'Philip Ingram! your education was awfully bad, and you are what might be expected from it'?"

"Nay, Sir, scarce that. I was thinking rather of that word, 'I am against the shepherds,'[17] and yet more of that other word of John, 'Therefore shall her plagues come in one day, ... for strong is the Lord God who judgeth her.'"[18]

"Spare me, please!" exclaimed Philip, springing up. "You never quote from the Revelation without a sermon after it. Urgent business requires my presence down-stairs. Mrs. Celia Ingram, your servant!"

And he shut the door, laughing; but the next minute he opened it again to say, "If Père Letellier should take it into his head to come here, send for me to keep you in countenance. You will find the bear in its den—Patient knows where."

"But, Philip, what do you expect people to do?"

It was not the advent of Père Letellier, but his own want of occupation, which, to use Philip's elegant simile, had drawn the bear out of its den. Père Letellier was gone some hours before, and Lady Ingram had shut herself up, desiring Thérèse to tell any one who asked for her that she had the vapors, and could see nobody; and Philip, thus thrown back on his own society or his sister's, had selected the latter as the pleasanter of the two.

"But what do you expect people to do?" was Celia's natural reply to Philip's remark that good people never did anything.

"Well, my dear, I can only say that if I were one of you good folks, I could not live as you do. If I believed—really, honestly believed—that all the people, or not all, say one-half, say one-tenth of the people around me, in this city alone, were going to perdition as fast as they could travel, and that I knew of something which would save them, if I could only persuade them to take it,—why, my dear Celia, I could never sit quietly on this sofa! I should want to go out instantly 'into the highways and hedges, and compel them to come in.'[19] It would be as cruel as helping oneself to an extra slice of plumcake in the presence of a starving wretch who had lived for a week on a handful of potato-parings."

"Philip, I am sure you have been reading the Bible. You have quoted it several times lately."

"I told you I had read it," answered Philip, shortly.

"Mr. Philip," said Patient, very gravely, "you have given me somewhat to meditate upon. Your words are very exercising. We do scarce follow sufficiently that word, 'Consider your ways.'[20] You are quite right, Sir, more shame for us!"

"Very well, then, you agree with me," said Philip. "Well, and here are all the good, charitably-disposed Catholics shutting themselves up in convents and telling their beads; and all the good, charitably-disposed Protestants sitting on sofas, reading their good books, and mourning to each other over the wickedness of the world. Now, is that really the best thing that either party can find to do?"

"Mr. Philip, I hope you don't mean to go to compare the poor blind souls of Papists, worshipping idols in those wicked monasteries, with enlightened Christian believers either in Scotland or England?" objected Patient, with a shade of rising indignation in her tone.

"I do not mean to say that the 'believers,' as you call them, may not be doing more good to their own souls than the monks and nuns: but if they sit still on their sofas, what more good are they doing the world than the monks are? Is it not the same thing under another name? Are they helping to lessen by one grain the heap of wickedness they mourn over?"

"I am afraid you are right, Philip," said Celia, thoughtfully.

"That is just the failing of you good folks," resumed he. "You hear of a poor family, shockingly destitute, and steeped in all manner of sin and wickedness; and you say to each other, 'Isn't it dreadful?' You talk them over—perhaps you pray them over; but at the best, you do anything but put on your hat and go and try to lift them out of the mire. Oh dear no! They are far too dirty and disagreeable for your delicate fingers. I am without, as you know; and on the principle that 'lookers-on see most of the game,' those things show more plainly to us than to you. Look at the men in our prisons. They are beyond you now. But was there no time when they were not beyond you? Did they pass, do you think, in five minutes from little children saying the Paternoster at their mother's knee, to the hardened criminals to whom you would not dare to speak? You should talk to Colville. He would put everything before you far better than I can."

A few days after this conversation, Celia made the acquaintance of her brother's solitary friend. Lady Ingram's reception took place on the Thursday subsequent; and that lady, who had not yet resumed her usual graciousness to Celia, nevertheless intimated her pleasure that her step-daughter should be present. As Celia sat quietly in her corner, moralizing to herself on the scene, Philip's voice beside her said—

"Celia, my dear, allow me to introduce you. Mr. Colville, Mrs. Ingram. Mrs. Ingram, Mr. Colville."

Celia lifted her eyes with much curiosity. Her first impression was that Philip's friend was a very thin long man, with very light hair and eyes of the palest blue, a stoop in the shoulders, and a noticeable nose. He and Philip remained standing by her chair.

"An interesting scene this," observed Mr. Colville, in a deep, hollow voice. "Pleasant to see men and women enjoying themselves. Life is short, and death certain. Let us be happy while we can."

"After death the judgment.'"[21] The words came suddenly from Celia's lips, and almost without her volition.

Mr. Colville smiled condescendingly.

"You are one of the old-fashioned thinkers," he said. "I shall be happy to show you how mistaken such a notion is. I always take a pleasure in disabusing young minds."

"Very generous of you," said Philip—Celia was not sure whether seriously or ironically.

"'Mistaken!'" she exclaimed, lifting her clear eyes to her opponent's, and thinking that her ears must have made some strange mistake. "'Tis a passage of Scripture."

"A fable, Madam," returned Mr. Colville, coolly. "Quite inconsistent with the character of God, who is a perfect Being; and most injurious to the minds of men. The soul, I assure you, is a mere quality of the body; it has no substance, yet is entirely material, and perishes with the body of which it is a quality."

"Sir, how can God's revelation be a fable?" was Celia's very grave reply. "And, without that revelation, what can we know of the character of God?"

"My dear Madam," replied Mr. Colville, with his pitying, patronizing smile, "these are quite obsolete, disproved notions. There can be no such thing as revelation; 'tis impossible. And there are no means of any kind by which man can understand the character of God. We know from nature that God is infinitely powerful, and infinitely wise. Of His moral character we can have no idea, except that He is a perfect Being. Whatever, therefore, is inconsistent with perfection, is inconsistent with God."

"Inconsistent with your notions of perfection, you mean," said Philip. "Doesn't it require a perfect creature to imagine perfection?"

"Then," pursued Mr. Colville, taking no notice of Philip, "you suppose that all Scripture is of Divine original. This is another mistake. The Gospel is of Divine original, and perhaps some portions of the Old Testament; but the Pentateuch was compiled by a most ignorant and unphilosophical man, a repellent, sanguinary law-giver—and the Epistles are the product of heated brains. Paul was a cabalistic Rabbi, a delirious enthusiast; Peter, a poor ignorant fisherman.[22] What could you expect from such persons? Entirely human, Madam, these parts of Scripture!"

"And you, Mr. Colville," said Celia, warmly, "dare to sit thus in judgment upon God! You presume to lay your human hand on different portions of His Book, and to say, 'This is from God, and this is from man!' Sir, at His bar you must one day stand, and by that Book you will have to be judged."

"Believe me, I quite honor your warmth and kindly feelings. Youth is enthusiastical—given to hero-worship. 'Tis a pity to set up for your hero a mere dead book. But perhaps you misunderstand me. I do not reject all Scripture. For the words and character of Jesus I have great respect. He was unquestionably a true philanthropist, and an enlightened man—a very excellent man. But"—

Celia had risen and stood before him. She forgot all about the lighted rooms and the crowds who might be watching and listening. "And no more?" she said, in a voice of suppressed intensity.

"More?" answered Mr. Colville. "What could you wish me to say more?"

"Mr. Colville, your words, complimentary as they might be if you were speaking of a man, are but an insult—an insult to Him in whom is life,[23] and who is the brightness of the Father's glory.[24] I cannot bear them!"

She would have passed on, but Colville detained her.

"My dear Madam, you entirely mistake. Suffer me but to show you"—

"Sir, I shall speak with you no more. 'He that biddeth you God-speed is the partaker of your evil deeds.'"[25]

And Celia made her way through the rooms and gained her own boudoir without another word to any one. But she had not been there for five minutes before Philip followed her.

"Upon my word, Celia!" said he, laughing, "I had no idea what an amount of undeveloped soldiery there was under that quiet manner of yours. You have fairly rendered Colville speechless—a state of things I never saw before. I beg to congratulate the successful general on the victory!"

"Philip, how can you like that odious man?"

"Well, my dear," responded Philip, "I am beginning rather to wonder at it myself. He has become insipid latterly. I used to think him a very ingenious fellow; I am beginning to suspect that he is only a showy donkey!"

"He is an Atheist," said Celia, in a tone of horror.

"Scarce that, my dear," answered Philip, quietly. "He does believe in a sort of God, but 'tis one of his own making."

"Will that deliver him in the day of the Lord's wrath?"[26] asked Celia in a low tone. "Philip, I hope I said nothing wrong. I did not mean to speak uncourteously or unchristianly. I hope I did not do it."

"My dear little scrap of scrupulousness! Do you suppose that a soldier in the heat of battle says 'Pray excuse me!' to the opposite man before he fires at him?"

"Ah! but the weapons of my warfare ought not to have been carnal.[27] St. Paul says, 'Speaking the truth in love.'[28] I am afraid there was not much love in what I said to-night."

"No, dear Celia, the truth was so hot that it burnt it up," said Philip, laughing. "Don't make yourself miserable. Colville will hardly break his heart over it. Indeed, I am not certain that he keeps one. Are you not coming down again? Well, then, good-night."

On questioning her counsellor Patient in a similar manner, Celia found her unable to see any error in her act. Perhaps the old fiery Covenanter spirit was too strong in her to temper the words which she spoke. That which to Celia was merely carrying out the apostolic injunction, "Be courteous,"[29] was in Patient's eyes "conferring with flesh and blood."[30]

"Nay, Madam," said she, "if Paul himself could say, 'If any man preach any other Gospel unto you than that ye have received, let him be accursed,'[31] are we to mince our words and dress the truth to make it dainty to the world and the Devil? Is it not written, 'If any man love not the Lord Jesus Christ, let him be Anathema Maran-atha'?"[32]

"You retired early last night," said Lady Ingram to Celia, as she sipped her chocolate on the following afternoon. "You were tired, I suppose?"

"No, Madam," said Celia, honestly; "I was angry."

Lady Ingram gave her usual sign of surprise or perplexity—a very slight elevation of her chiselled eyebrows.

"With whom, my dear?"

"With Mr. Colville, Madam."

"A very good family, child," said Lady Ingram, gravely. "A younger branch, it is true, but still an old family—allied to the Colvilles of Bassingbourne. They can trace their descent to the eleventh century."

"Madam, Mr. Colville and I were not disputing the length of our descent."

"When you do, my dear, remember that you are of a still older family than he. Hubert de Ingeramme went over to England with William the Conqueror, and before that his line had been seated at Gournay and Ingeramme from the days of Rollo. You must be careful to remember, child, that if there be no high titles in your house, you are very ancient indeed; and that, after all, is the real thing. There are many families in France who are merely Counts or Barons in respect of title, but whose lines are as old as the Crown itself. '*Familles en velours rouge cramoisi,*'[33] that is what some call them. And yours, my dear, is a crimson velvet family. Pray don't allow any one to dispute that."

"I am not in the least likely, Madam," was Celia's amused reply.

"That is right, my child!" resumed Lady Ingram, condescendingly. "I am rejoiced to see that you appreciate the importance of the subject. By the way, has Philip told you that he has received a commission from His Majesty?"

"Yes, Madam," said Philip's sister, sighing.

"My dear," answered his mother, "there is nothing to sigh about. 'Tis high honor to receive a commission from King James. The troops, I learn, march for Landrécies on the 19th—next Monday; and are to oppose Prince Eugene there about the 10th of next month. I propose, therefore, to travel to Landrécies, where I shall take apartments—small and inconvenient, I fear they will be: but I suppose you can put up with that? And then Philip can come and see us from time to time while the troops are there; and I shall be able to see that he powders his hair properly, and does not neglect the tying of his cravats. 'Twould never do that an Ingram should be unmodish, even in battle. Only think, if he were to go into action in a Steenkirk![34] I should never forgive myself. And he is far too careless in that respect."

"I can put up with anything that you can, Madam," said Celia, answering only one clause of her step-mother's speech.

"Very good, my dear. Then order Patient to be ready."

"Is Patient to go, Madam?"

"My dear!" said Lady Ingram, "do you think I mean to travel like a *bourgeoise*? Of course Patient will go. And be careful that you do not take too few gowns with you. I have to spur you, my *réligieuse*, or I really think you would scarce know the difference between silk and camlet. What a pity you were not born a Catholic! I will give the orders to Patient myself, that will be best. She is little better than you in such matters. I suppose, in her case, it arises from her being a Scotch-woman, and of no family. But how it ever came to be the case with you, an Ingram of Ingram, I really cannot understand. Those things generally run in the blood. It must be the people who brought you up. They did not look as if they knew anything."

"You think so much about family, Madam," said Celia, stung in the affections by this contemptuous notice of her dearest friends; "pardon me for telling you that the Passmores have dwelt at Ashcliffe for eight hundred years."

"My dear, you astonish me!" said Lady Ingram, with a faint glimmer of interest. "Then they really are respectable people! I assure you I am quite rejoiced to hear it. I did think there was something a little superior in the manner of the eldest daughter—something of repose; but you English are odd—so different from other people. Eight hundred years, did you say? That is quite interesting."

And Lady Ingram dropped another lump of sugar languidly into her cup of chocolate. Repose! thought Celia. Truly in Isabella's manners there was repose enough; but it had never occurred to the simple Passmores to regard it as enviable. On the contrary, they called it idleness in plain Saxon, and urged her by all means to get rid of it.

"Quite interesting!" repeated Lady Ingram, stirring up the sugar in a slow, deliberate style which Isabella would have admired. "Really, I did not know that the Passmores were a respectable family. I thought they were quite nobodies."

[1] Jonah iv. 9.

[2] Cor. ii. 11.

[3] Matt. vii. 14.

[4] John vi. 37.

[5] John x. 28.

[6] Sarah Duchess of Marlborough once called on a lawyer who happened to be from home. "I don't know who she was, Sir," said his clerk in informing him of the visit, "but she swore so dreadfully that she must be a woman of quality!"

[7] Ps. xxix. 10.

[8] Exod. xx. 7.

[9] Act of Contrition—"I most humbly entreat Thy pardon, O my God, for all the sins which I have committed against Thine adorable Majesty: I grieve for them bitterly, since Thou art infinitely good, and sin offendeth Thee. I detest these sins with all my heart, with the resolution to forsake them by the help of Thy grace."

Act of Faith—"My God, I firmly believe all the truths which the Church proposes to us, because it is Thou who hast revealed them."

[10] Matt. x. 37.

[11] Matt. vii. 13.

[12] These are true anecdotes.

[13] Ps. civ. 30.

[14] Gen. ii. 2.

[15] john v. 17.

[16] Isa. xliii. 13.

[17] Ezek. xxxiv. 10.

[18] Rev. xviii. 8.

[19] Luke xiv. 23.

[20] Hag. i. 5.

[21] Heb. ix. 27.

[22] The majority of Mr. Colville's expressions are taken *verbatim* from Lord Bolingbroke. The Modern Rationalist

arguments are mere *réchauffés* of those which did duty a hundred and fifty years ago.

[23] John i. 4.

[24] Heb. i. 3.

[25] 2 John 11.

[26] Zeph i. 18.

[27] 2 Cor. x. 4.

[28] Eph. iv. 15.

[29] 1 Pet. iii. 8.

[30] Gal. i. 6.

[31] Gal. i. 9.

[32] 1 Cor. xvi. 22.

[33] Madame Duplessis-Guénégaud thus described the House of Adhémar, from one branch of which the Princes of Orange were descended, while another was the stock of the Counts de Grignan.

[34] The Steenkirk, a peculiar twist of the ends of the cravat rather than a tie, is said to have taken its rise from the Duke of Monmouth's going hastily into action at the battle of Steenkirk with his cravat twisted out of his way in this manner. It was quite out of fashion in 1712, except among country people.

XI.

HOW PHILIP CAME BACK.

"The hour we see not, when, upsurging full,
Our cup shall outflow. God is merciful."

"Disengaged, Madam? I have just half an hour to spend with you. Positively the last time before I don my regimentals. And then hurrah for Landrécies! O Ned, I wonder where you are! I wish you would come back!"

"Do you travel with us, Philip?"

"No, thank you, Madam. That would be rather too spicy."

"You go with your regiment?"

"I have that honor."

"Mr. Philip," said Patient, as she noiselessly entered, "I have done your packing, and"—

"What a darling of a Covenanter you are, to take that off my hands!"

"And I have put a little Bible, Sir, along with your linen. Will you please to promise me, Mr. Philip, to read it?"

"Dear Patient," answered Philip, letting his lightness slip from him like a cloak, "I will read it. I have read it so much lately that I should feel almost lost without it, I assure you."

"Have you done aught but read it, Mr. Philip?" asked Patient, earnestly.

"As how?" queried Philip.

"Sir, I can conceive of none so awfully far off God and good as he that handles the bread of life but never eateth of it, he that standeth just outside the gate of the fold and never entereth therein. Have you felt it, Mr. Philip? have you believed it? have you prayed over it?"

There was no lightness about Philip's tone or manner as he answered, "I think, Patient, I have."

But Patient was not satisfied yet.

"Mr. Philip, my bairn," said she, "I do think that what you do, you'll do thoroughly—not half and half. I think you will know whether you do mean to follow the Lord or not. But 'tis one thing to mean to go, and another to set out on your journey; 'tis one thing to think you can leave all without trying, and another to leave all. And I'm no so sure, my dear bairn, whether you ken your own self, and whether you can leave all and follow Him. 'Tis rougher walking in the narrow way than on the broad road. It takes sore riving to get through the gate with some. Can you hold on? Can you set the Lord always before you, above all the jeering and scoffing, all the coldness and neglect of the world? For until the Lord is more to you than any in this world, you'll scarce be leaving all and following Him. Don't be deceived—don't be deceived! and oh, laddie dear, dinna deceive your ainsel'!"

"My dear old friend!" said Philip, looking up lovingly into Patient's face. "I will tell you the honest truth about myself. Celia, do you remember what I said to you the first time that I saw you?"

Celia remembered that well. It had pained her too much to be lightly forgotten.

"Well, that has all passed away. I believe that there is a God, and that the Bible is His revelation to man. Colville's philosophy merely disgusts me now. (I must say for him, though, that he was talking unusual nonsense the other night; he generally has something better to say than that.) Well, then, I believe, if I know what believing means, in Jesus Christ. Perhaps I *don't* know what believing means; I shall not feel astonished if you tell me so. I believe that He died to save sinners, that is, instead of sinners; but instead of what sinners I don't quite know. For I cannot help seeing that while all mankind are sinners, there is one class of sinners, called saints, who are quite different from the rest. My puzzle at present is what makes the difference. We all believe that Christ died for sinners, yet it seems to be only some of us that get any good from it. If you can explain this to me, do so."

"I must go back to eternity to explain that," said Patient. "Sir, ages back, ere the world had a beginning, the Lord God, who alone was in the beginning, Father, Son, and Spirit, covenanted the redemption of man.[1] Certain persons, whose names were written in the Book of Life,[2] were given of the Father to the Son,[3] unto whom, and to none other, the benefits of His redemption were to be applied.[4] 'No man,' quoth our Lord, 'can come to Me except the Father which hath sent Me draw him;[5] and also, 'All that the Father giveth Me shall come to Me.'[6] Therefore"—

"Stop, stop!" cried Philip. "Let me take all that in before you go on to secondly. Do you mean to say, Patient, that God, the loving and merciful God, who says He wills not the death of any sinner,[7] selected a mere handful of men whom He chose to save, and deliberately left all the rest to perish? Was that love? Was that like God?"

"Sir, we can only know from the Word what is or is not like God. He ruleth over all,[8] and who shall say unto Him, 'What doest Thou?'[9] And when all were sunk in sin, and He might justly have left all to perish, shall we quarrel with Him because He in His sovereign grace and electing love decided to whom the merit of His work, the free gift of God, should be applied?"

"That is Covenanting doctrine, I suppose," said Philip, dryly.

Celia saw breakers a-head.

"Dear Patient," she said, very gently, "are you not trying to feed Philip with rather too strong meat? Remember what our Lord said to His disciples, 'I have many things to say unto you, but ye cannot bear them now.'"[10]

"Speak you, then, Madam Celia," said Patient. "I have but one speech."

"Oh! you good folks don't always agree!" observed Philip, as if he had made a discovery.

"We quite agree," answered Celia. "I believe just what Patient does, but I don't think it is suited for you. She is trying to make you spell words of three syllables before you can say your alphabet perfectly; and I think it will be better to help you over the alphabet first. Dear Philip, those whom Christ saves are those whom He makes willing to accept His salvation. Are you willing?"

"Go your own way, Madam," said Patient, in a dissatisfied tone; "go your own way. But don't account me in agreement with the teaching of Arminius."

"My dear Patient, I know nothing about Arminius—neither who he is nor what he teaches," replied Celia, simply. "Does not God make His elect willing to accept His salvation?"

"Surely, Madam, surely," answered Patient, a little mollified. "But you spake of *will*, Madam. Now I never can accept the free-will views of that heretic Arminius."

"Fire away, Patient!" cried Philip, from the sofa; "I will lay five pounds on you. Well, really! I am rejoiced to find that the saints can quarrel like sinners! It makes a fellow feel himself less of an isolation."

This was exactly the sentiment which Celia was most unwilling to foster in Philip's mind. She paused a moment, and sent up a prayer for wisdom before she spoke again.

"Dear Philip, the saints after all are only a few of the sinners. Patient and I are both human, therefore open to sin and error. Don't take what we say, either of us; take what God says. He cannot mistake, and we may. Patient, you will not disagree with me in this?"

"Not a whit, Madam. And I ask your pardon if I spake unadvisedly with my tongue."

- 196 -

"And if I did," responded Celia, softly. "Least of all should we do it on such a subject as this."

"You did not," answered Philip. "It was the old bird that was the fighting cock!"

"Well, dear Philip," said Celia, turning to her brother, "this is the great question for you and me: Are we willing to accept Christ's work, and to place no reliance upon our own works? He will be all or nothing. We cannot save ourselves either wholly or in part. Our salvation is either done, or to do; and if it be yet to do, it can never be accomplished."

"Then what place do you find for good works in your system?"

"No place, as the efforts of the slave to set himself free;[11] every place, as the endeavor of the child to show his love to the reconciled father."[12]

"Well," said Philip, reflectively, "I found long ago that your view was the soil which grew the finest crop of them. Don't look at me so, Patient. Let me talk as I think; it is natural to my mind to express itself as I do. I don't mean anything wrong."

"The Lord will have that out of you, Mr. Philip, if you be His."

"Well," replied Philip, gravely, "I suppose He knows how."

"Ay, He knows how," answered Patient, sadly. "But don't you give Him more work in that way than you can help, Sir. The surgeon's knife may be very necessary, but it never can be otherwise than painful."

Celia did not quite agree with Patient here; but it was a secondary point, and she said nothing. Philip looked at his watch, and, declaring that he could not stay another minute, kissed Celia and Patient, saying, "*A Landrécies!*" as he left the room.

"I see a long, weary walk for Mr. Philip, Madam," remarked Patient, when he was gone. "If he be to reach the good City at all, 'twill sure be by a path of much affliction."

Celia was rather disposed to think the same.

Lady Ingram's expectation that she would be able to procure only small rooms at Landrécies was verified. The apartments to be obtained were both small and few. Lady Ingram and Celia occupied the same bed-chamber. Until this happened, Celia had no idea what a very artificial flower her handsome, stately step-mother really was. She now found that the fourth part of her hair, and nearly three-fourths of her bloom, were imparted. Every morning Lady Ingram sat for two hours under the hands of Thérèse, who powdered her hair, rouged her cheeks, applied pearl-powder to her forehead, tweezers to her eyebrows, and paint to her neck, fixing in also sundry false curls.

"My Lady," asked Patient, in her quietest manner, the first evening at Landrécies, which was the 12th of July, "if the Prince Eugene take us prisoners, what will become of us, if you please?"

"Prisoners!" repeated Lady Ingram. "Absurd, Patient! You speak as if you thought a defeat possible. The armies of the *Grand Monarque* and those of King James together to be routed by one Savoyard! Preposterous!"

"They were put to flight at Malplaquet, Madam" (which place Patient pronounced to rhyme with jacket); "and 'tis not so many days since the Prince took Le Quesnoy."[13]

"Patient Irvine, you are no better than a fool!" said Lady Ingram, turning round to give effect to her sentence.

"Very like, Madam," was the mild reply of Patient, who was employed in giving the last fold to her young lady's dress. "Indeed, 'tis but the act of a fool to reason beforehand. The Lord will dispose matters."

"Celia! I shall find you another attendant, now that you can speak French, and send Patient back to her sewing. Does she speak in this canting way to you?"

"Pray don't!" was Celia's alarmed reply to the first part of Lady Ingram's remark. "No more than I do to her, Madam," she answered to the second.

"I see!" said Lady Ingram, sarcastically. "A nice choice of an attendant I made for you! It was unavoidable at first, since she was the only woman in my house, except Thérèse, who could speak English; but I ought to have changed her afterwards. I might have known how it would be. When we return to Paris, I will provide you with a French woman."

"You will do the Lord's will, Madam," observed Patient, calmly.

"I will do my own!" cried Lady Ingram, more angrily than was her wont.

"Madam," was Patient's answer, "the Lord's will *will* be done; and in one sense, whether you choose it or not, you will have to do it."

"Leave the room! You are a canting hypocrite!" commanded her mistress, in no dulcet tones.

"Yes, my Lady," answered Patient, meekly, and obeyed.

"Now, if that woman had had the least spirit, she would have answered me again. A little more rouge here, Thérèse."

And Lady Ingram settled herself peacefully to her powderings, leaving Celia in a state very far from peace. She felt, indeed, extremely rebellious.

"Cannot I have my own choice in this matter?" she thought to herself. "Am I never to have my own way? Must I be forever the slave of this woman, who is neither my own mother nor one of the Lord's people? Shall I calmly let her take from me my only friend and counsellor? No! I will go back to Ashcliffe first; and if I break with Lady Ingram altogether, what matters it?" But the next minute came other thoughts. Patient had told her words of her grandfather's which she remembered,—"A soldier hath no right to change his position." And how could she put such an occasion to fall in her brother's way? Perhaps the Lord was drying up all the wells in order to drive her closer to the one perennial fountain. Ah! poor caged bird, beating against the cage! She little knew either how near she was to freedom, nor by what means God would give it to her.

The 21st of July dawned. Lady Ingram had risen a little earlier than usual, for she expected to see Philip, and had been grumbling all the previous evening at his non-appearance. He came in, dressed in full regimentals, about eleven o'clock, when his mother had been down for about an hour, and Celia for several hours.

"Good-morning and good-bye in one," he said, speaking hastily, and to both at once. "I have but ten minutes to stay. Marshal Villars has found a weak place in Prince Eugene's intrenchments at Denain, and he is going to draw his attention by an attack this morning on the Landrécies side, while we come up the other way and storm Denain this afternoon. Villars himself will be with us. Bentinck defends Denain with seventeen battalions and fourteen squadrons, mostly Dutch.[14] By the way, Le Marais has heard that Ned is in camp, but I have not come across him. You are sure to see him before long, if he be here."

"Philip!" said his mother, suddenly, "the tie of your cravat is quite a quarter of an inch on one side!"

"A quarter of a fiddle-stick, my dear Mother!" said Philip, laughing. "What do you think it will look like when I have been an hour in action! I hope they will let me head a charge. I expect to be made a Prince of the Empire at the very least! Good-bye, Mother."

"Adieu, my son," responded Lady Ingram, a little less languidly than usual. "Don't go into danger, Philip."

"What admirable advice to an officer of His Majesty's army!" returned Philip, kissing her. "Good-bye, little Celia. I have something to tell you when I come back."

Celia looked up from Philip's kiss into his eyes to see what it was. They were deeper and softer than usual, but she read nothing there.

"Good-bye, dear Philip. God keep you!" she said.

"And you—both," replied Philip, in a softened tone. "Adieu!" And he was gone.

All that day Celia could do nothing. She wondered to see Lady Ingram sit quietly knotting, as if the day of the battle of Denain were no more to her than other days. But the day passed like other days; they dined and drank chocolate, and the dusk came on, and Lady Ingram ceased knotting. She had been out of the room a few minutes when Patient put her head in at the door.

"Madam," she said, in her quiet, unmoved voice, "Sir Edward is below, and a strange gentleman with him. Will you speak with him while I find my Lady?"

Celia rose and went down into the dining-room, very curious to make the acquaintance of her unknown brother. But it was not the unknown brother upon whom her eyes first fell. She saw merely that he was there—a tall, dark, grave-looking man; but beside him stood a fair-haired man, a little older than himself, and with a cry of "Harry! dear, dear Harry!" Celia flew to him. Harry's greeting was quite as warm as Celia's, but graver.

"Who has won?" was her first question. She wondered afterwards that it should have been so.

"The allies," answered Harry, quietly. "I am Sir Edward's prisoner."

"A prisoner whom I yield to my sister, to be disposed of at her pleasure," said Edward, coming forward; and Celia, turning from Harry, greeted and thanked the real brother cordially, though a little shyly.

"Have you seen Philip?" she asked of both. Her apprehensions were beginning to subside.

We rarely know the supreme moments of our lives till they are past. We open laughing the letter which contains awful tidings; we look up brightly to see the unclosing of the door—

"Which lets in on us such disabling news,
We ever after have been graver."[15]

It was with a lightened heart, and almost a smile, that Celia asked if her brothers (as she considered both) had seen Philip; and full of apprehension as her heart had been all day, she did not guess the answer from the dead silence that ensued.

Harry was the first to speak, and he addressed himself to Sir Edward. "You, or I?" was his enigmatical question.

"You," answered Edward, shortly.

"Celia, darling!" began Harry, looking back at her with deep compassion in his eyes; and he got no further. And then she knew.

"O Philip, Philip!" broke in a bitter wail from the lips of the sister who had learned to love Philip so much. "Are you sure? Have you seen him?" she asked, turning first to Harry and then to Edward, hoping against hope that there might be some mistake.

"I have seen him," replied Edward; and her hope died away.

"Celia," resumed Edward, "listen, dear sister. I have seen Philip; there can be no mistake on that score. He will be brought here soon. But I have seen also something else, for which, knowing him as I do, I thank God so much that as yet I have hardly begun to grieve at all. He lies just where he fell at the head of his troops, after one of the finest and bravest charges that I ever witnessed in my life: his face turned to God and the foe. But this lay close to his heart. Look at it."

Celia took from her brother's hand the little book which he held out to her. She saw at once that it was a Testament, but the leaves were glued together with a terrible red, at which Celia shuddered as she tried to open them.

"The first leaf," was Edward's direction.

She recognized Philip's well-known hand as she turned to it. At the head of the fly-leaf Lady Ingram's name and address were faintly pencilled; and below were a few lines in darker and fresher lead. Celia dashed the intrusive tears from her eyes before she could read them.

"'Wherefore He is able to save to the uttermost them that come unto God by Him, seeing He ever liveth to make intercession for them.'[16] 'Lord, I believe; help Thou mine unbelief.'"[17]

The little book trembled in Celia's hand, and she broke into a fresh shower of uncontrollable weeping. Her companions allowed her to indulge her sorrow for a few moments in silence. Then Edward said gently, "Who shall tell his mother?"

"I will," she answered, ceasing her tears by a violent effort; and she left the room, and went up-stairs at once. Lady Ingram was seated at her knotting.

"Where have you been?" she asked, without looking at her step-daughter, for just then the knotting was at a difficult point, and required all her attention.

Instead of answering, Celia knelt down by her, and uttered one word—a word she had never used to her before.

"Mother!"

Lady Ingram dropped her work, and looked into Celia's face.

"My dear," she said, her voice slightly trembling, "you have bad news to tell me. At once, if you please—I do not like things broken gradually."

At once Celia told her: "Philip is killed."

With a wild shriek which rang through the house, Philip's mother flung up her arms—as Celia remembered that, once before in her life, Claude De L'Orient had done—and then fell back heavily and silently in her chair. Celia, ignorant and terrified, threw open the door and called for Patient and Thérèse. They came in together, the former quiet and practical, the latter screaming and wringing her hands.

"Eh, my faith! Madam is dead!" shrieked Thérèse.

"'Tis but a dwawm, Madam," was the decision of Patient. "Please to open the window. Thérèsa, cut her Ladyship's lace[18] whilst I fetch her water."

"But, my dear friend," remonstrated Thérèse, with an invocation in addition, "that will spoil her figure!"

"Go down-stairs and fetch a glass of water," said Patient, with a spice of scorn. "That's all *you* are fit for. Madam, will you please to hold her Ladyship's head while I get at her lace and cut it?"

Patient's remedies applied, Lady Ingram partly recovered herself in a few minutes. Edward was by her side when she again opened her eyes. They rested for an instant on him and on Celia, and closed again with a long tremulous sigh which seemed to come from her heart.

"If you will please to give me orders, Madam," said Patient, quietly, to Celia, "I think her Ladyship will be best in her bed, and she scarce seems knowledgeable to give orders herself. Will I and Thérèsa lay her there?"

Celia spoke to Lady Ingram, but received no answer, and she gave Patient the order. So Patient and Thérèse undressed the still figure and laid her to rest. Lady Ingram continued to sleep or swoon, whichever it were; she seemed occasionally sensible to pain, but not to sound, nor did she appear to know who was about her.

About ten o'clock, Celia, seated at her step-mother's bed-side, heard a regular tramp of soldiers' feet below, and knew too well what they must be bringing. A few minutes afterwards her brother softly entered the room.

"Celia, they have brought Philip here. Will you come and see him?"

She hesitated a minute, half for Lady Ingram, and half for herself.

"There is nothing painful or shocking, dear; I would not ask you if there were. Would you like to see him again or not?"

Celia rose and gave Edward her hand. He led her silently down to the dining-room, leaving her to go in the first by herself and kneel beside the still, white clay which only five hours earlier had been Philip Ingram.

Ah! if she only could have known, what might she not have said to him! Had she said enough? Had she done her duty?—her utmost? Had she pressed Christ and His salvation on him as she ought to have done? Where was Philip now?

"Oh, that *had!* how sad a passage 'tis!"[19]

Oh, that *might have been!* how much sadder!

Edward and Harry came in and stood by her.

"Can either of you tell me anything more?" she faltered, her eyes riveted on the calm, fixed, white face which would never tell anything more to her.

"I can," answered Harry Passmore, softly. "I heard his last words."

"O Harry, tell me!" pleaded Celia.

"I was stationed just opposite," he said, "and it was my regiment that received the charge. A shot killed the horse of the officer in command, and he too fell. I knew not whether he had received injury himself, and I was so much struck by his youth and bravery that I pressed forward to aid him. But as soon as I saw his face, I found that the shot had struck more than the horse. At this moment my adjutant spoke to me, calling me 'Colonel Passmore.' When he heard that, he saith from where he lay, 'Are you Harry Passmore of Ashcliffe?' 'Yes,' I said, wondering that he could know me. 'You are Celia's brother, then,' quoth he, with the ghost of a smile, 'and so am I. Take this to her. The address is on the fly-leaf.' I was so amazed that I could but utter, 'Are you Philip Ingram?' 'I am,' he saith, his breathing now very quick and short. 'Tell my mother gently. Take care of Celia.' His voice now failed him, and I bent my head close that I might hear anything more. I heard only as if he whispered to himself, 'The uttermost!' Then came a long sobbing sigh, and then all was over."

"God forbid that we should limit that uttermost!" murmured Edward, softly.

"O Edward!" sobbed his sister, "do you think he is safe?"

"My sister," he replied, very gently, "can I tell you more than God does? 'To the uttermost'[20] and 'he that believeth.'[21] But if you had known Philip as I knew him, you would feel with me that something must have happened to him, which had made an immense difference between what he was and is. I cannot think that something anything short of the redeeming love of Christ. God knows, dear, what are the boundaries of His uttermost. I can scarce think they are closer than our uttermosts."

"Yet outside the fold is outside," said Celia, falteringly.

"I did not mean for one moment to deny that," said he; "I expressed myself ill if you thought so. But we are told—'According to your faith be it unto you,'[22] and of what may come from 'faith as a grain of mustard-seed.'[23] And it seems to me that the words on that leaf had never been penned by such a hand as Philip's, unless his faith were at least equal to a grain of mustard-seed. Remember, dear heart, that in His hand who will not break the bruised reed, nor quench the smoking flax,[24] are the keys of Death and of Hell.[25] I can trust Him to do right, even to the brother I loved so well."

Lady Ingram returned to consciousness on the following day, but Thérèse reported that she was very weak and low, and desired to see no one but herself. On the Sunday morning she suddenly sent for Celia and Edward. They found her lying propped up by pillows, her eyes sunk and heavy, and her face very pale. She recognized her step-children with a faint smile.

"Come and kiss me, Edward," she said, in a low soft voice: "I have scarce seen you yet. And Celia, too. You loved him, both of you. Now listen to me, and I will tell you what I shall do. As soon as my health and strength admit, I shall take the veil at the convent of Sainte Marie de Chaillot. I have no more to live for. You are both old enough to take care of yourselves. And, after all, life in this world is not everything. I shall make my retreat, and after some years of penance and prayer, I trust I shall have grace to make my conversion. You, Edward—do you propose to remain in the army?"

"I do not think I shall, Mother."

"You will keep up your estates?"

"I should prefer living in England."

"And Celia; what will you do, my dear?"

"I shall go back to Ashcliffe if nobody want me. If Edward wish me to live with him I will willingly do so, especially in England; but even then I should like to pay a long visit to Ashcliffe before settling anywhere else."

"I should be very happy to have you with me, dear," said Edward, quietly, to this; "but I do not wish to be any tie to you. There is no necessity for your living with me, for I am about to marry. So pray do which you prefer."

"Whom are you about to marry, Edward?" asked Lady Ingram, turning to him with a look of some interest in her languid eyes.

"None whom you know, Mother. One with whom I met on my travels."

"I am glad you are marrying," she said, "And how is Celia to return to Ashcliffe?"

"Oh! with Harry," replied Celia, quickly.

"He is not at liberty yet," observed Edward, gravely.

"But you will set him free to go with me?" entreated his sister.

"I have nothing to do with it. You will, I suppose. I make you a present of my prisoner."

"Oh, thank you! If Harry's liberty depends on me, he shall have it directly."

"Edward," said Lady Ingram, "I have a favor to ask from you."

"Name it, and take it, Mother."

"Will you see that a small pension is settled on Thérèse; and, should she wish to continue in her present position, interest yourself in obtaining for her another situation?"

"I will attend to her interests as honestly and thoroughly as I think you would yourself."

"I do not recommend Patient to you, since she is already rather your servant than mine, and you will be careful of her, I know. Celia has a great liking for her: I dare say she will wish to take her to England."

"Do you object to that, Madam?" asked Celia.

"Not in the least," replied Lady Ingram.

"Do you?" continued Celia, this time addressing Edward.

"For a time, certainly not. I should not like to part with her altogether; but, on the other hand, I should not allow you to travel to England without a woman in your company. Patient shall go with you, and after my marriage let her return to me, wherever I may resolve to dwell."

"Thank you. You will write to me, then?"

"I will come to you, if you are willing to receive me. We have seen very little of each other yet."

"Very little," said Celia, rather sadly.

"Now, my children, leave me," requested Lady Ingram, faintly. "I am too weak to converse much. Send Patient to me."

Ten days later saw them journeying in company by easy stages to Paris; and ten days after that witnessed a solemn ceremony in the convent chapel of Sainte Marie de Chaillot, at which Queen Maria Beatrice, Madame de Maintenon, and a brilliant crowd of distinguished persons were present, when Claude Ingram took upon herself the white veil of a postulant. Edward and Celia were there, the latter with a slight misgiving whether she were not sanctioning idolatry to some extent, even by her appearance: a suspicion not laid to rest by the manifest disapproval and uncompromising speeches of Patient. "'Can a man take fire in his bosom, and his clothes not be burned?'"[26] asked she. But Celia was determined to see the last of Lady Ingram; and Edward promised to lead her out before anything objectionable began. To her it was an inexpressibly mournful ceremony. The different stages of the rites—the shearing off of the glossy hair, the taking of the vows, the white veil of the postulant—all seemed to her as so many epitaphs on the grave of a living woman. When the brother and sister went down to the guest-chamber to take leave of the novice, Celia was sobbing hysterically.

Lady Ingram parted from both with a very warm embrace. She appeared much softened.

"Farewell, my child!" she said to Celia. "And you will not live always in England? You will come and see me at least once more? And when you pray to God in your *prêches*, do not quite forget Soeur Marie Angélique."

Celia turned from the convent-gate with a sadder heart than she ever thought she could have felt at her parting from Claude Ingram.

Only for three days longer did she remain in Paris. The house was very painful to her now. In everything Philip lived again for her; and she became very anxious to get home to Ashcliffe. Of the warmth and cordiality of her reception there it never occurred to her to doubt. So on the 14th of August, Celia, Harry, and Patient left Paris on their way to England, escorted by Edward as far as Havre.

[1] Isa. xlviii. 16; Eph. i. 4.

[2] Rev. xvii. 8; xxi. 27.

[3] John x. 29; xvii. 6.

[4] Matt. xv. 13.

[5] John vi. 44.

[6] Ibid. 37.

[7] Ezek. xxxiii. 2; 2 Pet. iii. 9.

[8] Ps. ciii. 19.

[9] Eccles. viii. 4.

[10] John xvi. 12.

[11] Rom. xi. 6; Gal. ii. 16.

[12] Col. i. 10.

[13] Le Quesnoy was taken on the 3d of July.

[14] Sismondi, "*Histoire des Français*," vol. xxvii., p. 162. Lacretelle, "*Histoire de France pendant le XVIII. Siècle*," vol i. p. 43. The exact day of the battle is disputed. I have followed Lacretelle.

[15] Mrs. Browning's "Aurora Leigh."

[16] Heb. vii. 25.

[17] Mark ix. 24.

[18] Staylace—

"Oh, cut my lace asunder,
That my pent heart may have some scope to beat,
Or else I swoon with this dead killing news."
—Shakspeare, "Richard III.," act iv., sc. 1.

[19] Shakspeare, "All's Well that Ends Well," Act i. sc. 1.

[20] Heb. vii. 25.

[21] John iii. 36.

[22] Matt. ix. 29.

[23] Matt. xvii. 20.

[24] Isaiah xlii. 3.
[25] Rev. i. 18.
[26] Prov. vi. 27.

XII.

TRAITORS—HUMAN AND CANINE.

"Thy way, not mine, O Lord,
   However dark it be!
Lead me by Thine own hand,
   Choose out the path for me."

—DR. BONAR.

The *News-Letter* had just come in, posted from London, and Squire Passmore sat down in the parlor to read it. It was a warm, but wet, autumn afternoon. The embroidery frame was covered with a wrapper, and Isabella and her mother were tying up preserves and labelling them. Two large trays of them stood on the parlor-table, and Cicely came slowly in with another.

"Well, sure, that's main heavy!" said she. "If you please, Sir, is there aught by the post from Master Harry?" she added, with a courtesy.

"Nothing, Cicely, nothing," said the Squire, looking up from his newspaper. "I don't know what has come to the lad. He did scribble one line to let us know that he was not killed, but not a word have we had from him since."

"Mayhap he's a-coming," suggested Cicely.

"I wish he were," sighed Madam Passmore.

A merry laugh outside announced somebody, and the door sprang open to the united attacks of Pero and Lucy.

"Anything from Harry?" was her question too, and she received the same answer.

And "Anything from Harry?" asked Charley, sauntering in with his hands in his pockets.

"These are done, Cicely," said Madam Passmore. "Take them hence, and fetch another tray; and bid Dolly, if any should come on such a wet day, to have a care that she brings them not hither, but into the drawing-room—unless, of course, it were Harry," she added in a doubtful tone.

"Oh dear, Mother!" exclaimed Isabella, who had gone to the window, "here is a coach coming up but now."

Lucy was at the window in a second.

"Well, who is coming out?" she soliloquized. "An old woman—at least, no—she's not old, but she's older than I am"—

"You don't say so!" commented Charley, incredulously.

"Have done, Charley!—and the fattest little yellow dog—oh, such a funny one!—and—why, 'tis Harry! and Celia! Celia herself!"

An announcement which sent the whole family to the door at different paces, Lucy heading them. Celia felt herself obliged to greet everybody at once. Lucy was clinging to her on one side, and Charley on the other; Madam Passmore was before her, and the Squire and Isabella met her at the parlor-door.

"I am fain to see thee once more, child!" was the Squire's greeting; "but what a crinkum-crankum that woman has made of thee!"

"She looks quite elegant," said Isabella, kissing her with a little less languor than usual.

"Don't tease her, Charley; she is very tired," said Harry, when he could get in a word. "We have had a long stage to-day."

So Celia was established in an enormous easy-chair, and propped up with cushions, until she laughingly declared that she would require all the united strength of the family to help her out again; and Lucy was busy attempting to divest her of her out-door apparel, without having the least idea how to do it.

"Shall I take your hat and cloak up-stairs, Madam?" said Patient, entering with a general courtesy.

"Celia, what have you done with your yellow dog?"

"O dear!" cried Celia, in a tone of distress. "I was so taken up with you that I forgot her. Where is he, Patient?"

"'Tis a-sniffling and a-snuffling about, Madam," said Patient.

"Call her," replied Celia.

"Dog!" summoned Patient—for Patient scorned to pollute her lips with the heathen name which it had pleased Lady Ingram to bestow upon her pet. But Venus was accustomed to the generic epithet from Patient, and came trotting up at her call. Patient shut the little animal in and herself out. Venus waddled slowly up the room, sniffing at every member of the family in turn, until she came to Celia, at whom she wagged her curly tail and half her fat body, and coiled herself in peace upon a hassock at her feet.

"Celia," asked the Squire, "did you search all Paris, or offer a reward, for the ugliest dog that could be brought you?"

"By no means, Father. The dog is a bequest from my step-mother. It was her special pet, and I have not the conscience to discard it, if I had the heart."

"Is she dead, my dear? I see you are in black for some person," asked Madam Passmore.

The glad light died out of Celia's eyes, and her voice sank to a low, saddened tone.

"No, Mother; she has taken the veil at Chaillot. I am in black for Philip—my brother Philip—who died at Denain."

"Are you then come to us for good, my dear?" asked Madam Passmore, tenderly.

"For good, Mother, if you will have me, and I think you will. Only that I have promised to see my step-mother again, but my visit to her cannot last above a day, and will not be for some time to come."

"Have thee, my dear child!" murmured Madam Passmore, as if the reverse were the most preposterous notion of which she had ever heard.

"Do widows make nuns of themselves?" asked Charley. "I thought they were always girls, and that they walled them up alive when they had done with them!"

"And your woman, my dear?"

"I want to plead with you for her, Mother. She has been the best friend I have had—except Philip: and she is but lent to me for a time. She was my brother Edward's nurse, and when he wants her again he will come and fetch her. I thought you not mind my bringing her with me."

"What should I mind, my dear? If you have found her a true and faithful waiting-woman, and love her, let her by all means abide with you and serve you. Such are not to be picked up everywhere."

"My dear," asked the Squire, uneasily, "I hope they have not made a Tory of you, Celia?"

"I don't know, really, Father," was the answer. "I scarce think there is much difference between Whigs and Tories. They all seem to me devoid of honesty."

The Squire looked horror-struck.

"Nobody has made a Papist of me, if that be any consolation to you. I return as true a Protestant as I went."

"Is this woman a Tory?" gasped the Squire.

"Patient? No, Father," replied Celia, smiling, "she is a little on the other side of you. She calls Oliver Cromwell 'His Highness the Lord Protector,' and won't allow that King Charles was a martyr."

"Celia, child, thou hast been in ill company!" solemnly pronounced the Squire.

"I was afraid you would think so. But I thought I was bound to obey my step-mother in all things not wrong"—

"Surely, child, surely!" assented Madam Passmore.

"Therefore, Father—I hope you will forgive me, but I cannot in honesty keep it from you—I did not refuse her wish that I should be presented to Queen Mary."

The Squire gasped for breath. "Presented!" was the only word he could utter.

"I was afraid that it would vex you, when you came to know, dear Father," said Celia, very gently; "but you see, I was placed in such a position that I could not help vexing either you or my step-mother; and I thought that perchance I ought to obey that one in whose charge I was at the time. I did not like to go, I assure you; but I wished to do right. Do you think I did wrong, Father?"

"Now, John," said Madam Passmore, before the Squire could speak, "I won't have the child teased and made unhappy, in particular when she has only just come home. She meant to do right, and she did right as far as she knew. You must pocket your politics for once."

"Well, well, child," confessed the Squire at last, "we none of us do right at all times, I reckon, and thou art a good child in the main, and I forgive thee. I suppose there may be a few Tories who will manage to get into Heaven."

"I hope so," replied Celia, gravely.

"So do I, child—so do I; though I am a crusty old Whig at the best of times. But I do think they will have to leave their Toryism on this side."

When Celia went up-stairs, to give a longer and fuller greeting to old Cicely Aggett than she had the opportunity of doing before, she heard the unusual sound of voices proceeding from Cicely's little room. She soon found that Cicely and Patient were in close converse on a point of theology, and paused a moment, not wishing to interrupt them.

"Well, truly, I ben't so much troubled with pride as some other things," Cicely was saying. "You see, Mrs. Patient, I hasn't got nothing to be proud of. That's where it is. If I was a well-favored young damsel with five hundred pounds in my pocket, and a silk gown, and a coach for to ride in, well, I dare say I should be as stuck-up as a peacock. But whatever has an old sinner like me to be proud of? Why, I'm always doing somewhat wrong all day long."

"I am afraid I am a greater sinner than you, Mrs. Cicely," said Patient Irvine's quiet voice in answer. "You have nothing to be proud of, and you are not proud. I have nothing to be proud of, and I am."

"Well, surely, a white devil is the worst devil," responded Cicely.

"Aye, he is so," answered Patient. "If He was 'meek and lowly in heart'[1] which 'did no sin, neither was guile found in His mouth,'[2] what should we be who are for ever sinning? I tell you, Mrs. Cicely, some of the worst bouts of pride that ever I had, have been just the minute after I had been humbling myself before the Lord. Depend upon it, there is no prouder man in all the world than the man who is proud of his humility."

There was no audible answer from Cicely. Celia came softly forward.

"Eh, my dear!" cried old Cicely, looking up at her. "I am so fain to see you back as never was! Sit ye down a bit, Mrs. Celia, dear heart, and tell me how it has gone with you this long time."

"Very well, dear Cicely, as concerns the Lord's dealings with me, and very ill as concerns my dealings with Him."

"That's a right good saying, my dear. Ah! the good between Him and us is certain sure to be all on His side. We are cruel bad, all on us. And did you like well, sweetheart?"

"That she did not," said Patient, when Celia hesitated. "She has not had a bit of her own way since she left you."

Celia laughed, and then grew serious. "My own way is bad for me, Patient."

"I never knew one for whom it was not, Madam, except the few who were so gracious that the Lord's way was their way."

"Well, I'd lief be like that," said Cicely. "The King couldn't be no better off than so."

"So would I," Celia began; "but I am afraid that if I say the truth, it will be to add 'in everything but one.'"

"Now, my dear young lady," said Patient, turning to her, "don't you go to grieve in this way for Mr. Philip, as you have been doing ever since. I had no thought till then how he had twined himself round either your heart or mine. Do you think, my bairn, that the Lord, who laid down His life for him, loved him so much less than we?"

"O Patient! if it were only my loss!"

"Whose then, Madam?"

"I mean," said Celia, explanatorily, "if I could be sure that it was his gain."

Patient did not reply for a moment. "I ask your pardon, Madam," she said at length; "I did not know the direction in which your fears were travelling. The less, perhaps, that I had none to join them."

"I am surprised to hear you, Patient!" said Celia. "Only the last time that we saw him before he bade us adieu, you seemed to feel so doubtful about him."

"That was not the last time that I saw him, Madam. The next morn, ere he set out, I heard him conversing with Mr. Colville. They were on the stairs, and I was disposing of your linen above. Now I knew that all his life long the one thing which Mr. Philip could not bear was scorn. It was the thing whereof I was doubtful if he would not stand ill, 'and in time of temptation fall away.'[3] And that morn I heard Mr. Colville speaking to him in a way which, three months earlier, would have sent his blood up beyond anything I could name;—gibing, and mocking, and flouting, taunting him with listening to a parcel of old women's stories, and not being man enough to disbelieve, and the like—deriding him, yea, making him a very laughing-stock. And Mr. Philip stood his ground; John Knox himself could have been no firmer. He listened without a word till Mr. Colville had ended; and then he said, as quietly and gently as you could yourself, Madam,—'Farewell, Colville,' saith he; 'we have been friends, but all is over now betwixt you and me. I will be the friend of no man who is the enemy of Christ. He is more to me than you are—yes, more than all the world!' Madam, do you think I could hear that, and dare to dispute the salvation of a man who could set Christ above all the world? Now, you understand why I had no fear for Mr. Philip."

"He never said so much as that to me," replied Celia, with her eyes moist and glistening.

"He would have done so presently, Madam."

"But, Patient, it was so short a time after he had spoken so differently!"

"Ah, Madam! doth that offend you? The Lord can ripen His fruit very fast when He sees good, and hath more ways than one to do it. He knew that Mr. Philip's time was short. We can scarce tell how sweetly and surely He can carry the lambs in His bosom until we have been borne there with them."

The next morning Isabella brought forward her embroidery-frame, occupied just now by a brilliant worsted parrot and a couple of gorgeous peacocks, the former seated on a branch full of angles, the latter strutting about on a brown ground. The most important shade in the parrot's very showy tail was still wanting.

"Have you any work for me, Mother?" asked Celia. "I do not wish to sit idle."

"I can find you some, my dear. Here is a set of handkerchiefs and some cravats for Father, which all want hemming, and I have been obliged to work at them myself till now: Lucy scarce does well enough, and Bell is too busy with yonder birds."

"I will relieve you of those, Mother."

And Celia took the basket and established herself near the window.

"Mr. John Rowe to speak with Madam," was Dolly's announcement directly afterwards, and Madam Passmore left the room.

Charley and Lucy were learning their lessons. In other words, Charley was sitting with his Æneid and the Lexicon open on the table before him, bestowing his attention on everything in the room except those two volumes; while Lucy, seated at the window on a hassock, was behaving in much the same way to a slate.

"What a constant plague that man is!" said Isabella, as she sorted her wools. "There is no doing anything for him. I do believe he has been here every day for the last fortnight."

"Oh, I say!" commented Charley; "take that *cum grano salis*, Celia. I think he has been three times."

"Don't dispute with Bell, Charley; it doesn't signify."

"My dear, he won't dispute with me," observed Isabella, calmly, selecting different shades of scarlet. "I never dispute—it is too much trouble, takes my attention from my work."

She went on comparing her scarlets, and Charley, on receiving this rebuke, buried himself for five minutes in the adventures of Æneas. For a time all was silence except for the slight sound of Celia's needle and Lucy's slate-pencil.

"Where is Father?" inquired Madam Passmore, coming into the room with a rather troubled look.

Charley was up in a second. "He is in the stable; I saw him go. Shall I run and fetch him?"

"Ask him to come to me in the dining-room."

And both Charley and his mother disappeared.

"What is the matter now?" asked Lucy; but as nobody answered her, she went back to her arithmetic.

In about half an hour more, Madam Passmore entered, looking grave and thoughtful.

"Isabella, my child," she said, "I have something to tell thee."

Isabella looked up for a moment, and then went back to her wools. "Well, Mother?" she queried, carelessly.

"My dear, I will not disguise from thee that John Rowe's visit concerneth thee. He hath asked leave of thy father and me in order to his becoming thy servant. Now, dear child, neither I nor thy father desire to control thy choice; thou shalt speak for thyself. What sayest thou? Wilt thou marry John Rowe, or not?"

"My dear mother!" responded Isabella, still busy with the wools, "he will come to the wedding in a blue coat and a lilac waistcoat and lavender small-clothes!"

"I dare say, if thou art so particular, that he will dress in what color thou wouldst," said Madam Passmore, smiling. "But what is thy mind, child? Dost thou like him?"

"I don't care anything about him, but I cannot abide his suits," returned the young lady, comparing the skeins.

"Mother isn't asking you to marry his clothes, Bell!" exclaimed Charley.

"My dear, I am not asking her to marry him," said Madam Passmore; "I only wish to know her mind about it. If thou dost not care about him, child, I suppose thou wilt wish us to refuse his addresses?"

"No, I don't say that exactly," replied Isabella, undoing one of her two skeins.

"Then what dost thou wish, my dear?" inquired Madam Passmore, looking rather puzzled.

"Oh! do wait a minute, till I settle this red," said Isabella. "I beg your pardon, Mother—yes, that will do. Dear, 'tis quite a weight off my mind! Now then for this other matter."

"Child, the other matter imports rather to thee, surely, than the colors of thy worsteds!"

"I am sure it does not, Mother, asking your pardon. I have been all the morning over these reds. Well, as to John Rowe, I don't much mind marrying him if he will let me choose his suits, and give me two hundred pounds a year pin-money, and keep me a coach-and-pair, and take me up to London at least once in ten years. I don't think of anything else. Please to ask him."

"Don't much mind!" repeated her mother, looking dissatisfied and perplexed. "Bell, dear child, I fear thou dost not apprehend the import of that thou dost. 'Tis a choice for thy whole life, child! Do think upon it, and leave thy worsteds alone for a while!"

"If you want a downright answer, Mother, you shall have it," returned Isabella, with the air of one ending an unpleasant interruption. "I will marry John Rowe if he will keep me a coach-and-pair, and give me two hundred a year pin-money, and take me to London—say once every four years—I may as well do it thoroughly while I am about it—and of course let me drive in the Ring, and go to Ranelagh and Vauxhall, and see the lions in the Tower, and go to St. James's, and all on in that way. There! now that is settled."

Madam Passmore looked scarcely more satisfied than before, but she said, "Well, my dear, if that be thy wish, thou hadst better go and speak with John Rowe, and let him know thy conditions."

"O Mother! with all these worsteds on my lap!" deprecated Isabella, raising her eyebrows.

"Put them here, Bell," interposed Celia, holding her apron.

Isabella reluctantly disposed her worsteds and rose.

"I wish John Rowe were far enough!" she said, as she left the room.

"Dear, dear, child!" murmured Madam Passmore, looking doubtfully after her daughter.

"She is very like my step-mother," said Celia, quietly. "She reminds me of her many a time."

"Now then!" said Isabella, triumphantly re-entering. "I have sent him away, and told him he must not come teasing when I am busy. When I had just found the right shade of red! Look at this bracelet he has given me—pretty, is it not? He has promised all I asked, and to give me a black footman as well. I shall not repent marrying him, I can see."

"Is that happiness, my dear Isabella?"

"Happiness!" replied Bell, stopping in her business of transferring the wools from Celia's apron to her own. "Of course! Why, there are not above half a dozen families in the country that have black servants! I wonder at your asking such a question, Celia."

"I say, Bell," queried Charley, just before taking himself and Virgil out of the room, "I wonder which of you two is going to say the 'obey' in the service?"

"That boy's impertinence really gets insufferable," placidly observed Isabella, seating herself at the frame. "Now to finish my parrot's tail."

The wedding of John Rowe and Isabella Passmore was celebrated in the following spring. Thanks to the bride's taste and orders, the bridegroom's attire was faultless. The black footman proved so excessively black, and rolled the whites of his eyes to such an extent, that Lucy declared she could not believe that he was no more than an ordinary man. At the end of the summer, the absentees returned to Marcombe, and Isabella came over to Ashcliffe in her carriage, attended by her black Ganymede, in order to impress her relatives duly with a sense of her importance: herself attired in a yellow silk brocade almost as stiff as cardboard, with an embroidered black silk slip, and gold ornaments in her powdered hair. And once more Celia was vividly reminded of Lady Ingram.

"I am going to have the black baptized," the young lady languidly remarked. "I shall call him"—

"Othello," suggested Charley.

"Cassibelaunus—O Bell! do call him Cassibelaunus!"

"Nonsense, Lucy. I shall call him Nero."

"Then he is a Christian, my dear?" asked her mother.

"I don't think he knows anything about it," replied his mistress, with a short laugh. "But you know 'tis scarce decent to be attended by an unbaptized black; and he will be a Christian when 'tis done."

"I am not so sure of that, Bell," said Madam Passmore, quietly.

It was the first time that Madam Passmore had been known to express any individual opinion upon religious subjects.

"All baptized people are Christians," answered Mrs. John Rowe, a little more sharply than was respectful.

"All baptized are called Christians," corrected her mother. "I scarce think, Bell, that if thou hast left thy black completely untaught in matters of religion, that pouring a little water on his face will cause him to become suddenly learned. And whether it will suddenly cause anything else of a deeper nature may be to be questioned."

Celia listened with the greater interest because the tone of Madam Passmore's observations was alike unexpected and unprecedented.

"But, Mother," said Isabella, a little more deferentially as well as reverently, "the Holy Ghost is always given in baptism?"

"I was taught so, my dear. But I am come to feel unsure that God's Word saith the Holy Ghost is always given in baptism. And, Bell, I am not sure that He was so given to all my children."

"You mean me, I suppose, Mother?" asked Isabella, returning to her former tone.

"I fear so, my child," responded Madam Passmore, so sadly and so tenderly that Isabella could make no scornful answer. "I have feared, indeed, for months past that I have taught you all wrong. God amend it! Indeed, I hope He is Himself teaching some of you. But I did not mean thee only, Bell. I have as much fear for all of you, except Celia, and, perhaps, Harry. Have we feared God, child, as a family? Hath there not been mere form and habit even in our devotions? Have we not shown much unevenness, and walked unequally? Have we cared to serve or please Him at all? Ah, my children! these are grave questions, and I take bitter shame to myself to have lived as many years as I have, and never thought of them. God forgive you—and me!"

"Aye, to be sure, my dear!" said old Cicely upstairs, afterwards. "To be sure, Madam, she's a-coming home to the Lord. I see her reading the Book at odd times like, making a bit of a secret of it, very soon after you went; and by and bye, a little afore you came back, she came to make no secret of it; and since then I've seen many a little thing as showed me plain where she was a-going. And Master Harry, my dear, he reads the Book too—he does, for sure! Can't say nothing about Master, worse luck! Then Miss Lucy and Master Charley, you see, they're young things as hasn't got no thought of nothing. But as for Mrs. Bell"—

Celia quite understood, without another word. "O Cicely!" she said, many thoughts crowding on her mind, "surely I shall never distrust God again!"

"But you will, Madam," said Patient, looking up from her work. "Aye, many and many a time! 'Tis a lesson, trust me, that neither you nor I have learned yet. We are such poor scholars, for ever forgetting that though this very lesson be God's a-b ab, for us, we need many a rod to our backs ere we can spell it over. Aye, Madam, you'll not be out of school for a while yet."

"Celia," asked Madam Passmore that evening, "when do you expect your brother, my dear?"

"I don't know, indeed, Mother," replied Celia. "I expected him ere now. I know not what is keeping him. Surely he will be here before summer!"

Edward Ingram was not at Ashcliffe before summer.

The summer passed, and he did not come. The winter passed, and he did not come. Nay, the whole spring, and summer, and autumn, and winter of another year passed, and the third summer, of 1714, was fading into autumn—still Edward did not come.

But when the dusk was gathering on the 5th of August in that year, a horseman galloped into Ashcliffe village with news which he was carrying post-haste to Tavistock and Launceston—news which blanched in my a cheek and set many a man looking to his aims—which called forth muffled peals from the church-towers, and draped pulpits and pews in mourning, and was received with sadness and alarm in well-nigh every English home. For the one thread was snapped on which England's peace had hung—the one barrier standing between England and anarchy was broken. The last Stuart whom the nation acknowledged lay dead in Kensington Palace.

So long as Queen Anne lived, the embers of discord had been only smouldering. The Jacobites felt a half-satisfaction in the thought that the old line still held the sceptre; the Whigs rejoiced in their Whig and Protestant Queen. Not that the private political views of the Queen were very Whiggish ones. On the contrary, granted one thing—her own personal rule—she was at heart a Tory. For all the years of her reign she had been growing more and more a Tory. She would never have abdicated the sceptre; but very little indeed was wanted to make her say, when the cold grasp of the Angel of Death was laid upon her, "Let my brother succeed me." Such a speech would have given the Jacobites immense vantage-ground. For in 1714 the State was still the Sovereign, and "*La Royne le veut*" was sterling yet in England. This the partisans of the exiled family knew well; and to their very utmost, through their trusted agents, of whom Abigail Lady Masham was the chief, they strove to induce the Queen to utter such words. Her decease now was the signal for the division of the country into two sharply-defined parties. The Tories strove for King James, triennial Parliaments, removal of Popish disabilities, peace with France, free trade, and repeal of the union with Scotland. The Whigs battled as fiercely for King George, septennial Parliaments, Test and Corporation Acts, war with France, protection, and centralization.

A dreadful struggle was expected between these two parties before George Louis, Elector of Hanover, could seat himself on Anne Stuart's vacant throne. His character and antecedents were much against him. All who knew him personally were aware that he was a man of little intellect, and less morality. Moreover, from both demoralized parties there was a cry for money, and hands were eagerly stretched out to the Elector, less for the purpose of welcoming him than for the hope of what he might put into them. George Louis gave not a stiver. He had not many stivers to give; but what he had he loved too well to part with them either to Whigs or Tories. He sat quietly at Hanover, waiting for Parliament to vote him supplies, and for his disinterested supporters to secure his unopposed landing. Parliament—from a Whig point of view—did their duty, and voted liberal aids within a week or two after the Queen's death. James was up and doing at St. Germains, while George slumbered in his arm-chair at Herrenhausen. At length, on the 18th of September, the gentleman of doubtful, or rather undoubtful, morals, who was facetiously styled the Hope of England, condescended to land upon our shores. He formed his Cabinet, allowed himself to be crowned, dissolved Parliament, and leaving the country to take care of itself, returned to silence and tumblers of Hock.

The English people in the main were irreparably disgusted with the man of their choice. They were ready to welcome the grandson of their "Queen of Hearts," Elizabeth of Bohemia, but they looked for a royal Prince, a true Stuart, graceful and gracious. And here was a little stupid-looking man, who cared nothing about them, and was a stranger alike to their language, their customs, their manners, and their politics. A new edition of Charles II.'s vices, deprived of all Charles II.'s graces—this was their chosen King. Neither Celtic Cornwall nor Saxon Lancashire could bear the disappointment. West and North rose in insurrection. There were riots throughout England, and many a Dissenting chapel was levelled by the mob. The Riot Act was made perpetual, the Habeas Corpus Act suspended; a price of £100,000 was set upon the head of King James's exiled son; and his Hanoverian Majesty, meeting his Parliament on the 21st of September 1715, civilly requested the arrest of six Tory members of the House of Commons.

While all this was doing in England, in a quiet corner of Scotland a little cloud was rising, which had increased to goodly proportions by the 6th of September, when Lord Mar unfurled in Braemar the standard of King James the Third. On the 13th of November were fought the battles of Sheriffmuir and Prestonpans; and on the 22nd of December, a little group of seven men landed at Peterhead, one of whom was the royal exile, now generally known as the Chevalier de St. George. On the 7th of January 1716, he reached the ancient Palace of his forefathers at Scone; but by the 30th his cause was lost, and he retreated on Montrose, whence, on the 4th of February, quitting his native land, he returned to France.

The vengeance taken was terrible. Head after head fell upon the scaffold, and the throne of the House of Hanover was established only in a sea of blood.

On the evening of the 8th of March, the family at Ashcliffe were gathered in the parlor. The Squire was playing draughts with Harry, the ladies working, and Charley and Lucy engaged in the mutual construction of an elaborate work of art.

"Sea-coal any cheaper yet, Mother?" asked the Squire.

"Not yet," said Madam Passmore.

"Monstrous dear, is it not?" inquired Harry.

"Nothing to what it was in my young days," answered his father. "Forty or fifty years ago, at the time of the Dutch war, charcoals went up to one hundred and ten shillings the chaldron, and those were lucky who could get them even at that price."

"Was not that about the time of the Great Plague?"

"Yes—two or three years later."

"Then you remember the Plague, Father?"

"Remember it!" said the Squire, leaning back in his chair and neglecting his draughts. "Men don't forget such a thing as that in a hurry, my lad. Aye, I remember it."

"But there was no plague here, was there?"

"Not just in this village; but well-nigh all communication was stopped between Tavistock and Exeter, and in the King's highway the grass was growing. It was awful at Tavistock. The town was shut up and declared in a state of siege, and none allowed to approach nearer than three miles. Watchmen were appointed, the only men permitted to hold communication with the infected town; and when any provisions were needed, they made proclamation, and the neighboring villages brought such things as they asked to the high ground above Merrivale Bridge, where the cordon was drawn."

"And how did they pay for their provisions?"

"A pitful of vinegar was dug there, in some hole in Dartmoor,[4] and the money dropped into it. None in healthy places were allowed to touch money coming from infected places without that provision."

"Surely money could not carry the infection?"

"Money! aye, or anything else. You have scarce a notion how little would carry it. Harry, lad, throw another log on the fire; 'tis mightily cold."

Harry obeyed orders, resumed his seat, and the game between him and his father proceeded for a few minutes in silence.

"Hark!" cried Madam Passmore, suddenly, "what was that?"

"I heard nothing," said Lucy.

"What was it, Mother?" asked Harry, looking up.

"Some strange sound, as if one were about on the terrace," she answered in a suppressed voice. "There again! I am sure I hear a footstep on the gravel."

Charley rushed to the window, and endeavored to see through the darkness.

"'Tis as dark as pitch; I can see nothing at all!" observed that young gentleman.

"I will go out and see what it is," said Harry rising.

He took his sword from where it lay, and left the room.

"Bow-wow-wow-wow-wow!" said Venus, running after him, as her contribution to the family excitement.

Harry opened the front door, desiring Charley to guard it till his return, and Venus, after sniffing under it, rushed out of the house with him, barking loudly on the terrace, in a state of great perturbation. Harry came back after an absence of twenty minutes, during which the Squire had several times "wondered what on earth was keeping the boy."

"All right," he said, laying down his sword; "there are no robbers about."

"It has taken you a precious time to find it out," growled his father.

Harry sat down again to his game. "I walked round the terrace to make sure," he said.

"Which you might have done in five minutes," grumbled the Squire again. "Now then, 'tis your move."

Harry placed one of his three kings in dangerous proximity to his adversary's forces.

"Thank you, Sir," said his father, satirically, capturing the imperilled potentate.

Harry tried to retrieve himself, and succeeded in placing the second king in the same position.

"Harry, lad, what has come to you?" asked the Squire, looking at him. "You were playing better than usual till just now, but your walk round the terrace seems to have destroyed your skill."

"I beg your pardon, Sir," answered Harry, uncomfortably. "I will endeavor to play better."

And he carried out his attempt by placing in imminent peril his last remaining piece.

"Nay, nay," said his father, leaning back in his chair, "'tis no use going on, lad. Did you see a ghost on the terrace?"

"I did not, Sir, I assure you," returned Harry.

"Well, I wonder what is the matter with you," said the Squire. "Here, Lucy, come and let me see if you can do any better."

Lucy took her brother's vacated seat.

"Celia," said Harry, a quarter of an hour afterwards, turning to her, "would you mind bringing your needle and thread up-stairs? I want you to help me with something which I cannot well bring here."

"Oh yes, Harry, I will come with you," answered Celia, re-threading her needle, and following Harry out of the room with it in her hand.

Harry led her up-stairs, motioned her into her own room, and, much to her surprise, locked the door, and pocketed the key.

"Harry, something is the matter," she said.

"Something *is* the matter, Celia," repeated Harry. "I have brought you here to tell it you."

"What did you see on the terrace?" she asked, fearfully.

"Sir Edward Ingram," was the answer.

"Harry! where is he? why did you not tell me?"

"Nobody must know, Celia, except you and me—and, perhaps, Patient. But I would rather not tell even her if we can avoid it. Sir Edward is in hiding, having fled from Sheriffmuir, and a party of men have been riding him down, he says, since last night. They know he is somewhere in the neighborhood, and will most likely be here to search the house in an hour or less. I will readily risk my life for the man who saved it at Denain; and I know his sister will help me."

"But where can we hide him?" faltered Celia.

"Here," was Harry's short answer, opening the closet-door.

"In the closet? O Harry! that is not safe enough. They would find him in a minute."

"My dear little Celia, you don't know half the secrets of your own chamber. Look!"

A touch of the secret spring caused the panel-door to spring outward, and Celia's eyes to open very wide indeed.

"I never knew there was such a place!" she cried.

"I believe no one knows but myself, and now, you. I discovered this room five years ago, but I did not wish to alarm you, for I had reason to believe it was then inhabited. 'Tis one of the old priests' hiding-holes. Now, watch how the door is opened, and then contrive as best you can to procure food for Sir Edward. He says he is well-nigh famished. While you are with him, I will go to the outlet, where a passage leads to the garden, and remove the logs which I put at the door five years since, as silently as I can. Make haste, every minute may be priceless."

Celia ran down-stairs, feeling utterly bewildered by the position in which she was suddenly placed. Entering the larder, she possessed herself hastily of a large loaf and a jug of milk,—making some excuse—she scarcely knew what—to Patient, whom she found there; and discovered Harry and a lamp waiting for her at the closet-door. He had some carpenter's tools in the other hand. A hurried greeting was exchanged between Edward and Celia, who conversed in whispers until Harry returned, announcing that the passage was now open to the garden, and that, to avoid suspicion, both had better go down again to the parlor.

"You must talk in the night," he said.

Harry and Celia went back to the parlor. The latter sat down to her work, hardly seeing a stitch she set. They had not been down-stairs many minutes, when Lucy sprang up, triumphantly exclaiming that she had won the game; at the same moment the sound of horses' feet was audible outside, and a loud attack was made on the great bell which hung in front of the house.

"Open to His Majesty's troops!"

The cry could be distinctly heard in the parlor.

"Goodness me!" gasped Madam Passmore, dropping her work in terror.

The Squire had recourse to stronger language than this. Harry, whose composure seemed quite restored, went to the door and opened it with every appearance of haste.

"Oh!" said he, in a cordial tone, "how do you do, Wallace? Pray come in, my father will have infinite pleasure in making your acquaintance. Father, here is an old comrade of mine."

"Your servant, Mr. Passmore," said Captain Wallace, bowing, with his hat in his hand; "yours, ladies. I am very sorry for the ill errand I come on. There is a Jacobite hiding in this neighborhood, a Colonel in the rebel army, and a man of rank and influence—one Sir Edward Ingram. I am in charge to search all the houses hereabouts, and I am sure you will not take it ill of me if I ask leave not to omit yours, though the loyalty of Mr. Passmore of Ashcliffe must ever be above suspicion."

"Jacobites be hanged!" burst from the Squire. "Sir, you do me great honor. No Jacobites in my house—at least not if I know it. Pray search every corner, and cut all the cushions open if you like!"

"Thank you, Mr. Passmore. Only what I expected from a gentleman of your high character. I may begin at once?"

"By all means!"

Captain Wallace called in one of his men—leaving the others to guard the house outside—and after an examination of the parlor, they proceeded upstairs, Harry loyally volunteering to light them. In about an hour they returned to the parlor.

"Mr. Passmore," said Captain Wallace, "'tis my duty to question every person in the house, to make sure that this rebel has not been seen nor heard of. You do not object? A form, you know—in such a case as this, a mere form."

"Question away," said the Squire; "*I* have neither seen nor heard of him, and don't want to do either. Now for the ladies."

Madam Passmore answered the question with a quiet negative.

"It can scarcely be necessary to trouble the young ladies," gallantly remarked the Captain. "But if they please to say just a word"—

"We have seen and heard nothing at all, Sir," said Lucy, innocently replying for both; and the Captain did not repeat his question, neither he nor the Squire apparently noticing the suspicious silence of the elder sister.

"I must, if you please, ask leave to examine the servants."

Madam Passmore rang the bell, and ordered all the household up. They assembled in wonder, and each in turn responded to the Captain's queries by a simple denial of any knowledge on the subject. Patient stood last, and when Captain Wallace came to her, he accidentally put his first question in a different form from before.

"Do you know Sir Edward Ingram?"

"Ay do I," said she.

Celia listened with a beating heart. The innocent ignorance of Patient might work them terrible harm, which she would be the last person in the world to do wittingly.

"You know him?" repeated the Captain, in surprise.

"Do you think I shouldna ken the bairn I nursed?"

"Oh! you are his nurse, are you?"

"I was so, twenty-five years back."

"When did you see him last?"

"Four years past."

"Where?"

"At Havre, in France."

Celia breathed more freely

"Have you heard anything of his movements of late?"

"What do you mean?" inquired Patient, cautiously.

"Well, did you hear that he was likely to come into this neighborhood, or anything of that sort?"

"I cannot say I havena heard that," was the quiet answer.

"When did you hear that?"

"He was expecting to come four years past, but he didna come; and I heard a short space back that he might be looked for afore long." Patient spoke slowly and thoughtfully.

"Who told you that?"

"My kinsman, Willie M'Intyre."

"Are you a Scots woman?"

"Ay," said Patient, with a flash of light in her eyes.

"Humph!" muttered the Captain. "Difficult folks those mostly to get round. When did you see Willie M'Intyre?"

"An eight days or two since."

"Cannot you tell me the day?"

"I dinna keep a diary book," responded Patient, dryly.

"Whence had he come?"

"Whence should he come but from Scotland?"

"Where was he going?"

"I didna ask him."

Patient's information appeared to have collapsed all at once, and her Scotticisms to increase.

"What is Willie M'Intyre?"

"A harper."

"How long was it since he left Scotland?"

"You are a learned gentleman, Sir; ye ken better nor me how many days it would take."

"What else did he tell you about Sir Edward Ingram?"

"He told me he was looking unco sick when he saw him."

"Anything more?"

"I have na mair to say, Sir, without you have."

"You are a clever woman," involuntarily admitted the Captain, passing his hand across his forehead as if in thought. "Well, and when did he tell you to expect Sir Edward?"

"He didna tell me to expect him."

"What did he say about him?"

"The twa things I've told you."

"When did he say he was coming?" asked the Captain, impatiently.

"Afore lang."

"But *when*?"

"He didna name ony day."

Captain Wallace was no match for Patient, as might be seen.

"Have you seen Sir Edward since you saw M'Intyre?"

"No, Sir."

"Have you heard of his being here since then?"

"Being where?"

"Anywhere in this neighborhood."

Patient's answer came slowly this time, as if she were considering something before speaking. But it was, "No, Sir."

"Are you telling me the truth?" asked Captain Wallace, knitting his brows.

"I couldna tell ye aught else," answered Patient. "'Tis no lawful to do evil that good may come. But no good will come, Sir, of your hunting a man to death to whom Christ hath given power to become one of the sons of God."

"Oh dear! a Puritan!" murmured Wallace—"a Covenanter, for aught I know. Mr. Passmore, these are the most impracticable people you ever meet—these Puritans; particularly when they are Scots. There is not much loyalty among them; and what little there is is sacrificed to their religion at any moment."

"I'm loyal, Sir," said Patient, softly—"to any covenanted King: but needs be to the King of Kings the first."

"I fear you are a dangerous character," said Captain Wallace, severely. "I am surprised to meet with such an one in this house. However, you won't lie to me, being a Puritan—that is one good thing. They never tell lies. Now listen! Do you know where Sir Edward Ingram is at this moment?"

The "No Sir," came readily enough this time.

"Well, I suppose you can go," said Captain Wallace, doubtfully. "But I am not at all satisfied with you—mark that! Your witness is very badly given, and very unwillingly. I may want you again. If it should be needful to search the house a second time, I certainly shall do so. You have only just escaped being put under arrest now."

"I've told you the truth, Sir," said Patient, pausing. "I will tell you the truth any day. But if it were to come to this—that my dying could save you from finding my bairn Sir Edward, I wouldna haud my life as dear as yon bittie of thread upon the floor!"

She courtesied and departed.

"Ah! that shows what the woman is," said Captain Wallace, carelessly. "An enthusiast—a complete fanatic. Well, Mr. Passmore"—

"Sir," said the Squire, energetically, "I am by no means satisfied with this. The house shall be searched again, if you please, and I will join the party myself. Harry, fetch a longer candle—fetch two! That woman may have hidden the fellow anywhere! I'll have every corner looked into. There shall be no question of any hiding of Jacobites in my house. Charley, go and get a candle too. You girls have a lot of gowns and fallals in that closet in your room. Go and bundle them all out! Make haste!"

"Oh, I say, what fun!" remarked Charley, to whom any connection between the hunted man and his favorite sister never occurred.

Lucy left the room laughing to execute her father's behest, and Celia dared not but follow, lest her absence should be remarked. The two girls went hastily up-stairs, and at the top they found Patient standing.

"I'll help you, Mrs. Lucy," said she. And as Lucy passed on,—"You ken something, Madam Celia. Don't let those bloodhounds read it in your eyes, as I do. And be calm. The Lord reigneth, my bairn."

"Yes, dear Patient, I know," was Celia's faltering answer: and she went quietly into her own room.

[1] Matt. xi. 29.

[2] 1 Pet. ii. 22.

[3] Luke viii. 13.

[4] In the sunken circle which marked one of the habitations of the ancient Iberii, the aborigines of Britain. One of their villages stood above Merrivale Bridge, with a long avenue of stones (still visible), intersected here and there by circles, and at a little distance is a monolith.

XIII.

LADY GRISELDA'S RUBY RING

"He looketh upon us sweetly,
   With His well-known greeting, 'Peace!'
And He fills our hearts completely,
   And the sounds of the tempest cease;
But we know that the hour is come,
For one of us to go home."
                —B.M.

Celia found Lucy already engaged in emptying the closet. Patient came in and helped her until the bed was covered with cloaks and dresses. They heard the searchers coming slowly toward them on the other side of the passage, the Squire especially urging that not the smallest corner should be left unsearched. At length they tapped at the door for admittance. Charley came in first, holding his candle high above his head, as if his mission were to explore the ceiling.

"You be off!" said the Squire roughly, as soon as he saw Patient.

"Why, Father!" interposed Lucy, "she has only been helping us to move these things. You told us to make haste."

Lucy was unconsciously proving a useful ally.

"Wow!" came in a little smothered bark from somewhere, and Venus waddled from under the valance and the dresses overhanging it.

"Go down, Veny!" said Celia, adding apologetically, "she will get in the way."

She felt a terrible secret fear lest Venus should prove a more able searcher than any other of the party.

"I'll carry her out of the way,"—and suiting the action to the word, Lucy caught up the little dog and shut her outside.

A close examination was made of the room. Charley got into the closet, and held his candle up.

"Nothing there, thanks to the young ladies," said Captain Wallace, laughing, as he looked in.

"No—he'd be a clever fellow who could hide there," added the Squire, in blissful ignorance.

"Why, here's a nail," said Charley, "close to the wall. You'll tear your gowns on it. I'll pull it out."

Celia's very heart sank.

"Leave it just now, Charley," said Harry, coolly; "we shall want you and your candle."

Charley sprang down and rejoined the searching party. Outside the door they were also joined by Venus, who followed them into the next room, which had been the bed-chamber of Isabella. She picked out Captain Wallace, and followed close at his heels, paying no attention to anybody else. The room was searched like the others, the last thing which the Captain did being to look up the chimney. No sooner did he approach the fireplace than Venus gave an angry growl and made a futile attempt to bite him through his thick boots.

"What is the brute growling at?" demanded the Squire.

"I don't know, indeed," said Harry.

The growling continued so long as Captain Wallace was near the chimney, but nobody except Venus knew why. As soon as the party turned from Isabella's room to Henrietta's, which was the next, Venus trotted back to Celia. At the close of the inspection, both Captain Wallace and Squire Passmore were forced to acknowledge that no trace of any hidden fugitive could be discovered. They went down-stairs.

Five minutes later Harry came lightly up again, and called to Celia, who was helping Lucy to replace the dresses in the closet. She found him in Isabella's chamber.

"Let us look at this chimney, Celia," he said. "It must be very near the hiding-place. What made Veny growl?"

He had brought a small ladder from the housemaid's closet, with which he mounted as far as he could go inside the wide old chimney. When he came down, he looked pale and excited.

"Celia, we must get him out of the house. If either Wallace or my father should think of returning to see the cause of Veny's growling, he will infallibly be discovered. The chimneys join, and every sound from one room can be heard in the other. Venus is wiser than we are. The dog knew, though I did not, that there was a shorter passage to the concealed chamber from Bell's chamber than from yours."

"What shall we do?" whispered Celia.

"Go down-stairs, and fetch from the buttery such provisions as you can take to Sir Edward, of any portable kind. Converse with him if you will, but let it be in the lowest tones; and if you hear any noise in this chamber be as mute as mice. I will go down and set my father and Wallace at some game, and get my mother to prepare Henrietta's chamber for him, as it is too late for him to think of leaving to-night now. Then I shall go and have a horse ready saddled as near as is safe. When the clock strikes nine, lead Sir Edward down to the well door. You cannot miss it, if only you keep going down. I will meet you with a lantern at the well, at nine or as soon after as possible."

"Is the well low enough, with all this rain?"

"Water up to the ankles, but he will not care for that."

Harry and Celia left the room softly, departing on their several errands.

"Wallace," said the former, coming into the parlor, "do you think it is necessary to keep your men on guard outside? 'Tis a bitter cold night, and if they may come into the kitchen, the poor fellows would be none the worse for a hot supper."

"I do not think it is necessary," said the Captain.

Captain Wallace having called the men in, Harry took them to the kitchen, and desired Molly the cook-maid to give them as good a supper as she could, with hot ale, for which Robert was despatched to the cellar. This done, Harry went up-stairs to his own room. Silently opening his window—which, fortunately for his project, was at the north-east corner of the house, away from both parlor and kitchen—he climbed down the lime-tree which stood close beside it, and took his way noiselessly to the stable. Meanwhile Celia, who had concealed in her pocket and by means of the dressing-gown over her arm, two standing pies, came back to her own room, and descended to the concealed chamber.

"See what I have brought you!" she said to the fugitive. "The troops are here, and have searched the house twice, and Harry thinks that we must get you away to-night. He will have a horse ready for you, and will meet you at the well at nine o'clock. Do you mind going through a foot of water?"

"I should be a Sybarite if I did," smiled Edward in reply. "Celia, I am bringing you into danger, and I am very sorry for it. I begin to think now that it was but a cowardly act to seek shelter here; yet when a man is riding for life he scarce pauses to choose his course."

"You have brought me into no danger, dear, into which I did not choose to be brought," she answered. "But if they found you, Edward, what would they do to you?"

"What they did but a few days since on Tower Hill to my friend Lord Derwentwater,"[1] he said, gravely.

Celia shuddered as the agony and ignominy of that horrible scaffold came up before her eyes.

"They will not do it without the Lord's permission," added he, quietly. "Celia, I am in grave doubt whether I have done right in this matter. Not that I could ever see it right to fight against King James, nor that I doubt which would have been the right side to take at the time of the Revolution. I cannot quite see—what I know would be Patient's view, and is the view of many good men—that we had no right to fight for a Popish King. I do not judge those who thought so—to our own Master we all stand or fall. But I see the matter in another light. It was not that King James, being a Papist, was made King out of his turn, but that, being heir to the throne, he became a Papist. I see an immense difference between the two. God, not we, made him our King; God made the present King James his son, knowing that he would be brought up a Papist. What right had we to cast him off? Now the case is altered; he is cast off; and, considering the danger of Popery, have I, *now*, any right to bring him in again? This is my difficulty; and if I can leave England in safety, I do not think I shall draw my sword in the Jacobite cause again, though I never could take the oath of allegiance to any other King. I will never dare to attempt the prevention of the Lord's will, if only I can be certain what the Lord's will is in this matter."

"Well, I do not see the question quite as you do. It seems to me that they were right to cast off a Popish King. But we have no time to discuss politics to-night. You will leave England, then, at once?"

"There is no hope of life otherwise. The Elector of Hanover and his Ministers can have no mercy for us who fought at Sheriffmuir."

"And when am I likely to see you again, Edward?"

"When the Heavenly Jerusalem descendeth out of Heaven from God," he answered, softly.

"No sooner?" responded Celia, tearfully.

"God knoweth," he said. "How do I know? I have a fancy sometimes—a foreboding, if you will—that my life will not be long. So much the better. Yet I do not wish to be longing selfishly for rest ere the Lord's work for me is done. Look here, Celia! Look well at this ring, so that you will know it again in any place after any lapse of time."

He drew the ring from his finger and passed it to her. It was an old-fashioned gold ring, set with a single ruby. Inside it was engraved in obsolete spelling, a "posy"—

"In thys my chance
I doe rejoyce."

"I shall know this again," said Celia, returning the ring after a close inspection. "'Tis an old jewel."

"A family heirloom," said Edward. "Our mother was married with that ring. It came into out family as the wedding-ring of Lady Grissel Fleming, our grandmother. I will endeavor to contrive, dear Cicely, that by some means this ring shall reach your hands after my death. When you next see it in the possession of any but myself, it will signify to you that I have entered into my rest."

"Edward, where is your wife?" asked Celia, suddenly.

A spasm of pain crossed Edward's face.

"I have no wife," he said. "The Lord had more need of my Flora than I had, and two summers past He said unto her, 'Come up higher.' I am almost glad now that she was spared this. I saw her but twice after I parted from you at Havre. And I do not think it will be long now ere I shall see her again."

"You seem to like the prospect, Edward," said Celia, remonstratingly.

"Have I so very much to live for, my sister? I can do no good to you, especially now that we must be parted; and my sole object in life is to do and suffer all the will of God. Do you wonder if I wish at times that it would be the Lord's will to summon me home?"

There was a short pause, broken by Edward's sudden exclamation, "Celia!"

She looked up to see what was coming.

"How long have you known of this chamber?"

"Harry said he had known of it for five years; I never heard a word about it before to-night."

"Did he suspect that it was occupied?"

"I think he said it was, or had been, shortly before he discovered it."

"Would you like to know by whom?"

"Very much. Why, Edward, how do you know?"

"There is not time to explain that; but I can tell you that Father Stevens, a Jesuit priest, was in hiding here for some time, and for about two months, Gilbert Irvine."

"What were they doing here? and how did they get their provisions?"

"What Stevens was doing I cannot say; but Gilbert's object was you. He was sent here by my mother to make himself acquainted with you by sight, and to discover all he could about you and your friends here. As to provisions, he catered for himself in the village and elsewhere; but on two or three occasions, when he dared not venture out, and was very hard bestead, he supplied himself from Mr. Passmore's larder."

"How did he get there?"

"Through your room."

"Edward!"

"It was a bold move, and might have cost him dear if you had awoke."

"Do you mean to say that he did it while Lucy and I were sleeping in the room?"

"Yes," said Edward, with his grave smile.

Celia sent her memory back to the time, and a dim vision gradually revealed itself to her of one winter night when, awaking suddenly, she had fancied she heard mice in the wainscot, and the next morning the black cat had suffered at the hands of Molly for the absence of a partridge and a cold chicken from the buttery.

"But how came my step-mother to know anything about this hidden chamber?"

"Through Stevens, who at one time was among her confessors. Oh! the priests know their old hiding-places, though the owners may have lost the tradition of them."

"Have you seen my Lady Ingram of late?"

"Within the last six months."

"How does she at Chaillot?"

"The nuns say she is killing herself with austerities, and she looks as though she might be. She has her salvation to make, you see."

"What a dreadful delusion!" sighed Celia.

"One of man's hundred usurpations of the prerogative of God. If man may not save himself wholly, he will save himself in part; he will do anything rather than let Christ do everything. 'Tis just the world, the flesh, and the devil, in a peculiar shape, and of a very fair color. 'Puffed up by his fleshly mind,'[2] saith St. Paul of this manner of mortifying of the flesh. The subtlest serving of the devil lies, I think, in this kind of renouncing of the world. And the world, in whatever shape, 'passeth away, and the lust thereof; but he that doeth the will of God abideth forever.'"[3]

As Edward spoke the last word, the old clock in the hall struck nine. Both rose, and Edward, drawing Celia to him, kissed his last farewell.

"God be brother and sister to you, dear," he said, "and keep thee in all thy ways;[4] set thee in the secret place of the Most High, that thou mayest abide under the shadow of the Almighty.[5] Christ be with thee! Amen!"

They went softly down to the door opening into the well, outside of which was Harry with a ladder. There was another figure there beside Harry's, but the moonlight was not sufficient to show who it might be.

"Say farewell to Patient for me," said Edward. "I wish I could have seen her. Adieu!"

In another minute Edward was safely landed. As soon as he touched the ground, the second figure came forward and threw its arms round his neck.

"Eh, my bairn! my bairn!" sobbed a voice which both Edward and Celia knew well. "I could never bear to let you go but a word. The Lord bless thee and guide thee! My ain bit laddie, that I nursed!"

Edward returned the embrace very warmly. Patient had always been far more of a mother to him than Lady Ingram. He seemed disposed to hesitate for a moment, but Harry urged him away, and motioned to Celia to return. She left the three on the outside of the well. Harry and Edward hastening to the place where the horse waited, and Patient, silent and motionless, watching her darling pass from her sight.

Celia was early down-stairs the next morning. Harry met her in the hall, and contrived to whisper along with his morning kiss, "All right." Further communication was impossible, for the Squire was just behind them, and the three entered the parlor together. They found Captain Wallace looking out of the window.

"Good-morning, Captain," said the Squire. "I suppose you have heard nothing of your man?"

"Nothing whatever, Mr. Passmore."

"Well, I'll have the house searched again by daylight. First thing after breakfast"—

"Your energy is most laudable, Mr. Passmore; but really, after two previous searches—is it necessary?"

"Necessary or unnecessary, it shall be done, Sir," said the Squire, warmly. "No man on earth shall have the shadow of reason for suspecting any concealment of rebels in Ashcliffe Hall. You will do me the favor to accompany me, and Harry and Charley shall come too."

"I shall be most happy, Sir," responded Harry.

"'Tis splendid fun!" commented Charley. "I only wish we could find him!"

The search took place, and not a corner was left an examined, except only the undiscovered hiding-place, which alone needed examination. The Squire pressed Captain Wallace to be his guest for another day, and so, for a different reason, did his eldest son. Captain Wallace accepted the offer, after a decent show of reluctance to save his conscience. Harry no longer pressed him to stay after the following morning, and he left the next day.

"Father," said Harry, in the evening, "I fear I am about to draw your displeasure upon me, but I have done what I thought right, and I must bear it. Sir Edward Ingram left this house at nine o'clock yesterday evening."

"Left this house!" cried the Squire and Madam Passmore, in a breath—the former adding some very powerful language, which shall not be reproduced here.

"Left the house," Harry repeated, calmly.

The Squire exploded a second time, telling his son, among other equally pleasant assertions, that he was a disgrace to his family and his country, and would come to the gallows before he was much older.

"Father," was Harry's dignified reply, "I am sorry for nothing, except that I have angered you. This man whom Wallace was seeking is a gentleman and a Protestant, and at the battle of Denain he saved my life, and gave me my liberty without ransom. Would you, as a man of conscience and honor, have advised me to give him up after that?"

The Squire growled something inaudible.

"Father!" said Celia, rising in her turn, very white and trembling, "this was my brother whom we concealed in your house last night. I will take half, or more than half, of whatever blame is due. Harry concealed him, but it was in my bed-chamber, and I brought him food, and assisted in his escape. Could I have delivered up my brother to death—the only brother I have left? Father, have you the heart to say so?"

"No, my dear!" said Madam Passmore, pouring a little oil upon the turbulent waters; "no, I am sure he never would—never!"

Madam Passmore's gentle deprecation of his wrath appeared to set the Squire free to explode a third time.

"Lucy!" he exclaimed, turning to his wife, in one of the severest tones he had ever used to her, "I am a Whig, and my father was a Whig before me, and my grandfather fought for King Charles at Edgehill and Naseby: and I have brought up these children to be Whigs, and if they aren't, 'tis a burning shame! A murrain on the day that sent my Lady Ingram here after our Celia! But, hang it all! how can I help it?" said the Squire, suddenly breaking down. "If this fellow be Celia's brother, and have saved Harry's life, as a man of honor I could not bid them do otherwise than try to save his—no, not if he were the Pope himself! 'Tis not nature for a man to take sides against his own children. Botheration!" he concluded, suddenly veering round again; "that isn't what I meant to say at all. I intended to be very angry, and I have only been an old fool—that's what I am!"

"You are a dear old father, who can't be cross when he thinks he ought to be—that's what you are!" said Lucy, coaxingly.

"Get along with you, hussey!" returned the Squire, shaking his fist at her in a manner which Lucy very well knew was more than half make-believe. "And pray, Colonel Passmore, after allowing me to search the house three times and find nothing, I should like, if you please, to know where you hid your refugee?"

"You shall see that, Father," said Harry, rising.

And he led the way to the hiding-place, followed by the whole family, Cicely bringing up the rear when she heard the noise they made. Each member expressed his or her amazement in a characteristic manner.

"Oh, my buttons! isn't that capital!" said Charley. "I wish I had known last night! It would have been ten times better fun!"

"I think you enjoyed yourself sufficiently," returned his brother, gravely.

"What a horrid, dark hole, Harry!" said Lucy.

"I never knew of such a place here!" exclaimed his mother.

"Well, Mr. Henry Falkland Passmore, you are an uncommon cool hand!" asserted his father. "And who helped you to get your Jacobite safely away, I wonder?"

"Celia and Patient Irvine."

"Did Patient know where he was, Harry?" asked his mother, gravely.

"Not when Wallace questioned her. I told her afterwards."

But the astonishment of the whole group faded before that of old Cicely Aggett.

"Well, I do declare!" was what she said. "If ever anybody did! No, nobody couldn't never have guessed the like of this—that they couldn't! I've lived in this house three-and-thirty years come Martlemas, and I never, never did see nor hear nothing this like in all my born days! Only just to think! And them things I took for rats and ghostesses was Papishes? Eh, but I'd a cruel deal rather have a hundred rats and mice nor one of them wicked Papishes, and ghostesses too, pretty nigh! Well, to be sure, my dears, the Lord has preserved us wonderful! and 'tis uncommon thankful we'd ought to be."

"You will sleep to-night, Madam, I trust," said Patient, that evening, as she bound up Celia's hair.

"And you, my poor Patient!" said Celia. "I fear you slept not much last night."

"No, Madam," answered Patient, quietly; "I watched unto prayer."

"Well, I hope Edward is quite safe by this time," sighed Celia.

"You will never see him again, Madam," said Patient, solemnly.

"Patient!" exclaimed Celia, in sudden terror lest she might have heard some bad news.

"Best, my bairn," said Patient, reading her thought in her face. "I have heard nothing. But 'tis borne in upon me—'tis borne in upon me. The Lord hath said unto me, 'He shall surely die.'"

Celia listened in awe and wonder. "Patient, you are not a prophetess!" she said.

"Ah, Madam! I think more than one of us hath been a prophet where our heart's beloved are concerned. Was it not revealed unto Alexander Peden that he should die in Scotland? And did he not say unto the captain of the ship appointed to carry him unto the American plantations, 'The ship is not launched that shall carry me thither?'"

"And where did he die?"

"In Scotland, Madam, as the Lord had showed him; and they laid his dust on the Gallows' Hill of the city. I reckon the Lord can see it as easily there as in the kirkyard. It is a kirkyard now. One after another came and laid their dead beside Peden, and from a gallows' hill 'tis become a burying-place.[6] It was said, indeed, that Mr. Renwick saw further than many, but he was not known unto me, and I can say nought thereanent. But that, 'The secret of the Lord is with them that fear Him'[7] may be a deeper word than we ken. And as to

George Wishart, all knew that he was called to be a prophet of the Lord, and John Knox likewise; but there were giants in their days. We be smaller men now. Yet the Lord is the same now as then, and He doeth whatsoever He will. 'Tis not the worthiness nor holiness of the man that maketh a prophet, but the breath and Spirit of the Lord within him. And I, being less than the least of all His, do know of a surety that I shall never see Master Edward any more."

Patient's lips quivered, and some seconds passed ere she could speak again.

"Ay, the will of the Lord be done!" she said, presently. "'He knoweth them that are His,'[8] and He will not let us fail of a meeting in our Father's house. Rest, my bairn; you need it!"

Two months afterwards came a letter to Squire Passmore, bearing neither date nor signature. Though Edward's hand was unknown to her, Celia claimed the precious paper at once.

"DEAR SISTER,—Last night I landed at Corunna. I shall be safe for the present, and the Lord is ever with me. Thank better than I could all who helped me. You will know from whom this comes. Love to both of you. God keep you!"

Celia carried the paper to Patient, whom she guessed to be included with herself in the "both of you."

"Thank you, Madam!" said Patient, when she had read it. "'Tis a comfort to hear that he is in safety. Yet I cannot forget that the Lord hath showed unto me that he shall die in the flower of his age."

The 5th of June 1721, was Celia's thirtieth birth-day. She was seated at work in the parlor with Madam Passmore and Lucy, when a ring at the great bell summoned Robert to the front door, and was followed by his announcement of "Mr. Colville." Celia looked up in surprise to see if Philip's friend had sought her out. No; this was certainly not her pantheist adversary. He was a smaller and slighter man, with a much pleasanter expression of face than his namesake, yet with the same pale blue eyes and flaxen hair, and some resemblance in the features.

"Mrs. Ingram?" he asked, a little doubtfully, with a smile and a low bow. "Mrs. Celia Ingram?"

Celia rose to receive him, wondering all the time who he was and what he wanted with her.

"That is my name, Sir," she said, a little timidly. "I once knew a Mr. Colville in Paris"—

"Who was my brother," said the visitor, in explanation. "It was Arthur Colville whom you met in Paris. I am David Colville. I have been commissioned to give something into your hands, and none other's, the signification of which I believe you know. I received it at Barcelona on the 18th of January last."

And he drew a pocket-book from his breast-pocket, out of which he took and held forward to Celia something which brought a pang to her heart and a cry of pain to her lips. It was the Ingram heirloom, Lady Griselda's ruby ring, which was to be the signal to Edward Ingram's sister that he had entered into his rest.

"When was this?" she faltered at last.

"At Barcelona, on the 18th of January," David Colville repeated. "I had met him, for I also was journeying in Spain, three weeks before. I saw the end was near, and I stayed with him and tended him till he died."

"Where is he buried?"

"The Spaniards allow no burial to heretics, Madam—not more than they allow to a horse or a dog. He lies in a quiet meadow near the inn at Barcelona. I took care of that."

"Thank you!" murmured Celia; "but no burial-service—O Edward!"

The soft answer from David Colville almost startled her—"'Thy brother shall rise again.'"[9]

"Yes, I know," she said. "And you, Mr. Colville—you do not share your brother's philosophical views?"

"God forbid!" was the uncompromising reply. "I have yet hope that Arthur may see the error of his ways."

"May I ask if Mr. Arthur Colville is well?"

"I have not seen him for many years," said David. "Madam, may I ask, in my turn, if Patient Irvine be yet here? I think she would remember me as an old playmate of Ned and Philip, in the days long ago when we were all boys at Paris."

Patient received David Colville very affectionately, and his news very quietly.

"I knew it would be so," she said. "'With Christ, which is far better.'"[10]

David Colville left an agreeable impression of himself on the minds of both Celia and Patient when he shook hands with them at parting.

There was sore mourning for Edward Ingram at Ashcliffe.

"If it would please the Lord to ask me also!" sighed Patient.

"No, dear Patient! I want you," said Celia, lovingly.

"So long as you really want me, Madam, I shall be kept here; but the Lord knoweth better than you what you need, and our work is done when He calleth us. Yet so much, there! My father, my mother, Roswith, Mr. Grey, and Lady Magdalene, and Mr. Philip, and now my ain bairn Maister Edward"—and Patient broke down.

"Now, Patient, my dear!" said Cicely, from her chair, for she was infirm now—"now Patient, my dear, don't you go to fret over the Lord's mercies. Can't you see, child, that He is but taking all your jewels to keep them safer than you can, and that He'll give them all back to you up yonder? 'Tis such a short time here—such a short time!"

"Ay, I ken that," said Patient; "but you're a deal further on than I am, Cicely."

"Why, my dear, if you mean I shall die sooner, I don't know who told you; and if you mean that I know more about the Lord than you, I'm sure 'tis the first time I've heard of it. Maybe, children, we can't tell which of us is the furthest—the Lord knows. The one nearest Him is the furthest on."

"And we are always straying from Him," said Celia, sighing. "It scarce seems in us to keep always near Him."

"When you were a little babe, my dear," said Cicely, "I remember, if you were frighted at aught, you used to make-believe to throw your bits of arms about my neck, and cling close to me; but after all, it warn't your clinging as kept you from falling, but me holding of you. We are all as babes in the Lord's arms, my dear. 'Tis well, surely, for us to keep clinging to Him; but, after all, it ben't that as holds us—'tis His keeping of us. It ben't always when we are looking at Him that He is closest to us. He may be nearest when we can't see Him; and I'm sure of one thing, child,—if the Good Shepherd didn't go a-seeking after the lost sheep, the lost sheep would never turn of itself and come home to the Good Shepherd;—it would only go farther and farther in the great wilderness, until it was wholly lost. 'He calleth His own sheep by name'—ben't that it?—'and leadeth them out.'[11] Deary me! what was we a-talking about? It seems so natural like to get round to Him."

Celia smiled sadly as Philip's remark occurred to her—"There you come round to your divinity!"

For eleven years longer George Louis of Hanover sat on the throne of England. Every year he sank lower and lower in the estimation of his subjects. When he first landed, in 1714, in tones more deep than loud, England had demanded her Queen, and had no answer. Now, through these thirteen years, she had seen her King, chosen out of all the Princes of Europe, living apart from every member of his family, and keeping up a Court which only the complete demoralization of her nobles made them not ashamed to visit. And though very dimly and uncertainly, yet reports did reach England of a guarded prison in Hanover, and of a chapel in it where, every Communion Sabbath, a white-robed prisoner knelt down before the holy table, and, laying her hand upon it, solemnly protested in the presence of God that she had done no wrong deserving of that penalty. And England began to wonder if she had spoken well in summoning to her helm the husband and gaoler of this woful, white-robed captive. If the grand question of Protestantism had not been at stake—if she could have retained that and yet have had back her old line—the throne of George Louis would have trembled and fallen under him. Not "The Fifteen," nor "The Forty-five," brought so near a second Restoration as the evil and miserable life of that crowned sinner from Hanover.

So early as 1716, George had persuaded Parliament to repeal that clause of the Act of Settlement which made obligatory the perpetual residence of the Sovereign: and no sooner had the clerk[12] said *Le Roy le veut* to the repeal, than George set out for Hanover, with extreme delight at his release. After that, he spent as little time in England as was possible.

On the 7th of June 1727, George Louis landed from England on the Dutch shores. He was travelling onwards towards Osnabrück, when, on the night of the 11th, an unknown hand threw a letter into his carriage. The King, who was alone, opened it in the expectation of seeing a petition. There were only a few lines in the letter, but they came from the dead, and were written as with fire. What met his eyes was a summons from Sophia Dorothea of Zelle, written on her death-bed in the preceding November at Ahlden, calling on him in God's name to meet her before His tribunal within a year and a day. The King was intensely superstitious. What more happened in that carriage where he sat solitary, holding in his hand the open letter from his dead wife, none ever knew: but when the carriage stopped at the gates of the Palace of Osnabrück, George Louis was dead.

There were no mourners. Least of all could England mourn for the man who had so bitterly disgraced her, and had made her feel ashamed of her choice before all the world. On the contrary, there were bonfires and bell-ringings and universal rejoicings for the accession of George Augustus, whom England welcomed with hope in her heart that he would restore the honor which his father had laid in the dust.

A vain hope, and a groundless joy.

It is on that summer day, the 11th of June 1727, that I take leave of the Passmores. A quiet family party—Lucy growing into another and a livelier Celia; Charley toning down into a second Harry; Isabella, when she condescends to shine upon Ashcliffe in her glories of carriage and Nero, being the only discordant element. She and John Rowe get on very well, by reason of the lady being mistress, and John her obedient servant. Squire and Madam Passmore have grown more white and infirm; and on one quiet summer night in the preceding year, without sound or forewarning, the angels of God came down from heaven to bear Cicely Aggett home to the Father's house. But Patient lives on, for her work is not yet over.

On that afternoon Celia and Harry had rung the bell at the gate of Sainte Marie de Chaillot, and had asked for an interview with Soeur Marie Angélique. And in the guest-chamber there came to them a pale, slender, worn-looking woman in a nun's garb, who assured them, as she had done before on several occasions, that she was making her salvation; that she trusted she had by this time nearly expiated all her sins, and that a very short time in Purgatory would suffice to purify her. Only once during the interview did her stoic calmness give way, and that was when she said of the Purgatory she anticipated, "And there I shall see Philip!" And Celia felt that nearly all she could do was to pray earnestly that this wandering sheep might see Philip elsewhere. Then they took leave of Claude Ingram, and she went back to the convent chapel, and tried to make a little more of her salvation by kneeling on the cold stones and repeating interminable Litanies and Ave Marias. So we leave her to her hard task—hardest of tasks in all the world—to stand before God without a Mediator, to propitiate the Judge by the works of the law. For "without shedding of blood is no remission."[13]

The summer evening is drawing to a close, as outside the convent Harry and Celia pause to watch the sunset.

"How beautiful God has made this world!" says one of the travellers. "How much more beautiful it must be in that other land very far off,[14] the Heavenly Jerusalem, where is no need of the sun,[15] for the Lord is their everlasting light."[16]

And the answer, associated to her with the dead lips of Edward, comes in Celia's quietest and softest tones—

"For 'the world passeth away, and the lust thereof; but he that doeth the will of God abideth forever.'"[17]

[1] James Ratcliffe, Earl of Derwentwater, eldest son of Francis, first Earl and Lady Mary Tudor, natural daughter of Charles II.; beheaded on Tower Hill, February 24, 1716.

[2] Col. ii. 18.

[3] 1 John ii. 17.

[4] Ps. xci. 11.

[5] Ibid. 1.

[6] A fact.

[7] Ps. xxv. 14.

[8] 2 Tim. ii. 19.

[9] John xi. 23.

[10] Phil. i. 23.

[11] John x. 3.

[12] George Louis of Hanover was the first who resigned to a mere official the grandest act of the royal prerogative. Before his accession, the Kings of England "sceptred" every Act of Parliament, and the royal assent was really given, every bill being solemnly presented to the Sovereign in person, seated on the throne. Anne Stuart was the last Sovereign who dared on her own personal responsibility to say, *La Royne s'avisera.*

[13] Heb. ix. 22.

[14] Isaiah xxxiii. 17.

[15] Rev. xxi. 23.

[16] Isaiah lx. 20.

[17] 1 John ii. 17.

www.ingramcontent.com/pod-product-compliance
Ingram Content Group UK Ltd.
Pitfield, Milton Keynes, MK11 3LW, UK
UKHW031348260325
456749UK00003B/562